Essential Algorithms:
A Practical Approach to
Computer Algorithms

Essential Algorithms: A Practical Approach to Computer Algorithms

Joe Oswald

Larsen & Keller
www.larsen-keller.com

Essential Algorithms: A Practical Approach to Computer Algorithms
Joe Oswald
ISBN: 978-1-64172-151-6 (Hardback)

 Larsen & Keller

Published by Larsen and Keller Education,
5 Penn Plaza,
19th Floor,
New York, NY 10001, USA

Cataloging-in-Publication Data

Essential algorithms : a practical approach to computer algorithms / Joe Oswald.
   p. cm.
Includes bibliographical references and index.
ISBN 978-1-64172-151-6
1. Algorithms. 2. Computer algorithms. I. Oswald, Joe.
QA9.58 .E87 2019
511.8--dc23

For more information regarding Larsen and Keller Education and its products, please visit the publisher's website www.larsen-keller.com

Table of Contents

Permissions

Index

Preface

An algorithm is a specification of instructions for solving a class of problems by performing calculations and performing automated reasoning tasks and data processing. It describes a computation which when executed takes a finite number of successive states to produce an output. It is written in software in computer systems to produce output from a given input. Algorithms can be classified on the basis of implementation, design paradigm, optimization problems, etc. into a number of varied types. Some algorithm types are recursion, deterministic and non-deterministic, logical, randomized algorithms, etc. This book provides comprehensive insights into computer algorithms. It attempts to understand the varied kinds of computer algorithms and their practical applications. For someone with an interest and eye for detail, this textbook covers the most significant topics in this field.

To facilitate a deeper understanding of the contents of this book a short introduction of every chapter is written below:

Chapter 1, An algorithm is a logical framework designed for the solution of a class of problems. A computer algorithm is written for generating an intended output from a given input. This chapter elucidates in detail the principal topics of randomized algorithm, deterministic and non deterministic algorithm, external memory algorithm and online algorithms and competitive analysis in order to provide an understanding of computer algorithms. **Chapter 2**, The computational complexity of an algorithm is a measure of the amount of resources that is needed for running it. Complexity may be classified into various types, such as worst-case complexity, average-case complexity, time complexity and space complexity. This chapter has been carefully written to provide an easy understanding of computational complexity of an algorithm through the elucidation of the chief aspects of computational complexity theory, Big O notation, asymptotic computational complexity, analysis of algorithms, etc. **Chapter 3**, Sorting algorithm is an algorithm in computer science that arranges elements of a list in a specific numerical or lexicographical order. Sorting when done in an efficient way optimizes the efficiency of other algorithms. The diverse topics covered in this chapter on comparison sort,comb sort, insertion sort, shellsort, selection sort, etc. will help in providing a better perspective about sorting algorithm. **Chapter 4**, An understanding of graph algorithms is vital for a holistic understanding of computer algorithms. This chapter discusses in extensive detail the varied graph algorithms, such as Hopcroft–Karp algorithm, Edmonds' algorithm, Borůvka's algorithm, Bellman–Ford algorithm, etc. **Chapter 5**, Parallel algorithm is an algorithm that can be executed one piece at a time on different processing devices and thereafter combined to produce the desired result. A distributed algorithm is a type of parallel algorithm that is designed to operate on hardware that is constructed from interconnected processors. All the diverse aspects of parallel and distributed algorithms, such as algorithm structures, algorithm models, matrix-matrix multiplication, etc. have been carefully analyzed in this chapter.

I owe the completion of this book to the never-ending support of my family, who supported me throughout the project.

Joe Oswald

Computer Algorithms and its Types

An algorithm is a logical framework designed for the solution of a class of problems. A computer algorithm is written for generating an intended output from a given input. This chapter elucidates in detail the principal topics of randomized algorithm, deterministic and non deterministic algorithm, external memory algorithm and online algorithms and competitive analysis in order to provide an understanding of computer algorithms.

Algorithm

An algorithm is a procedure or formula for solving a problem, based on conductiong a sequence of specified actions. A computer program can be viewed as an elaborate algorithm. In mathematics and computer science, an algorithm usually means a small procedure that solves a recurrent problem.

Algorithms are widely used throughout all areas of IT (information technology). A search engine algorithm, for example, takes search strings of keywords and operators as input, searches its associated database for relevant web pages, and returns results.

The word algorithm derives from the name of the mathematician, Mohammed ibn-Musa al-Khwarizmi, who was part of the royal court in Baghdad and who lived from about 780 to 850. Al-Khwarizmi's work is the likely source for the word algebra as well.

Types of Algorithm

Algorithms can be classified into 3 types based on their structures:

1. Sequence: this type of algorithm is characterized with a series of steps, and each step will be executed one after another.

2. Branching: this type of algorithm is represented by the "if-then" problems. If a condition is true, the output will be A, if the condition is false, the output will be B. This algorithm type is also known as "selection type".

3. Loop: for this type, the process might be repeatedly executed under a certain condition. It is represented by "while" and "for" problems. But make sure the process will end after a number of loops under the condition. This algorithm type is also known as "repetition type".

Example

A very simple example of an algorithm would be to find the largest number in an unsorted list of numbers. If you were given a list of five different numbers, you would have this figured out in no time, no computer needed. Now, how about five million different numbers? Clearly, you are going to need a computer to do this, and a computer needs an algorithm.

Below is what the algorithm could look like. Let's say the input consists of a list of numbers, and this list is called L. The number L1 would be the first number in the list, L2 the second number, etc. And we know the list is not sorted - otherwise, the answer would be really easy. So, the input to the algorithm is a list of numbers, and the output should be the largest number in the list.

The algorithm would look something like this:

Step 1: Let Largest = L1

This means you start by assuming that the first number is the largest number.

Step 2: For each item in the list:

This means you will go through the list of numbers one by one.

Step 3: If the item Largest:

If you find a new largest number, move to step four. If not, go back to step two, which means you move on to the next number in the list.

Step 4: Then Largest = the item

This replaces the old largest number with the new largest number you just found. Once this is completed, return to step two until there are no more numbers left in the list.

Step 5: Return Largest

This produces the desired result.

Notice that the algorithm is described as a series of logical steps in a language that is easily understood. For a computer to actually use these instructions, they need to be written in a language that a computer can understand, known as a programming language.

Algorithm Engineering

When the design of new algorithms is applied in practical terms, the related discipline is known as algorithm engineering. The two functions are frequently carried out by the same people, although larger organizations (such as Amazon and Google) employ specialized designers and engineers, given their level of need for new and specialized algorithms. Like the design process, algorithm engineering frequently involves computer science accreditation, with a strong background in mathematics: where they exist as a separate, specialized profession, algorithm engineers take the conceptual ideas of designers and create processes from them that a computer will understand. With the steady advancement of digital technology, dedicated engineers will continue to become more and more common. It consists of the design, analysis, experimental testing and characterization of robust algorithms: it is mainly concerned with issues of realistic algorithm performance, and studies algorithms and data structures by carefully combining traditional theoretical methods together with thorough experimental investigations.

There are many potential benefits involved in this approach. First of all, it promotes and fosters bridges toward key algorithmic applications. Furthermore, experimenting with algorithms and data structures has already proven to be a crucial step in many circumstances, such as in the case of heuristics for very hard combinatorial problems, design of test suites for a variety of problems, and for proposing new conjectures that may be of theoretical interest as well. Indeed, experimentation can provide guidelines to realistic algorithm performance whenever standard theoretical analyses fail. In our experience, experimentation is a very important step in the design and analysis of algorithms, as it tests many underlying assumptions and tends to bring algorithmic questions closer to the problems that originally motivated the work. Last, but not least, providing leading edge implementations of algorithms is also a key step for a successful technology transfer of algorithmic research.

There has been a substantial work on the efficient implementation and practical evaluation of algorithms, both from the theoretical and from the experimental side.

Algorithmic problems on massive data sets arise in many large scale applications. In this scenario, traditional algorithms and computational models do not seem to be fairly adequate. Indeed, they are not able to account for the major bottleneck that occurs while dealing with massive amounts of data, which lies in the communication between fast internal memory and slower external storage devices, such as disks and CD-ROMs. The situation is likely to become even more dramatic in the future, as current technological advances are increasing CPU speeds at annual rates of 40–60% while disk transfer rates are only increasing by 7–10% annually.

The use of parallel processors further widens this gap. The main approach used to optimize performance in these cases is to bypass the virtual memory system, and to engineer algorithms so that they can explicitly manage data placement and movement. These algorithms are referred to as external memory algorithms. They are designed and analyzed in a more accurate and realistic model of the memory system: the parallel disk model. Recently developed by Vitter and Shriver, this model captures the main properties of multiple disk systems by taking into account the following parameters: the number of elements N in the problem instance, the number of elements M that can fit into main memory, the number of elements B per block, the number D of disk drives available, and the number P of CPUs. In typical I/O subsystems in use today, $M \approx 109, B \approx 103, D \approx 102$, while large-scale problem instances can be in the range $N \approx 1010$ to $N \approx 1015$. In this model, the primitive operation is a swap of B elements from internal memory with B consecutive elements in external memory, and at most D such operations (one per disk) are allowed during each I/O; the main measures of performance are the number of I/O operations performed, the internal (parallel) computation time, and the amount of disk storage. The parallel disk model is a good generic programming model that facilitates the design of external memory algorithms. The implementation, engineering and experimental evaluation of the performance of these algorithms can benefit from several tools and software platforms that have been developed recently. Among these, we cite the transparent parallel I/O environment (TPIE) developed by Vengroff.

Many I/O-efficient algorithms, paradigms and techniques have been designed, engineered and experimented. For a more complete view, we refer the interested reader to the excellent survey of Vitter. Among the general techniques proposed, we cite external sorting , matrix computations, external memory algorithms for computational geometry, for graph problems, and the buffer trees of

Arge, a rather general technique which is able to transform an internal-memory tree data structure into an external-memory structure.

Another area in which the need for well-engineered algorithms is crucial relates to numerical stable implementations. Indeed, developing robust and stable implementations has been an important task in many numerical applications, and its importance has become more recognized even in non-numerical disciplines such as the design of combinatorial algorithms and computational geometry. In these areas, several issues on numerical properties of existing algorithms have been recently raised, and as a consequence of a severe engineering effort, major revisions in the practical evaluation and design of algorithms have been proposed. In particular, two computational models, which are considered more realistic than traditional computational models, have been considered: the variable precision arithmetic model, where one is mainly concerned with the number of digits required to compute the exact solution to the problem, and the fixed precision arithmetic model, where one is concerned more with round-off errors. Both models have been considered as a good compromise between their inherent complexity and their adherence to real-world situations, and for this reason have been widely adopted. The fixed precision model is typical of numerical analysis, and indeed sophisticated techniques have been developed by numerical analysts for bounding round-off errors in this model. However, in some cases a rigorous analysis seems difficult to obtain, and the only information can be obtained from experimental evidence, whenever this is available.

In order to compensate the lack of precise information available on the numerical stability properties of many algorithms, several techniques for performing comparative analysis in both models (variable and fixed precision) have been introduced. For instance, in techniques of this kind have been introduced for fast parallel matrix inversion algorithms, and it is shown that for many algorithms available in the literature for this problem, the number of digits that are required to achieve computational precision can be extremely high. Thus, although these algorithms provide theoretically interesting and brilliant solutions, they seem doomed to fail serious engineering tests.

One crucial ingredient for experimentation has already proved to be the development of software platforms, such as the already mentioned TPIE. However, also the need for general-purpose algorithmic software libraries is becoming more pervasive. Indeed, implementing complex algorithmic code from scratch can be extremely time consuming, error-prone, and requires expert knowledge in algorithmics: in this scenario, a library allows the implementer to rely on flexible, already tested (and hopefully validated) software modules, which can be easily reused in new implementations. This seems to be confirmed by the substantial amount of work done recently on the integration of algorithmic code into software packages. Among the existing algorithmic software libraries, we cite LEDA (Library of Efficient Data types and Algorithms), which is perhaps one of the more mature and widespread products, and it is becoming a de facto standard in the implementation of discrete and combinatorial algorithms. Besides libraries, there are also algorithm repositories, which contain collections of known implementations for combinatorial problems. Although not as reusable as library modules, such implementations have shown to be another important tool in engineering algorithms, as they provide standard (and/or benchmark) implementations which are very useful in performance evaluations.

Finally, another contribution of algorithm engineering consists in the development of methodologies, standards and benchmarks for the experimental evaluation of algorithms. This is particularly important, as it provides scientific guidelines for setting up, organizing, and interpreting algorithmic experiments, and for comparing results obtained from different experiments. There has been much work in this direction, and in particular, the Center for Discrete Mathematics & Computer Science (DIMACS) has greatly contributed to methodologies and to test suites for a variety of problems with its series of implementation challenges.

Future Challenges

There are several aspects of algorithm engineering which we believe should require more attention in the near future. In particular, we believe that the aim of providing solid, well-engineered and tested algorithms that the computing community at large can really use, can only be met with a proper blend of algorithmic and software research. This is perhaps one of the major challenges to be faced in the next years, and preliminary work in this direction shows that it might benefit from closer interactions and cross-fertilization between the algorithmic and software communities. It might also require developing a completely new set of tools and techniques, as the software community has not been devoting much attention to issues that arise when developing software which is intricate but not necessarily large, as the typical algorithmic software is.

Algorithm engineering is by now an emerging discipline, gaining momentum and credibility throughout the whole research community. There is already strong evidence that it is developing its own standards of quality and methodologies, that it will further crystallize from the current efforts over the next few years, and that it will lead to much improved theory of algorithms, (re)usable implementations, algorithmic libraries, and more impact and technology transfers outside our own community.

Algorithm Design

An algorithm is a series of instructions, often referred to as a "process," which is to be followed when solving a particular problem. While technically not restricted by definition, the word is almost invariably associated with computers, since computer-processed algorithms can tackle much larger problems than a human, much more quickly. Since modern computing uses algorithms much more frequently than at any other point in human history, a field has grown up around their design, analysis, and refinement. The field of algorithm design requires a strong mathematical background, with computer science degrees being particularly sought-after qualifications. It offers a growing number of highly compensated career options, as the need for more (as well as more sophisticated) algorithms continues to increase.

Conceptual Design

At their simplest level, algorithms are fundamentally just a set of instructions required to complete a task. The development of algorithms, though they generally weren't called that, has been a popular habit and a professional pursuit for all of recorded history. Long before the dawn of the modern computer age, people established set routines for how they would go about their daily tasks, often writing down lists of steps to take to accomplish important goals, reducing the risk of forgetting something important. This, essentially, is what an algorithm is. Designers take a similar approach to the development of algorithms for computational purposes: first, they look at a problem. Then, they outline the steps that would be required to resolve it. Finally, they develop a series of mathe-matical operations to accomplish those steps.

From Small Tasks to Big Data

A simple task can be solved by an algorithm generated with a few minutes, or at most a morning's work. The level of complexity runs a long gauntlet, however, arriving at problems so complicated that they have stymied countless mathematicians for years — or even centuries. Modern computer confronts problems at this level in such areas as cyber-security, as well as big data handling — the efficient and thorough sorting of sets of data so large that even a standard computer would be un-able to process them in a timely fashion.

Divide and Conquer Algorithm

Divide and Conquer is an algorithmic design paradigm. A typical Divide and Conquer algorithm solves a problem using following three steps.

1. *Divide:* Break the given problem into subproblems of same type.

2. *Conquer:* Recursively solve these subproblems

3. *Combine:* Appropriately combine the answers

Following are some standard algorithms that are Divide and Conquer algorithms.

1) Binary Search is a searching algorithm. In each step, the algorithm compares the input element x with the value of the middle element in array. If the values match, return the index of middle. Otherwise, if x is less than the middle element, then the algorithm recurs for left side of middle element, else recurs for right side of middle element.

2) Quicksort is a sorting algorithm. The algorithm picks a pivot element, rearranges the array elements in such a way that all elements smaller than the picked pivot element move to left side of pivot, and all greater elements move to right side. Finally, the algorithm recursively sorts the subarrays on left and right of pivot element.

3) Merge Sort is also a sorting algorithm. The algorithm divides the array in two halves, recursively sorts them and finally merges the two sorted halves.

4) Closest Pair of Points The problem is to find the closest pair of points in a set of points in x-y plane. The problem can be solved in $O(n^2)$ time by calculating distances of every pair of points and comparing the distances to find the minimum. The Divide and Conquer algorithm solves the problem in $O(nLogn)$ time.

5) Strassen's Algorithm is an efficient algorithm to multiply two matrices. A simple method to multiply two matrices need 3 nested loops and is $O(n^3)$. Strassen's algorithm multiplies two matri-ces in $O(n^{2.8974})$ time.

6) Cooley–Tukey Fast Fourier Transform (FFT) algorithm is the most common algorithm for FFT. It is a divide and conquer algorithm which works in $O(nlogn)$ time.

7) Karatsuba algorithm for fast multiplication it does multiplication of two n-digit numbers in at most $3n^{\log_2 3} \approx 3n^{1.585}$ single-digit multiplications in general (and exactly $n^{\log_2 3}$ when n is a power of 2). It is therefore faster than the classical algorithm, which requires n^2 single-digit products. If $n = 2^{10} = 1024$, in particular, the exact counts are $3^{10} = 59{,}049$ and $(2^{10})^2 = 1{,}048{,}576$, respectively.

We use recurrences to analyze the running time of such algorithms. Suppose T_n is the number of steps in the worst case needed to solve the problem of size n. Let us split a problem into $a \geq 1$ sub-problems, each of which is of the input size $\frac{n}{b}$ where b > 1. Observe, that the number of subproblems a is not necessarily equal to b. The total number of steps T_n is obtained by all steps needed to solve smaller subproblems $T_{n/b}$ plus the number needed to combine solutions into a final one. The following equation is called divide-and-conquer recurrence relation

$$T_n = aT_{n/b} + f(n)$$

As an example, consider the mergesort:

- divide the input in half

- recursively sort the two halves

- combine the two sorted subsequences by merging them.

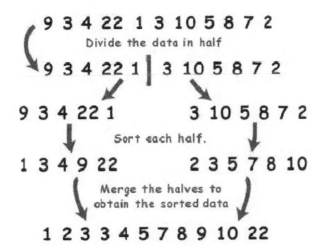

Let T(n) be worst-case runtime on a sequence of n keys:

If $n = 1$, then $T(n) = \Theta(1)$ constant time

If $n > 1$, then $T(n) = 2T(n/2) + \Theta(n)$

here $\Theta(n)$ is time to do the merge. Then

$$T(n) = 2T_{(n/2)} + \Theta(n)$$

Other examples of divide and conquer algorithms: quicksort, integer multiplication, matrix multiplication, fast Fourier trnsform, finding conver hull and more.

There are several techniques of solving such recurrence equations:

- the iteration method
- the tree method
- the master-theorem method
- guess-and-verify

Tree Method

We could visualize the recursion as a tree, where each node represents a recursive call. The root is the initial call. Leaves correspond to the exit condition. We can often solve the recurrence by looking at the structure of the tree. To illustrate, we take this example

$$T(n) = 2T\left(\frac{n}{2}\right) + n^2$$
$$T(1) = 1$$

Here is a recursion tree that diagrams the recursive function calls

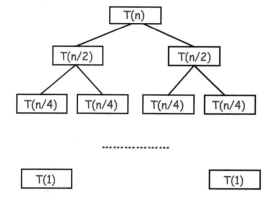

Using a recursion tree we can model the time of a recursive execution by writing the size of the problem in each node.

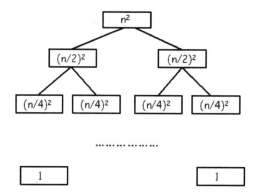

Using a recursion tree we can model the time of a recursive execution by writing the size of the problem in each node.

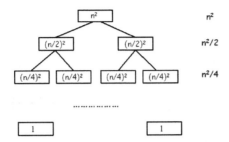

The last level corresponds to the initial condition of the recurrence. Since the work at each leaf is constant, the total work at all leaves is equal to the number of leaves, which is

$$2^h = 2^{\log_2 n} = n$$

To find the total time (for the whole tree), we must add up all the terms

$$T(n) = n + n^2 \left(1 + \frac{1}{2} + \frac{1}{4} + \frac{1}{8} + \ldots \right) = n + n^2 \sum_{k=0}^{-1+\log_2 n} \left(\frac{1}{2}\right)^k$$

The sum is easily computed by means of the geometric series

$$\sum_{k=0}^{h} x^k = \frac{x^{h+1} - 1}{x - 1}, x \neq 1$$

This yields

$$T(n) = 2n^2 - 2n + n = 2n^2 - n$$

$$RSolve\left[\left\{T[n] == 2T[n/2] + n^2, T[1] == 1\right\}, T[n], n\right]$$

$$\left\{\left\{T[n] \rightarrow n(-1 + 2n)\right\}\right\}$$

Example:

Solve the recurrence

$$T(n) = 3T\left(\frac{n}{4}\right) + n$$

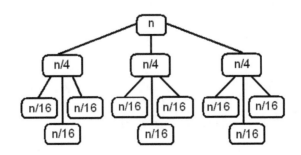

The work at all levels is

$$n\left(1+\frac{3}{4}+\frac{9}{16}+\ldots\right)$$

Since the height is $log_4 n$, the tree has $3^{\log_4 n}$ leaves. Hence, the total work is given by

$$T(n) = n \sum_{k=0}^{-1+\log_4 n} \left(\frac{3}{4}\right)^k + 3\log_4^n T(1)$$

By means of the geometric series and taking into account

$$3^{\log_4 n} = n \log_4{}^3$$

the above sum yields

$$T(n) = 4n - 4n\log_4{}^3 T(1) = O(n)$$

Master Theorem

The master theorem solves recurrences of the form

$$T(n) = aT\left(\frac{n}{b}\right) + f(n)$$

For a wide variety of function $f(n)$ and $a \geq 1, b > 1$. Here is the recursive tree for the above equation

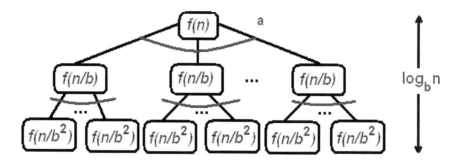

It is easy to see that the tree has $a^{\log_b n}$ n leaves. Indeed, since the height is $\log_b n$, and the tree branching factor is a, the number of leaves is

$$a^h = a^{\log_b n} = a^{\frac{\log_a n}{\log_a b}} = n^{\frac{1}{\log_a b}} = n^{\log_b a}$$

Summing up values at each level, gives

$$T(n) = f(n) + a f\left(\frac{n}{b}\right) + a^2 f\left(\frac{n}{b^2}\right) + \ldots + n\log_b a \, T(1)$$

Therefore, the solution is

$$T(n) = n^{\log_b a} T(1) + \sum_{k=0}^{-1+\log_b n} a^k f\left(\frac{n}{b^k}\right)$$

Now we need to compare the asymptotic behavior of $f(n)$ with $n \log_b a$. There are three possible cases.

$$T(n) = \begin{cases} \Theta\left(n^{\log_b a}\right) & if\ f(n) = O\left(n^{\log_b a}\right) \\ \Theta\left(n^{\log_b n}\right) & if\ f(n) = \Theta\left(n^{\log_b a} \log^k n\right), k \geq 0 \\ \Theta(f(n)) & if\ f(n) = \Omega\left(n^{\log_b a}\right) \end{cases}$$

The following examples demonstrate the theorem

Case 1: $T(n) = 4T\left(\frac{n}{2}\right) + n$

We have $f(n) = n$ and $n^{\log_b a} = n \log_2 4 = n^2$, therefore $f(n) = O(n^2)$. Then the solution is $T(n) = \Theta(n^2)$ by case 1.

Case 2: $T(n) = 4T\left(\frac{n}{2}\right) + n^2$

In this case $f(n) = n^2$ and $f(n) = \Theta(n^2)$. Then $T(n) = \Theta(n^2 \log n)$ by case 2.

Case 3: $T(n) = 4T\left(\frac{n}{2}\right) + n^3$

In this case $f(n) = n^2$ and $f(n) = \Omega(n \log_b a) = \Omega(n^2)$. Then $T(n) = \Theta(n^3)$ by case 3.

Karatsuba Algorithm

The Karatsuba algorithm is a fast multiplication algorithm. It was discovered by Anatoly Karatsuba in 1960 and published in 1962. It reduces the multiplication of two n-digit numbers to at most $n^{\log_2 3} \approx n^{1.585}$ single-digit multiplications in general (and exactly $n^{\log_2 3}$ when n is a power of 2). It is therefore faster than the classical algorithm, which requires n^2 single-digit products. For example, the Karatsuba algorithm requires 3^{10} = 59,049 single-digit multiplications to multiply two 1024-digit numbers (n = 1024 = 2^{10}), whereas the classical algorithm requires $(2^{10})^2$ = 1,048,576 (a speedup of 17.75 times).

The Karatsuba algorithm was the first multiplication algorithm asymptotically faster than the quadratic "grade school" algorithm. The Toom–Cook algorithm is a faster generalization of Karatsuba's method, and the Schönhage–Strassen algorithm is even faster, for sufficiently large n.

Multiplication of Large Integers

The brute force approach ("grammar school" method)

$$\begin{array}{ccc} 1 & 2 & 3 \\ & 4 & 5 \\ \hline 6 & 1 & 5 \\ 49 & 2 & \\ \hline 5 & 53 & 5 \end{array}$$

We say that multiplication of two n-digits integers has time complexity at worst $O(n^2)$.

We develop an algorithm that has better asymptotic complexity. The idea is based on divide-and-conquer technique.

Consider the above integers and split each of them in two parts

$$123 = 12 *10 + 3$$
$$45\ = 4\ *10 + 5$$

and then multiply them:

$$123 * 45 = (12 * 10 + 3)(4 * 10 + 5) =$$
$$12 * 4 * 10^2 + (12 * 5 + 4 * 3) * 10 + 3 * 5$$

In general, the integer which has n digits can be represented as

$$num = x * 10^m + y$$

Where

$$m = \text{floor}\left(\frac{n}{2}\right)$$

$$x = \text{ceiling}\left(\frac{n}{2}\right)$$

$$y = \text{floor}\left(\frac{n}{2}\right)$$

Example

$$154\,517\,766 = 154451 * 10^4 + 7766$$

Consider two n-digits numbers

$$num_1 = x_1 * 10^P + x_0$$
$$num_2 = y_1 * 10^P + y_0$$

Their product is

$$num_1 * num_2 = x_1 * y_1 10^{2P} + (x_1 * y_0 + x_0 * y_1) * 10^P + x_0 * y_0$$

Just looking at this general formula you can say that just instead of one multiplication we have 4.

Where is the advantage?

numbers x_1, x_0 and y_1, y_0 have twice less digits.

Worst-case Complexity

Let THnL denote the number of digit multiplications needed to multiply two n-digits numbers.

The recurrence (since the algorithm does 4 multiplications on each step)

$$T(n) = 4T\left(\frac{n}{2}\right) + O(n), T(c) = 1$$

By ignoring multiplications by a base, we get

$$T(n) = 4^{\log_2 n} = n^2$$

The algorithm is still quadratic.

Karatsuba Algorithm

$$\text{num}^1 * \text{num}^2 = x_1 * y_1 * 10^{2p} + (x_1 * y_0 + x_0 * y_1)10^p + x_0 * y_0$$

The goal is to decrease the number of multiplications from 4 to 3. We can do this by observing that

$$(x_1 + x_0) * (y_1 + y_0) = x_1 * y_1 + x_0 * y_0 + (x_1 * y_0 + x_0 * y_1)$$

It follows that

$$\text{num}_1 * \text{num}_2 = x_1 * y_1 * 10^{2p} + ((x_1 + x_0) * (y_1 + y_0) - x_1 * y_1 - x_0 * y_0) * 10^p + x_0 * y_0$$

and it is only 3 multiplications. The total number of multiplications is given by (we ignore multiplications by a base)

$$T(n) = 3T\left(\frac{n}{2}\right) + O(n), \quad T(c) = 1$$

Its solution is

$$T(n) = 3^{\log_2 n} = n^{\log_2 3} = n^{1.58...}$$

Toom-Cook 3-Way Multiplication

The key idea of the algorithm is to divide a large integer into 3 parts (rather than 2) of size approximately $n/3$ and then multiply those parts.

Here is the equation of for the total number of multiplications

$$T(n) = 9T\left(\frac{n}{3}\right) + O(n), \ T(c) = 1$$

and the solution

$$T(n) = 9^{\log_3 n} = n^2$$

Let us reduce the number of multiplications by one

$$T(n) = 8T\left(\frac{n}{3}\right) + O(n)$$

$$T(n) = 8^{\log_3 n} = n^{\log_3 8} = n^{1.89...}$$

No advantage. This does not improve the previous algorithm, that runs at $O(n^{1.58})$ How many multiplication should we eliminate?

Let us consider that equation in a general form, where parameter $p > 0$ is arbitrary

$$T(n) = pT\left(\frac{n}{3}\right) + O(n)$$

$$T(n) = p^{\log_3 n} = n^{\log_3 p}$$

Therefore, the new algoritnm will be faster than $O(n^{1.58})$ if we reduce the number of multiplications to five

$$T(n) = 5\log_3 n = \log_3 5 = n^{1.47...}$$

This is an improvement over Karatsuba. Is it possible to reduce a number of multiplications to 5? Yes, it follows from this system of equations:

$$x_0 y_0 = Z_0$$
$$12(x_1 y_0 + x_0 y_1) = 8Z_1 - Z_2 - 8Z_3 + Z_4$$
$$24(x_2 y_0 + x_1 y_1 + x_0 y_2) = -30Z_0 + 16Z_1 - Z_2 + 16Z_3 - Z_4$$
$$12(x_2 y_1 + x_1 y_2) = -2Z_1 + Z_2 + 2Z_3 - Z_4$$
$$24 x_2 y_2 = 6Z_0 - 4Z_1 + Z_2 - 4Z_3 + Z_4$$
$$Z_0 = x_0 y_0$$
$$Z_1 = (x_0 + x_1 + x_2)(y_0 + y_1 + y_2)$$
$$Z_2 = (x_0 + 2x_1 + 4x_2)(y_0 + 2y_1 + 4y_2)$$
$$Z_3 = (x_0 - x_1 + x_2)(y_0 - y_1 + y_2)$$
$$Z_4 = (x_0 - 2x_1 + 4x_2)(y_0 - 2y_1 + 4y_2)$$

Kernelization

In computer science, a kernelization is a technique for designing efficient algorithms that achieve their efficiency by a preprocessing stage in which inputs to the algorithm are replaced by a smaller input, called a "kernel". The result of solving the problem on the kernel should either be the same as on the original input, or it should be easy to transform the output on the kernel to the desired output for the original problem.

Kernelization is often achieved by applying a set of reduction rules that cut away parts of the instance that are easy to handle. In parameterized complexity theory, it is often possible to prove that a kernel with guaranteed bounds on the size of a kernel (as a function of some parameter associated to the problem) can be found in polynomial time. When this is possible, it results in a fixed-parameter tractable algorithm whose running time is the sum of the (polynomial time) kernelization step and the (non-polynomial but bounded by the parameter) time to solve the kernel. Indeed, every problem that can be solved by a fixed-parameter tractable algorithm can be solved by a kernelization algorithm of this type.

Example: Vertex Cover

A standard example for a kernelization algorithm is the kernelization of the vertex cover problem by S. Buss. In this problem, the input is an undirected graph G together with a number k. The output is a set of at most k vertices that includes the endpoint of every edge in the graph, if such a set exists, or a failure exception if no such set exists. This problem is NP-hard. However, the following reduction rules may be used to kernelize it:

1. If $k > 0$ and k is a vertex of degree greater than k, remove v from the graph and decrease k by one. Every vertex cover of size k must contain v since otherwise too many of its neighbors would have to be picked to cover the incident edges. Thus, an optimal vertex cover for the original graph may be formed from a cover of the reduced problem by adding v back to the cover.

2. If v is an isolated vertex, remove it. An isolated vertex cannot cover any edges, so in this case v cannot be part of any minimal cover.

3. If more than k^2 edges remain in the graph, and neither of the previous two rules can be applied, then the graph cannot contain a vertex cover of size k. For, after eliminating all vertices of degree greater than k, each remaining vertex can only cover at most k edges and a set of k vertices could only cover at most k^2 edges. In this case, the instance may be replaced by an instance with two vertices, one edge, and $k = 0$, which also has no solution.

An algorithm that applies these rules repeatedly until no more reductions can be made necessarily terminates with a kernel that has at most k^2 edges and (because each edge has at most two endpoints and there are no isolated vertices) at most $2k^2$ vertices. This kernelization may be implemented in linear time. Once the kernel has been constructed, the vertex cover problem may be solved by a brute force search algorithm that tests whether each subset of the kernel is a cover of the kernel. Thus, the vertex cover problem can be solved in time $O(2^{2k^2} + n + m)$ for a graph with n vertices and m edges, allowing it to be solved efficiently when k is small even if n and m are both large.

Although this bound is fixed-parameter tractable, its dependence on the parameter is higher than might be desired. More complex kernelization procedures can improve this bound, by finding smaller kernels, at the expense of greater running time in the kernelization step. In the vertex cover example, kernelization algorithms are known that produce kernels with at most $2k$ vertices. One algorithm that achieves this improved bound exploits the half-integrality of the linear program relaxation of vertex cover due to Nemhauser and Trotter. Another kernelization algorithm achieving that bound is based on what is known as the crown reduction rule and uses alternating path arguments. The currently best known kernelization algorithm in terms of the number of vertices is due to Lampis (2011) and achieves $2k - c\log k$ vertices for any fixed constant c.

It is not possible, in this problem, to find a kernel of size $O(\log k)$, unless P = NP, for such a kernel would lead to a polynomial-time algorithm for the NP-hard vertex cover problem. However, much stronger bounds on the kernel size can be proven in this case: unless coNP $\subseteq$ NP/poly (believed unlikely by complexity theorists), for every $\epsilon > 0$ it is impossible in polynomial time to find kernels with $O(k^{2-\epsilon})$ edges. It is unknown for vertex cover whether kernels with $(2-\epsilon)k$ vertices for some ϵ would have any unlikely complexity-theoretic consequences.

There is no clear consensus on how kernelization should be formally defined and there are subtle differences in the uses of that expression.

Downey-Fellows Notation

In the Notation of Downey & Fellows (1999), a *parameterized problem* is a subset $L \subseteq \Sigma^* \times \mathbb{N}$ describing a decision problem.

A kernelization for a parameterized L problem is an algorithm that takes an instance $L \subseteq \Sigma^* \times \mathbb{N}$ and maps it in time polynomial in $|x|$ and k to an instance (x', k') such that

- (x, k) is in L if and only if (x', k') is in L,

- the size of x' is bounded by a computable function f in k, and

- k' is bounded by a function in k.

The output (x', k') of kernelization is called a kernel. In this general context, the *size* of the string x' just refers to its length. Some authors prefer to use the number of vertices or the number of edges as the size measure in the context of graph problems.

Flum-Grohe Notation

In the Notation of Flum & Grohe a *parameterized problem* consists of a decision problem $L \subseteq \Sigma^*$ and a function $\kappa : \Sigma^* \to \mathbb{N}$, , the parameterization. The *parameter* of an instance x is the number $\kappa(x)$.

A kernelization for a parameterized problem L is an algorithm that takes an instance with parameter x and maps it in polynomial time to an instance y such that

- x is in L if and only if y is in L and

- the size of y is bounded by a computable function f in k.

Note that in this notation, the bound on the size of y implies that the parameter of y is also bounded by a function in k.

The function f is often referred to as the size of the kernel. If $f = k^{O(1)}$, it is said that L admits a polynomial kernel. Similarly, for $f = O(k)$, the problem admits linear kernel.

Kernelizability and Fixed-parameter Tractability are Equivalent

A problem is fixed-parameter tractable if and only if it is kernelizable and decidable.

That a kernelizable and decidable problem is fixed-parameter tractable can be seen from the definition above: First the kernelization algorithm, which runs in time $O(|x|^c)$ for some c, is invoked to generate a kernel of size $f(k)$. The kernel is then solved by the algorithm that proves that the problem is decidable. The total running time of this procedure is $g(f(k)) + O(|x|^c)$, where $g(n)$ is the running time for the algorithm used to solve the kernels. Since $g(f(k))$ is computable, e.g. by using the assumption that $f(k)$ is computable and testing all possible inputs of length $f(k)$, this implies that the problem is fixed-parameter tractable.

The other direction, that a fixed-parameter tractable problem is kernelizable and decidable is a bit more involved. Assume that the question is non-trivial, meaning that there is at least one instance that is in the language, called I_{yes}, and at least one instance that is not in the language, called I_{no}; otherwise, replacing any instance by the empty string is a valid kernelization. Assume also that the problem is fixed-parameter tractable, ie., it has an algorithm that runs in at most $f(k) \cdot |x|^c$ steps on instances (x,k), for some constant c and some function $f(k)$. To kernelize an input, run this algorithm on the given input for at most $|x|^{c+1}$ steps. If it terminates with an answer, use that answer to select either I_{yes} or I_{no} as the kernel. If, instead, it exceeds the $|x|^{c+1}$ bound on the number of steps without terminating, then return (x,k) itself as the kernel. Because (x,k) is only returned as a kernel for inputs with $f(k) \cdot |x|^c > |x|^{c+1}$, it follows that the size of the kernel produced in this way is at most $\max\{|I_{yes}|, |I_{no}|, f(k)\}$. This size bound is computable, by the assumption from fixed-parameter tractability that $f(k)$ is computable.

More Examples

- Vertex Cover: The vertex cover problem has kernels with at most $2k$ vertices and $O(k^2)$ edges. Furthermore, for any $\varepsilon > 0$, vertex cover does not have kernels with $O(k^{2-\varepsilon})$ edges unless . The vertex cover problems in -uniform hypergraphs has kernels with $O(k^d)$ edges using the sunflower lemma, and it does not have kernels of size $O(k^{d-\varepsilon})$ unless coNP $\subseteq$ NP/poly..

- Feedback Vertex Set: The feedback vertex set problem has kernels with $4k^2$ vertices and $O(k^2)$ edges. Furthermore, it does not have kernels with $O(k^{2-\varepsilon})$ edges unless coNP $\subseteq$ NP/poly.

- k-Path: The k-path problem is to decide whether a given graph has a path of length at least k. This problem has kernels of size exponential in k, and it does not have kernels of size polynomial in k unless coNP $\subseteq$ NP/poly.

- Bidimensional problems: Many parameterized versions of bidimensional problems have linear kernels on planar graphs, and more generally, on graphs excluding some fixed graph as a minor

Iterative Compression

Iterative Compression is a tool that has recently been used successfully in solving a number of problems in the area of Parameterized Complexity. This technique is used to solve the Odd Cycle Transversal problem, where one is interested in finding a set of at most k vertices whose deletion makes the graph bipartite. Iterative compression was used in obtaining faster FPT algorithms for Feedback Vertex Set, Edge Bipartization and Cluster Vertex Deletion on undirected graphs. Recently this technique has led to an FPT algorithm for the Directed Feedback Vertex Set problem [4], one of the longest open problems in the area of parameterized complexity. The main idea behind iterative compression for parameterized algorithms is an algorithm which, given a solution of size $k+1$ for a problem, either compresses it to a solution of size k or proves that there is no solution of size k. This is known as the compression step of the algorithm. Based on this compression step, iterative (and incremental) algorithms for minimization problems are obtained. The most technical part of an FPT algorithm based on iterative compression is to show that the compression step can be carried out in time $f(k).n^{O(1)}$, where f is an arbitrary computable function, k is a parameter and n is the length of the input.

The presence of a solution of size $k+1$ can provide important structural information about the problem. This is one of the reasons why the technique ofiterative compression has become so powerful. Structures are useful in designing algorithms in most paradigms. By seeing so much success of iterative compression in designing fixed parameter tractable algorithms, it is natural and tempting to study its applicability in designing exact exponential time algorithms.

The goal of the design of moderately exponential time algorithms for NP complete problems is to establish algorithms for which the worst-case running time is provably faster than the one of enumerating all prospective solutions, or loosely speaking, algorithms better than brute-force enumeration. For example, for NP-complete problems on graphs on n vertices and m edges whose solutions are either subsets of vertices or edges, the brute-force or trivial algorithms basically enumerate all subsets of vertices or edges. This mostly leads to algorithms of time complexity 2^n or 2^m, modulo some polynomial factors, based on whether we are enumerating vertices or edges. Almost all the iterative compression based FPT algorithms with parameter k have a factor of 2^{k+1} in the running time, as they all branch on all partitions (A, D) of a $k+1$ sized solution S and look for a solution of size k with a restriction that it should contain all elements of A and none of D. This is why, at first thought, iterative compression is a quite useless technique for solving optimization problems because for $k = \Omega(n)$, we end up with an algorithm having a factor 2^n or 2^m in the worst-case running time, while a running time of 2^n or 2^m (up to a polynomial factor) often can be achieved by (trivial) brute force enumeration. Luckily, our intuition here appears to be wrong and with some additional arguments, iterative compression can become a useful tool in the design of moderately exponential time algorithms as well. We find it interesting because despite of several exceptions (like the works of Bj̈orklund et al.), the area of exact algorithms is heavily dominated by branching algorithms, in particular, for subset problems. It is very often that an (incremental) improvement in the running time of branching algorithm requires an extensive case analysis, which becomes very technical and tedious. The analysis of such algorithms can also be very complicated and even computer based. The main advantage of iterative compression is that it provides combinatorial algorithms based on problem structures. While the improvement in the running time compared to (complicated) branching algorithms is not so impressive, the simplicity and elegance of the arguments allow them to be used in a basic algorithm

Dovetailing

Dovetailing, in algorithm design, is a technique that interweaves different computations, performing them essentially simultaneously. Algorithms that use dovetailing are sometimes referred to as dovetailers.

Consider a tree that potentially contains a path of infinite length: if a depth-first search is performed in this environment, the search may move down an infinite path and never return, potentially leaving part of the tree unexplored. However, if a breadth-first search is used, the existence of an infinite path is no longer a problem: each node is visited in a branching manner according to its distance from the root, so an infinite path will only impact the part of the search travelling down that path.

We can regard this tree as analogous to a collection of programs; in this case, the depth-first approach corresponds to running one program at a time, moving to the next only when the current program has finished running. In the case where one of the programs runs for an infinite amount of time, this transition will never happen. The breadth-first approach of visiting each child on the same level of the tree corresponds to dovetailing, where a single step is performed for every program before moving to the next. Thus, progress is made in each program, regardless of the potential existence of a program of infinite runtime.

In the case of an infinite number of programs, all potentially infinitely long, neither the breadth-first nor depth-first would be sufficient to ensure progress on all programs. Instead, the following technique can be used: perform the first step of the first program; next, perform the first step of the second program and the second step of the first program; next, perform the first step of the third program, the second step of the second program, and the third step of the first program; and so on.

We could dovetail the depth-first (no dovetailing) and breadth-first (full dovetailing) mechanism of combining algorithms. This recursive application of the dovetailing algorithm to itself leads to an infinite number of new algorithms, each involving slightly less total dovetailing.

Dovetailing in Turing machines

Dovetailing (in carpentry) is a way of connecting two pieces of wood by interleaving them. Dovetailing is an interleaving technique for simulating many (in fact, infinite number of) TM together. Here, we would like to interleave an infinite number of simulations, so that if any of them stops, our simulation of all of them would also stop. Consider the language

$$J = \left\{ \langle M \rangle \big| M \text{ accepts at least one string in } \sum{}^* \right\}$$

It is tempting to design our recognizer for J as follows.

algBuggyRecog $(\langle M \rangle)$

$x = \in$

while True do

        simulated M on x $\left(\text{using } U_{TM}\right)$

        if M accepts then

                halt and accept

      x ← next string in lexicographic order

Unfortunately, if M never halts on one of the strings, this process will get stuck before it even reaches the string that M does accept. So we need to run our simulations in parallel. Since we cannot start up an infinite number of simulations all at once, we use the following idea.

Dovetailing is the idea of running k simulations in parallel, but keep dynamically increasing k. So, for our example, suppose that we store all our simulations on tape $\circledast_T$ and x lives on some other tape. Then our code might look like:

alg DovetailingRecog $(\langle M \rangle)$

    $x = \in$

while True do

On $\circledast_T$, start up the simulation of M on x Advance all simulations on $\circledast_T$ by one step. if any simulation on $\circledast_T$ accepted then halt and accept

    $x \leftarrow Next(x)$

Here Next (x) yields the next string in the lexicographic ordering. In each iteration through the loop, we only start up one new simulation. So, at any time, we are only running a finite number of simulations. However, the set of simulations keeps expanding. So, for any string w $w \in \sum^*$, we will eventually start up a simulation on w.

Increasing Resource Bounds

The effect of dovetailing can also be achieved by running simulations with a resource bound and gradually increasing it. For example, the following code can also recognize J.

Increasing resource bound

for i = 0, 1, . . .

- Generate the first i strings (in lexicographic order) in $\sum^*$

- On tape T, start up simulations of M on these i input strings

- Run the set of simulations for i steps.

- If any simulation has accepted, halt and accept

- Otherwise increment i and repeat the loop

Each iteration of the loop does only a finite amount of work: i steps for each of i simulations. However, because i increases without bound, the loop will eventually consider every string in $\sum$* and will run each simulation for more and more steps. So if there is some string w which is accepted by M, our procedure will eventually simulate M on w for enough steps to see it halt.

Pseudocode

Pseudocode is a detailed yet readable description of what a computer program or algorithm must do, expressed in a formally-styled natural language rather than in a programming language. Pseudocode is sometimes used as a detailed step in the process of developing a program. It allows designers or lead programmers to express the design in great detail and provides programmers a detailed template for the next step of writing code in a specific programming language.

Because pseudocode is detailed yet readable, it can be inspected by the team of designers and programmers as a way to ensure that actual programming is likely to match design specifications. Catching errors at the pseudocode stage is less costly than catching them later in the development process. Once the pseudocode is accepted, it is rewritten using the vocabulary and syntax of a programming language. Pseudocode is sometimes used in conjunction with computer-aided software engineering-based methodologies.

It is possible to write programs that will convert a given pseudocode language into a given programming language.

Foundational Elements of Pseudocoding and Coding

The first assumption is that the program runs from top to bottom in a continuous sequence. Think of it like a recipe.

```
Step 1

Step 2

...

Step N
```

Selection

There are going to be points in the program where you will want to divert the flow based on some sort of condition. In that case, just like in English, you'll use an IF statement to tell it where to go if one thing is true and then an ELSE to tell it what to do if the condition is not met. People don't always use "Else" in daily English anymore, but it's the same as "Otherwise".

You can also choose between multiple options by combining the two into one ELSE IF. Here's an example which you may be familiar with if you've been to an amusement park where they only allow children above certain heights to ride the roller coasters:

```
PROGRAM CheckChildHeightBeforeEntry

    IF the child is taller than 4 feet

        give the child a high-five

        Allow the child to enter the ride

    ELSE IF the child is between 3'10" and 4 feet tall

        IF the parents give permission

            Allow the child to enter the ride

        ELSE

            Prevent the child from entering the ride

        END

    ELSE

        Prevent the child from entering the ride

    END

END
```

In the example above, we used indentation to show you where one batch of instructions ends and the next part of our expression begins. We also use "END" to show when each IF statement has finished (even though it's redudnant with the indentation). We've also decided to capitalize all the important keywords like "IF" to make them easier to see. And we wrapped the whole thing in the words PROGRAM and END to identify the boundaries of the script.

The point isn't to stick with an exact style; it's to be as clear as possible so the reader knows what's going on.

Here's the same example with some slightly more formal syntax:

```
PROGRAM CheckChildHeightBeforeEntry

    IF(the child is taller than 4 feet) THEN

        Give the child a high-five;

        Allow the child to enter the ride;

    ELSE IF(the child is between 3'10" and 4 feet tall) THEN

        IF(the parents give permission) THEN

            Allow the child to enter the ride;

        ELSE

            Prevent the child from entering the ride;
```

```
        END

    ELSE

        Prevent the child from entering the ride;

    END

END
```

Iteration

Imagine that you need to perform the same set of instructions many times, relying on feedback from each time to decide whether you're ready to finish yet. The most common way to do that is by using the words WHILE and DO and also specifying a condition. As long as the condition is true, you will keep looping back through your code. Once it's done, the program continues executing as normal.

Let's say you want to fill in a hole:

```
PROGRAM FillInAHole

    WHILE(the hole is not full) DO

        Get a shovel full of dirt

        Empty the shovel onto the hole

    END

    Relax with an ice cold lemonade

END
```

There are a few different ways of writing iterators that will show up again when you start learning code, for instance just saying TIMES:

```
PROGRAM ThreeCheers

    Print "Three Cheers."

    3 TIMES DO

        Print "Hip Hip Hooray."

    END

END
```

Or maybe you want to iterate through each item in a batch of things. A good keyword for that would be EACH, and you would just have to specify which bunch of things to iterate through:

```
PROGRAM CleanTheFridge

    for EACH item in the fridge DO
```

```
    IF(the item is rotten) THEN

        throw away the item

    ELSE

        put the item back in the fridge

    END

  END

  Make Dinner

END
```

Flowchart

A flowchart is a diagram that depicts a process, system or computer algorithm. They are widely used in multiple fields to document, study, plan, improve and communicate often complex processes in clear, easy-to-understand diagrams. Flowcharts, sometimes spelled as flow charts, use rectangles, ovals, diamonds and potentially numerous other shapes to define the type of step, along with connecting arrows to define flow and sequence. They can range from simple, hand-drawn charts to comprehensive computer-drawn diagrams depicting multiple steps and routes. If we consider all the various forms of flowcharts, they are one of the most common diagrams on the planet, used by both technical and non-technical people in numerous fields. Flowcharts are sometimes called by more specialized names such as Process Flowchart, Process Map, Functional Flowchart, Business Process Mapping, Business Process Modeling and Notation (BPMN), or Process Flow Diagram (PFD). They are related to other popular diagrams, such as Data Flow Diagrams (DFDs) and Unified Modeling Language (UML) Activity Diagrams.

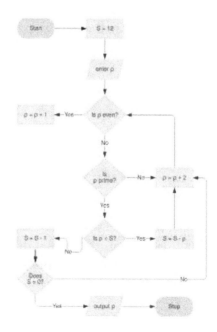

Flowchart Symbols

Here are some of the common flowchart symbols.

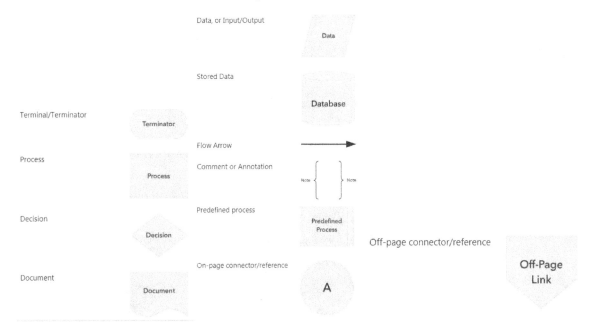

Flowcharts for Computer Programming/Algorithms

As a visual representation of data flow, flowcharts are useful in writing a program or algorithm and explaining it to others or collaborating with them on it. You can use a flowchart to spell out the logic behind a program before ever starting to code the automated process. It can help to organize big-picture thinking and provide a guide when it comes time to code. More specifically, flowcharts can:

- Demonstrate the way code is organized.
- Visualize the execution of code within a program.
- Show the structure of a website or application.
- Understand how users navigate a website or program.

Often, programmers may write pseudocode, a combination of natural language and computer language able to be read by people. This may allow greater detail than the flowchart and serve either as a replacement for the flowchart or as a next step to actual code.

Related diagrams used in computer software include:

- Unified Modeling Language (UML): This is a general-purpose language used in software engineering for modeling.
- Nassi-Shneiderman Diagrams: Used for structured computer programming. Named after Isaac Nassi and Ben Shneiderman, who developed it in 1972 at SUNY-Stony Brook. Also called Structograms.

- DRAKON charts: DRAKON is an algorithmic visual programming language used to produce flowcharts.

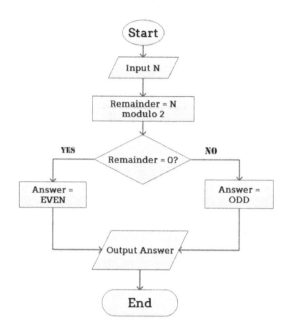

General Rules for Flowcharting

- All boxes of the flowchart are connected with Arrows. (Not lines)

- Flowchart symbols have an entry point on the top of the symbol with no other entry points. The exit point for all flowchart symbols is on the bottom except for the Decision symbol.

- The Decision symbol has two exit points; these can be on the sides or the bottom and one side.

- Generally a flowchart will flow from top to bottom. However, an upward flow can be shown as long as it does not exceed 3 symbols.

- Connectors are used to connect breaks in the flowchart. Examples are:

  - From one page to another page.

  - From the bottom of the page to the top of the same page.

  - An upward flow of more then 3 symbols

- Subroutines and Interrupt programs have their own and independent flowcharts.

- All flow charts start with a Terminal or Predefined Process (for interrupt programs or subroutines) symbol.

- All flowcharts end with a terminal or a contentious loop.

Flowcharting uses symbols that have been in use for a number of years to represent the type of operations and/or processes being performed. The standardised format provides a common method for people to visualise problems together in the same manner. The use of standardised symbols makes the flow charts easier to interpret, however, standardizing symbols is not as important as the sequence of activities that make up the process.

Some Examples of Flowcharts

Now, we will discuss some examples on flowcharting. These examples will help in proper understanding of flowcharting technique. This will help you in program development process.

Problem: Find the area of a circle of radius r

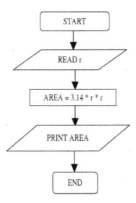

Problem: Convert temperature Fahrenheit to Celsius.

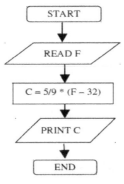

Problem: Flowchart for an algorithm which gets two numbers and prints sum of their value

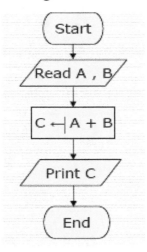

Problem: Algorithm for find the greater number between two numbers.

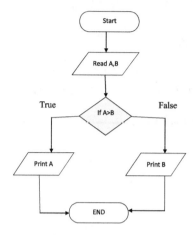

Problem: Flowchart for the problem of printing even numbers between 9 and 100:

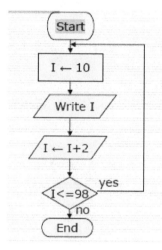

Problem: Flowchart for the problem of printing odd numbers less than a given number. It should also calculate their sum and count.

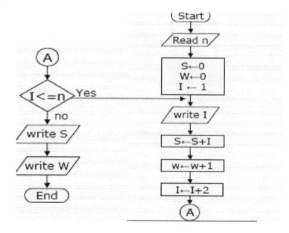

Problem: Flowchart for the calculate the average from 25 exam scores.

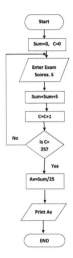

Advantages of Using Flowcharts

As we discussed flow chart is used for representing algorithm in pictorial form. This pictorial representation of a solution/system is having many advantages. These advantages are as follows:

1) Communication: A Flowchart can be used as a better way of communication of the logic of a system and steps involve in the solution, to all concerned particularly to the client of system.

2) Effective analysis: A flowchart of a problem can be used for effective analysis of the problem.

3) Documentation of Program/System: Program flowcharts are a vital part of a good program documentation. Program document is used for various purposes like knowing the components in the program, complexity of the program etc.

4) Efficient Program Maintenance: Once a program is developed and becomes operational it needs time to time maintenance. With help of flowchart maintenance become easier.

5) Coding of the Program: Any design of solution of a problem is finally converted into computer program. Writing code referring the flowchart of the solution become easy.

Randomized Algorithm

An algorithm that uses random numbers to decide what to do next anywhere in its logic is called Randomized Algorithm.. For example, in Randomized Quick Sort, we use random number to pick the next pivot (or we randomly shuffle the array). And in Karger's algorithm, we randomly pick an edge.

Some randomized algorithms have deterministic time complexity. For example, this implementation of Karger's algorithm has time complexity as O(E). Such algorithms are called Monte Carlo Algorithms and are easier to analyse for worst case. On the other hand, time complexity of other randomized algorithms (other than Las Vegas) is dependent on value of random variable. Such Randomized algorithms are called Las Vegas Algorithms. These algorithms are typically analysed for expected worst case. To compute expected time taken in worst case, all possible values of the used random variable needs to be considered in worst case and time taken by every possible value needs to be evaluated. Average of all evaluated times is the expected worst case time complexity. Below facts are generally helpful in analysis os such algorithms.

For example consider below a randomized version of Quick Sort.

A Central Pivot is a pivot that divides the array in such a way that one side has at-least 1/4 elements.

```
// Sorts an array arr[low..high]

randQuickSort(arr[], low, high)

1. If low >= high, then EXIT.

2. While pivot 'x' is not a Central Pivot.

   (i)    Choose uniformly at random a number from [low..high].

          Let the randomly picked number number be x.

   (ii)   Count elements in arr[low..high] that are smaller

          than arr[x]. Let this count be sc.

   (iii)  Count elements in arr[low..high] that are greater

          than arr[x]. Let this count be gc.

   (iv)   Let n = (high-low+1). If sc >= n/4 and

          gc >= n/4, then x is a central pivot.

3. Partition arr[low..high] around the pivot x.

4. // Recur for smaller elements

   randQuickSort(arr, low, sc-1)

5. // Recur for greater elements

   randQuickSort(arr, high-gc+1, high)
```

The important thing in our analysis is, time taken by step 2 is $O(n)$.

The probability that the randomly chosen element is central pivot is 1/2. Therefore, expected number of times the while loop runs is 2. Thus, the expected time complexity of step 2 is $O(n)$.

In worst case, each partition divides array such that one side has $n/4$ elements and other side has $3n/4$ elements. The worst case height of recursion tree is $\log_{3/4} n$ which is $O(\log n)$.

```
T(n) < T(n/4) + T(3n/4) + O(n)

T(n) < 2T(3n/4) + O(n)

Solution of above recurrence is O(n Log n)
```

Las Vegas Algorithm

A randomized algorithm is called a Las Vegas algorithm if it always returns the correct answer, but its runtime bounds hold only in expectation.

In Las Vegas algorithms, runtime is at the mercy of randomness, but the algorithm always succeeds in giving a correct answer.

Randomized Quicksort Analysis

Recall that the randomized quicksort algorithm picks a pivot at random, and then partitions the elements into three sets: all the elements less than the pivot, all elements equal to the pivot, and all elements greater than the pivot.

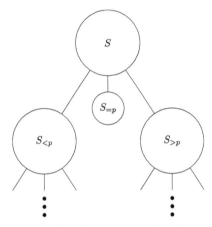

We analyze the runtime using charging. In the computation tree shown above, we count the number times each element appears. The sum over all elements is equal to the sum of the sizes of all the sets in the computation tree, which is proportional to the runtime.

Claim: The number of times an element appears in sets in the computation tree is $O(\log_n)$ in expectation.

Each set S in the computation tree has three children. Let S=p be child set with elements equal to the pivot. Let $S_{>p}$ and $S_{<p}$ be defined similarly. We color the tree edges to these children as follows:

- Color the edge to S$_{=p\ red}$.

- Color the edge to the larger of $S_{>p}$ and $S_{<p}$ black.

- Color the edge to the smaller of   and $S_{<p}$ blue.

Now, we trace the path of some element e through the computation tree, and count the number of edges of each color along the path.

- The number of red edges is 1. Only the last edge can be red.

- The number of blue edges is at most $\log_2 n$, since the smaller of $S_{>p}$ and $S_{<p}$ has at most

$$\frac{1}{2} \cdot |S|$$

- The number of black edges, using the definitions we have given, could be large.

What is the probability that an edge is black? That is, given that $e \in S$, what is the probability that the next edge in $e's$ path is black? Suppose e is the smallest element in the array

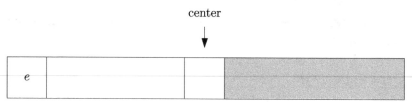

For this element, any pivot in the right half of the array, illustrated with the shaded region in the image above, will cause $e's$ next edge to black. Therefore, the probability that the next edge is black in this case is roughly $\frac{1}{2}$.

However, consider some element e near the center of the array

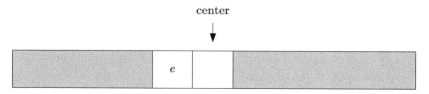

The shaded region shows which pivots will cause the next edge in $e's$ path to be black. For this element, the probability that the next edge is black is nearly 1. The probability will be high for all elements near the center of the array.

We need to modify our definition of black edges and blue edges to fix the problem. If $\left|S_{>P}\right| > \frac{3}{4}\left|S\right|$, color the edge to $S_{>p}$ black. Otherwise, color the edge to $S_{<p}$ blue. We color the edge to $S_{>p}$ using identical rules. Note that now it is possible for both edges to be blue (but not both to be black). We have the following:

- The number of red edges is still 1.

- The number of blue edges is at most $log_{4/3} n$.

To calculate the probability of an edge being black, we split the array into four equal parts:

If the pivot is selected from the shaded quadrants, one of the edges will be blue and the other will be black. If the pivot is selected from the non-shaded quadrants, both edges will be blue. Therefore, regardless of which element $e \in S$ we pick, the probability that the next edge on $e's$ path is black is at most $\frac{1}{2}$.

Now, we can bound the number of black edges in a path. Let X_i a random variable, equal to the number of black edges between the ith and the $(i+1)$ st blue edge.

$$\mathbb{E}[X_i] \leq \frac{1}{Psuccess} \leq \frac{1}{1/2} = 2$$

By linearity of expectation, we have

$$E[\textit{total number of black edges}] = \mathbb{E}\left[\sum_i X_i\right] = \sum_i \mathbb{E}[X_i] \leq 2(\log_{4/3} n) = O(\log n)$$

We now need to bound the total running time, T. Let T_e be the amount of running time charged to e (which is proportional to the number of sets e appears in).

$$\mathbb{E}[T] = \mathbb{E}\left[\sum_e T_e\right] = \sum_e \mathbb{E}[T_e] = \sum_e O(\log n) = O(n \log n)$$

Monte Carlo Algorithm

A randomized algorithm is called a Monte Carlo algorithm if it may fail or return incorrect answers, but has runtime independent of the randomness.

The game, Wheel of Fortune, can be played using a Monte Carlo randomized algorithm. Instead of mindfully choosing letters, a player (or computer) picks randomly letters to obtain a solution, as shown in the image below. The more letters a player reveals, the more confident a player becomes in their solution. However, if a player does not guess quickly, the chance that other players will guess the solution also increases. Therefore, a Monte Carlo algorithm is given a deterministic amount of time, in which it must come up with a "guess" based on the information revealed; the best solution it can come up with. This allows for the possibility of being wrong, maybe even a large probability of being wrong if the Monte Carlo algorithm did not have sufficient time to reveal enough useful letters. But providing it with a time limit controls the amount of time the algorithm will take, thereby decreasing the risk of another player guessing and getting the prize. It is important to note, however, that this game differs from a standard Monte Carlo algorithm as the game has one correct solution, whereas for a Monte Carlo algorithm, the 'good enough' solution is an acceptable output.

Estimation of Pi using Monte Carlo Algorithm

One of the basic examples of getting started with the Monte Carlo algorithm is the estimation of Pi.

The idea is to simulate random (x, y) points in a 2-D plane with domain as a square of side 1 unit. Imagine a circle inside the same domain with same diameter and inscribed into the square. We then calculate the ratio of number points that lied inside the circle and total number of generated points.

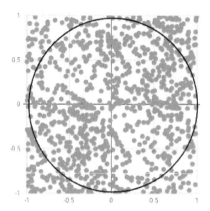

Random points are generated only few of which lie outside the imaginary circle

We know that area of the square is 1 unit sq while that of circle is $\pi * (\frac{1}{2})^2 = \frac{\pi}{4}$. Now for a very large number of generated points,

$$\frac{\text{area of the circle}}{\text{area of the square}} = \frac{\text{no. of points generated inside the circle}}{\text{total no. of points generated or no. of points generated inside the square}}$$

that is,

$$\pi = 4 * \frac{\text{no. of points generated inside the circle}}{\text{no. of points generated inside the square}}$$

The beauty of this algorithm is that we don't need any graphics or simulation to display the generated points. We simply generate random (x, y) pairs and then check if $x^2 + y^2 \leqslant 1$. If yes, we increment the number of points that appears inside the circle. In randomized and simulation algorithms like Monte Carlo, the more the number of iterations, the more accurate the result is. Thus, the title is "Estimating the value of Pi" and not "Calculating the value of Pi". Below is the algorithm for the method:

The Algorithm

1. Initialize circle_points, square_points and interval to 0.

2. Generate random point x.

3. Generate random point y.

4. Calculate d = x*x + y*y.

5. If d <= 1, increment circle_points.

6. Increment square_points.

7. Increment interval.

8. If increment < NO_OF_ITERATIONS, repeat from 2.

9. Calculate pi = 4*(circle_points/square_points).

10. Terminate.

```cpp
/* C++ program for estimation of Pi using Monte
   Carlo Simulation */
#include <bits/stdc++.h>

// Defines precision for x and y values. More the
// interval, more the number of significant digits
#define INTERVAL 10000
using namespace std;

int main()
{
    int interval, i;
    double rand_x, rand_y, origin_dist, pi;
    int circle_points = 0, square_points = 0;

    // Initializing rand()
    srand(time(NULL));

    // Total Random numbers generated = possible x
    // values * possible y values
    for (i = 0; i < (INTERVAL * INTERVAL); i++) {

        // Randomly generated x and y values
        rand_x = double(rand() % (INTERVAL + 1)) / INTERVAL;
        rand_y = double(rand() % (INTERVAL + 1)) / INTERVAL;
```

```cpp
        // Distance between (x, y) from the origin
        origin_dist = rand_x * rand_x + rand_y * rand_y;


        // Checking if (x, y) lies inside the define
        // circle with R=1
        if (origin_dist <= 1)
            circle_points++;


        // Total number of points generated
        square_points++;


        // estimated pi after this iteration
        pi = double(4 * circle_points) / square_points;


        // For visual understanding (Optional)
        cout << rand_x << " " << rand_y << " " << circle_points
            << " " << square_points << " - " << pi << endl << endl;


        // Pausing estimation for first 10 values (Optional)
        if (i < 20)
            getchar();
    }


    // Final Estimated Value
    cout << "\nFinal Estimation of Pi = " << pi;


    return 0;
}
```

Reservoir Sampling

Reservoir sampling is a family of randomized algorithms for randomly choosing k samples from a list of n items, where n is either a very large or unknown number. Typically n is large enough that the list doesn't fit into main memory. For example, a list of search queries in Google and Facebook.

So we are given a big array (or stream) of numbers (to simplify), and we need to write an efficient function to randomly select k numbers where $1 <= k <= n$. Let the input array be *stream[]*.

A simple solution is to create an array *reservoir[]* of maximum size k. One by one randomly select an item from *stream[0..n-1]*. If the selected item is not previously selected, then put it in *reservoir[]*. To check if an item is previously selected or not, we need to search the item in *reservoir[]*. The time complexity of this algorithm will be $O(k^2)$. This can be costly if k is big. Also, this is not efficient if the input is in the form of a stream.

It can be solved in $O(n)$ time. The solution also suits well for input in the form of stream. The idea is similar to this post. Following are the steps.

1) Create an array *reservoir[0..k-1]* and copy first k items of *stream[]* to it.

2) Now one by one consider all items from *(k+1)th* item to nth item.

a) Generate a random number from 0 to i where i is index of current item in *stream[]*. Let the generated random number is j.

b) If j is in range 0 to $k-1$, replace *reservoir[j]* with *arr[i]*

Following is implementation of the above algorithm.

- C/C++

```
// An efficient program to randomly select k items from a stream of items


#include <stdio.h>
#include <stdlib.h>
#include <time.h>


// A utility function to print an array
void printArray(int stream[], int n)
{
    for (int i = 0; i < n; i++)
        printf("%d ", stream[i]);
    printf("\n");
```

```
}


// A function to randomly select k items from stream[0..n-1].
void selectKItems(int stream[], int n, int k)
{
    int i;  // index for elements in stream[]


    // reservoir[] is the output array. Initialize it with
    // first k elements from stream[]
    int reservoir[k];
    for (i = 0; i < k; i++)
        reservoir[i] = stream[i];


    // Use a different seed value so that we don't get
    // same result each time we run this program
    srand(time(NULL));


    // Iterate from the (k+1)th element to nth element
    for (; i < n; i++)
    {
        // Pick a random index from 0 to i.
        int j = rand() % (i+1);


        // If the randomly  picked index is smaller than k, then replace
        // the element present at the index with new element from stream
        if (j < k)
            reservoir[j] = stream[i];
    }


    printf("Following are k randomly selected items \n");
    printArray(reservoir, k);
```

```
}


// Driver program to test above function.

int main ()

{

    int stream[] = {1, 2, 3, 4, 5, 6, 7, 8, 9, 10, 11, 12};

    int n = sizeof (stream) /sizeof (stream[0]);

    int k = 5;

    selectKItems (stream, n, k);

    return 0;

}
```

Output:

```
Following are k randomly selected items

6 2 11 8 12

Output will differ every time as it selects and prints random elements
```

Time Complexity: O(n)

Working

To prove that this solution works perfectly, we must prove that the probability that any item *stream[i]* where $0 <= i < n$ will be in final *reservoir[]* is k/n. Let us divide the proof in two cases as first k items are treated differently.

Case 1: For last *n-k* stream items, i.e., for *stream[i]* where $k <= i < n$

For every such stream item *stream[i]*, we pick a random index from 0 to i and if the picked index is one of the first k indexes, we replace the element at picked index with *stream[i]*

To simplify the proof, let us first consider the *last item*. The probability that the last item is in final reservoir = The probability that one of the first k indexes is picked for last item = k/n (the probability of picking one of the k items from a list of size n)

Let us now consider the *second last item*. The probability that the second last item is in final *reservoir[]* = [Probability that one of the first k indexes is picked in iteration for *stream[n-2]*] X [Probability that the index picked in iteration for *stream[n-1]* is not same as index picked for *stream[n-2]*] = $[k/(n-1)]*[(n-1)/n] = k/n$.

Similarly, we can consider other items for all stream items from *stream[n-1]* to *stream[k]* and generalize the proof.

Case 2: For first k stream items, i.e., for *stream[i]* where $0 <= i < k$

The first k items are initially copied to *reservoir[]* and may be removed later in iterations for *stream[k]*to *stream[n]*.

The probability that an item from *stream[0..k-1]* is in final array = Probability that the item is not picked when items *stream[k]*, *stream[k+1]*, ... *stream[n-1]* are considered = $[k/(k+1)] \times [(k+1)/(k+2)] \times [(k+2)/(k+3)] \times ... \times [(n-1)/n] = k/n$

Deterministic and Non Deterministic Algorithm

Algorithm is deterministic if for a given input the output generated is same for a function. A mathematical function is deterministic. Hence the state is known at every step of the algorithm. For instance if you are sorting elements that are strictly ordered (no equal elements) the output is well defined and so the algorithm is deterministic. In fact most of the computer algorithms are deterministic. Undeterminism usually appears when you have some parallelization or some equal elements that are only equal according to some non-full criteria.

A nondeterministic algorithm can provide different outputs for the same input on different executions. Unlike a deterministic algorithm which produces only a single output for the same input even on different runs, a nondeterministic algorithm travels in various routes to arrive at the different outcomes. Nondeterministic algorithms are useful for finding approximate solutions, when an exact solution is difficult or expensive to derive using a deterministic algorithm.

One example of a nondeterministic algorithm is the execution of concurrent algorithms with race conditions, which can exhibit different outputs on different runs. Unlike a deterministic algorithm which travels a single path from input to output, a nondeterministic algorithm can take many paths, with some arriving at the same outputs, and others arriving at different outputs. This feature is mathematically used in nondeterministic computation models like nondeterministic finite automaton.

A nondeterministic algorithm is capable of execution on a deterministic computer which has an unlimited number of parallel processors. A nondeterministic algorithm usually has two phases and output steps. The first phase is the guessing phase, which makes use of arbitrary characters to run the problem. The second phase is the verifying phase, which returns true or false for the chosen string. There are many problems which can be conceptualized with help of nondeterministic algorithms including the unresolved problem of P vs NP in computing theory. Nondeterministic algorithms are used in solving problems which allow multiple outcomes. Every outcome the nondeterministic algorithm produces is valid, regardless of the choices made by the algorithm during execution.

External Memory Algorithm

External memory (EM) algorithms are designed for computational problems in which the size of the internal memory of the computer is only a small fraction of the problem size.

A good EM algorithm makes full use of the resources at its s disposal. This includes s consideration of the following factors:

1. the disk blocking factor B, as described above,

2. the available internal memory, captured by the parameter M, the number of data items that fit into internal memory,

3. the ability to perform I/O concurrently to all D available disk drives,

4. full utilization of all p available processors, and

5. efficient use of the communication bandwidth available between processors.

Model

External memory algorithms are analyzed in the external memory model.

The external-memory model was introduced by Aggarwal and Vitter in 1988, and is sometimes also known as the I/O model or disk access model (DAM). It captures a two-layered memory hierarchy. The model is based on a computer with a CPU connected directly to a fast cache of size M, which is connected to a much larger and slower disk.

Both the cache and disk are divided into blocks of size B; the cache thus holds $\frac{M}{B}$ blocks, while the disk can hold many more. The CPU can only operate directly on the data stored in cache. Algorithms can make memory transfer operations, which read a block from disk to cache, or write a block from cache to disk. The cost of an algorithm is the number of memory transfers required; operations on cached data are considered free.

Clearly any algorithm that has running time $T(N)$ in the RAM model can be trivially converted into an external-memory algorithm that requires no more than $T(N)$ memory transfers, by ignoring locality.

We want to do better than this. Ideally, we would like to achieve $\frac{T(N)}{B}$, but this optimum is often hard to achieve.

Searching

The ideal search tree structure for the external-memory model is a B-tree with branching factor $\Theta(B)$, such that each node fits in a block. This allows us to perform Insert, Delete, and Search operations using $O(\log_{B+1} N)$ memory transfers and $O(\log N)$ time in the comparison model.

This is an optimal bound for the external-memory comparison-model searching, as an information theoretic argument shows. Suppose that we wish to discover where some element x is located in an array of n elements. Expressing the answer (e.g. as an index into the array) requires at least $\lg(N+1)$ bits. Each time a block is transferred, it reads at most $\Theta(B)$ elements, learning where x fits into these B elements. This provides no more than $O\big(\lg(B+1)\big)$ bits of information.

Since we need to determine $\lg(N+1)$ bits of information, at least $\dfrac{\lg(N+1)}{O(\lg(B+1))} = \Omega(\lg_{B+1} N)$ memory transfers are required.

Sorting

The natural companion to the searching problem is sorting. In the RAM model, we can sort N elements by inserting them into a B-tree and performing N Delete-Min operations. This gives us $O(N \lg N)$ runtime, which we know to be optimal. We can do the same in the external-memory model, and perform sorting in $O(n \lg_{B+1} N)$ memory transfers. But this is not optimal.

We can do better with $\dfrac{M}{B}$-way mergesort, which divides a sorting problem into $\dfrac{M}{B}$ subproblems, recursively sorts them, and merges them.

This gives us a cost of $O\left(\dfrac{N}{B} \log_{\frac{M}{B}} \dfrac{N}{B}\right)$ memory transfers. In fact, this is optimal: it can be shown by a similar information-theoretic argument to the one above that sorting N elements in the comparison model requires $\Omega\left(\dfrac{N}{B} \log_{\frac{M}{B}} \dfrac{N}{B}\right)$ memory transfers.

Permutation

The permutation problem is, given N elements and a permutation, to rearrange the elements according to that permutation. We can do this in $O(N)$ memory transfers by moving each element to its new position, ignoring locality.

We can also solve the problem with $O\left(\dfrac{N}{B} \log_{\frac{M}{B}} \dfrac{N}{B}\right)$ memory transfers by sorting the elements, sorting the permutation, and then applying the permutation in reverse. This gives us a bound of

$$O\left(\min\left(N, \dfrac{N}{B} \log_{\frac{M}{B}} \dfrac{N}{B}\right)\right)$$

In the indivisible model, where elements cannot be divided between blocks, there is a matching lower bound. It remains an open problem whether one can do better in a general model.

Buffer Trees

B-trees are optimal for searching, but cannot be used as the basis for an optimal sorting algorithm.

The buffer tree [2] is a data structure that provides Insert, Delete, Delete-Min, and Batched-Search operations using $O\left(\dfrac{1}{B} \log_{\frac{M}{B}} \dfrac{N}{B}\right)$ amortized memory transfers per operation.

(Notice that this bound is usually o(1), so it has to be amortized.) Batched-Search is a delayed query: it performs a search for a particular value in the tree as it appears at a particular time, but does not give the results immediately; they become available later, after other operations have been performed.

Cache-Oblivious Model

The cache-oblivious model is a variation of the external-memory model introduced by Frigo, Leiserson, Prokop, and Ramachandran in 1999. In this model, the algorithm does not know the size M of its cache, or the block size B. This means that it cannot perform its own memory management, explicitly performing memory transfers. Instead, algorithms are RAM algorithms, and block transfers are performed automatically, triggered by element accesses, using the offline optimal block replacement strategy. Though the use of the offline optimal block replacement strategy sounds like it would pose a problem for practical applications, in fact there are a number of competitive block replacement strategies (FIFO, LRU, etc.) that are within a factor of 2 of optimal given a cache of twice the size.

Though the algorithm does not know the size M of its cache, we will routinely assume that $M \geq c.B$ for any constant c, i.e. that the cache can hold at least c blocks. (In practice, however, the algorithms we consider will not require c to be very large at all.)

From a theoretical standpoint, the cache-oblivious model is appealing because it is very clean. A cache-oblivious algorithm is simply a RAM algorithm; it is only the analysis that differs. The cache-oblivious model also works well for multilevel memory hierarchies, unlike the external-memory model, which only captures a two-level hierarchy. Since a cache-oblivious algorithm provides the desired result for any cache size and block size, it will work with every cache and block size at each level of the hierarchy, thus giving the same bound overall.

B-tree: A cache-oblivious variant of the B-tree provides the Insert, Delete, and Search operations with $O\left(\log_{B+1} N\right)$ memory transfers, as in the external-memory model.

Sorting: As in the external-memory model, sorting N elements can be performed cache-obliviously using $O\left(\dfrac{N}{B}\log_{\frac{M}{B}}\dfrac{N}{B}\right)$ memory transfers. Note, however, that this requires the tall-cache assumption: that $M = \Omega(B^{1+C})$. The external-memory sorting algorithm does not require this to be the case. The tall-cache assumption is necessary.

Priority queue: A priority queue can be implemented that executes the Insert, Delete, and De-lete-Min operations in $O\left(\dfrac{1}{B}\log_{\frac{M}{B}}\dfrac{N}{B}\right)$ memory transfers.

Static Search Trees

How to construct a static search tree that can perform searches using $O\left(\log_{B+1} N\right)$ memory transfers? We do this by constructing a complete binary search tree with the N elements stored in sorted order.

In order to achieve the desired memory transfer bound, we will store the tree on disk using a representation known as the van Emde Boas layout. It uses the van Emde Boas idea of dividing the tree at the middle level of edges, giving a top subtree of $\sqrt{N}$ elements, and $\sqrt{N}$ subtrees of N elements each. We recursively lay out each of the $\sqrt{N}+1$ subtrees, then concatenate them, ensuring that each subtree is stored consecutively.

Claim: Performing a search on a search tree in the van Emde Boas layout requires $O\left(\log_{B+1} N\right)$ memory transfers.

Proof: We can stop our analysis when we reach a subtree that has size less than B : the algorithm will continue, but since the subtree fits entirely within one block, it will fit in the cache, and no further memory transfers will be required. So consider the level of recursion that "straddles" B: the whole structure at that level has size greater than B :, but each subtree has size at most B . Each subtree requires at most two memory transfers to access (it can fit in one block, but it might actually need to be stored in two blocks if it is "out of frame" with the block boundaries.)

Since we are considering the level that straddles B, each subtree must have height at least $\frac{1}{2}\lg B$: : otherwise two levels of these subtrees would have height less than $\lg B$, and thus contain less than B elements, violating the definition of the level that straddles B. So we will need to access $\dfrac{1gN}{\frac{1}{2}\lg B} = 2\log_B N$ subtrees.

Each subtree access can be done in 2 memory transfers, so we need no more than $4\log_B N$ memory transfers to perform a search.

This technique can be generalized to trees whose height is not a power of 2, and non-binary trees of constant degree (except for degree 1, of course).

Ordered File Maintenance

Before we proceed to describe how to make these search trees dynamic, we will need a result to use as a black box.

The ordered file maintenance (OFM) problem is to store N elements in order in an array of size O (N). This array can have gaps, but any two consecutive elements must be separated by at most O(1) gaps. An ordered file maintenance data structure must support two operations: to Insert an element between two other elements, preserving the order of the array, and to Delete an element.

Our black box can accomplish these two operations by rearranging $O\left(lg^2 N\right)$ consecutive elements, amortized.

Dynamic Search Trees

Now we can turn to how to build a dynamic search tree. This description follows that of [5], a simplification of.

We store our elements in an ordered file structure, then build a static search tree "on top" of the ordered file structure: the leaves correspond to the array slots in the ordered file structure (including blank spaces where there are gaps in the ordered file array). The search tree invariant is that each internal node stores the maximum value of its children (ignoring the blank spaces due to empty slots).

This structure allows us to perform searches with $O\left(lg_{B+1} N\right)$ memory transfers in the standard way. Performing an insertion is a bit more complicated. We begin by performing a Search to find the predecessor or successor of our new element, and thus find out where to insert it into the ordered file maintenance structure. Performing the OFM insert changes $O(\lg^2 N)$ cells. Then, for all of these cells, we update the corresponding leaves of the search tree, and propagate the changes upward in a post-order traversal of the changed leaves and their ancestors.

Claim 2: If k cells in the ordered file structure are changed, the cost of updating the corresponding leaves and ancestors in the $O\left(\lg_{B+1} N + \dfrac{k}{B}\right)$ search tree memory transfers.

Proof. As before, consider the level of detail straddling B. Consider the bottom two levels of subtrees (each of size at most B). We are performing updates in a post-order traversal of the tree.

For the bottom two levels, this is essentially a scanning over the subtrees, each of which fits in one block: we perform the updates in one subtree at the bottom level, then move up to the subtree at the next higher level to perform some updates before moving on to the next subtree at the bottom level. So as long as our cache is big enough to hold six blocks at once (for a block of the ordered file maintenance structure, the subtree at the bottom level, and the subtree at the second-from-bottom level — actually two each, since we do not know where the block boundaries are and may be "out of frame" as before), we need $O\left(\dfrac{k}{B}\right)$ memory transfers to update the bottom two levels.

Now we consider the updates above the bottom two levels. The larger subtrees composed of the bottom two levels have size $J > B$ since we are considering the level of detail that straddles B. This means that after the bottom two levels, J leaves are reduced to one node, so there are $O\left(\dfrac{K}{J}\right) = O\left(\dfrac{K}{B}\right)$ elements to be traversed until the least common ancestor has been reached. We can afford one memory transfer per element. Then, after the least common ancestor has been reached, there are $O(\lg_{B+1} N)$ elements on the path to the root. So the total cost is $O\left(\lg_{B+1}^{N+\frac{K}{B}}\right)$ memory transfers.

We now have a tree that can perform Insert operations in $O\left(\lg_{B+1} N + \dfrac{\lg^2 N}{B}\right)$ amortized memory transfers (and Delete operations with the same cost, in a similar way), and searches in $O(\lg_{B+1} N)$ memory transfers.

To eliminate the $O\left(\dfrac{\lg^2 N}{B}\right)$ factor, we can use indirection. We cluster elements into groups of $O(\lg N)$ elements, and store the minimum of the group in the ordered file maintenance structure and search tree as before. Now performing a Insert operation requires rewriting an entire group, but this costs $O\left(\dfrac{\lg N}{B}\right) = O(\lg_B N)$ memory transfers. If the size of a group grows too large after O (lg N) Inserts, we may need to split the group, but we can amortize away the cost of this in the standard way. Now the cost of a update operation is $O\left(\lg_{B+1} N + \dfrac{lgN}{B}\right) = O(\lg_{B+1} N)$ amortized memory transfers.

Online Algorithms and Competitive Analysis

An online algorithm is one that can process its input piece-by-piece in a serial fashion, i.e., in the order that the input is fed to the algorithm, without having the entire input available from the start. Contrasting to this is an Offline algorithm.

For example, the common selection sort requires all items to be given first to be able to sort, hence Offline. While insertion sort could be an example of online algorithms as it works with 2 elements at a time. Because it does not know the whole input, an online algorithm is forced to make decisions that may later turn out not to be optimal which is the case in insertion sort.

The K-server problem is another example of online algorithms as each request arrives, the algorithm must determine which server to move to the requested point.

Further online algorithm examples would be for: Stock markets, paging, resource allocation, robotics for exploring unknown terrains such as the rovers on mars.

In contrast, an offline algorithm is given the whole problem data from the beginning and is required to output an answer which solves the problem at hand. In operations research, the area in which online algorithms are developed is called online optimization.

In online optimization the input is modeled as a finite request sequence r_1, r_2, ... which must be served and which is revealed step by step to an online algorithm. The way in which the request sequence is served, depends on the specific online paradigm. The two most common models are the sequence model and the time stamp model.

Let ALG be an online algorithm. In the sequence model requests must be served in the same order in which they occur. More precisely, when serving request r_j, the online algorithm ALG does not know of requests r_i with $i > j$ (or the total number of requests). When request r_j is presented it must be served by ALG according to the specific rules of the problem. The serving of r_j incurs a cost and the overall goal is to minimize the total service cost. The decision by ALG of how to serve r_j is irrevocable. Only after r_j has been served, the next request r_j+1 becomes known to ALG.

In the time stamp model each request has a arrival or release time at which it becomes available for service. The release time $t_j \geq 0$ is a nonnegative real number and specifies the time at which request r_j is released (becomes known to an online algorithm). An online algorithm ALG must determine its behavior at a certain moment t in time as a function of all the requests released up to time t and of the current time t. Again, we are in the situation that an online algorithm ALG is confronted with a finite sequence r_1, r_2, ... of requests which is given in order of non-decreasing release times and the service of each request incurs a cost for ALG. The difference to the sequence model is that the online algorithm is allowed to wait and to revoke decisions and that requests need not be served in the order of their occurrence.

Waiting incurs additional costs, typically depending on the elapsed time. Previously made decisions may, of course, only be revoked as long as they have not been executed.

Some of the example online problems are:

- Resource management in operating systems: Paging is a classical online problem where a two-level memory system has to be maintained which consists of a small fast memory and a large slow memory. The main aim is to keep actively referenced pages in fast memory without any knowledge of future requests for the pages.

- Data structures: Consider a data structure such as a linear linked list or a tree. This structure has to be maintained dynamically so that a sequence of accesses to elements can be served at low cost. Future access patterns are unknown.

- Scheduling: It consists of scheduling a sequence of jobs on a set of machines in order to optimize a given objective function. The jobs arrive one by one and no prior knowledge about the future requests is provided. They have to be scheduled immediately.

- Networks: Many online problems in this area arise in the context of data transmission. The problem can be, for instance, to dynamically maintain a set of open connections between network nodes without knowing which connections are needed in the future.

The quality of online algorithms is usually evaluated using competitive analysis. The idea of competitiveness is to compare the output generated by an online algorithm to the output produced by an optimal offline algorithm.

Analysis of Online Algorithms

Online problems had been studied already explicitly or implicitly during the nineteen-seventies and nineteen-eighties. However, broad systematic investigation only started when Sleator and Tarja suggested comparing an online algorithm to an optimal offline algorithm, thus laying the foundations of competitive analysis. An online algorithm ALG is called c-competitive if the objective function value of the solution produced by ALG on any input sequence is at most c times that of an optimal offline algorithm on the same input. Here, the "optimal offline algorithm" has complete knowledge about the whole input sequence.

Observe that in the above definition there is no restriction on the computational resources of an online algorithm. The only scarce resource in competitive analysis is information as quoted by Krumke. Competitive analysis of online algorithms can be imagined as a game between an online player and a malicious offline adversary. The online player uses an online algorithm to process an input which is generated by the adversary. If the adversary knows the (deterministic) strategy of the online player, he can construct a request sequence which maximizes the ratio between the player's cost and the optimal offline cost. For randomized algorithms we have to define what kind of information about the online player is available to the adversary.

Competitive Analysis

In competitive analysis, the output generated by an online algorithm is compared to the output generated by an optimal offline algorithm. An optimal offline algorithm already knows the entire input data and thus can result into an optimal output, whereas such is not the case with an online algorithm. The better an online algorithm approximates the optimal solution, the more competitive the algorithm is said to be.

The competitive ratio of an online algorithm for an optimization problem is simply the approximation ratio achieved by the algorithm, that is, the worst-case ratio between the cost of the solution found by the algorithm and the cost of an optimal solution.

Online algorithms can be either deterministic or randomized. The competitive analysis of deterministic online algorithm is straightforward whereas the randomized case is craftier. The competitive ratio of a randomized online algorithm A is defined with respect to an adversary. An adversary can be defined as a pair (Q, S), where Q is the requesting component, responsible for creating the request sequence, and S is the servicing component, which is an algorithm responsible for answering all requests created by Q. The nature of these components will determine the type of adversary-oblivious, adaptive-online or adaptive-offline adversary.

- Oblivious Adversary: The oblivious adversary has to generate a complete request sequence in advance, before any requests are served by the online algorithm. The adversary is charged the cost of the optimum offline algorithm for that sequence.

- Adaptive Online Adversary: This adversary may observe the online algorithm and generate the next request based on the algorithm's (randomized) answers to all previous requests. The adversary must serve each request online, i.e., without knowing the random choices made by the online algorithm on the present or any future request.

- Adaptive Offline Adversary: This adversary also generates a request sequence adaptively. However, it is charged the optimum offline cost for that sequence.

Extensions of Competitive Analysis

Competitive analysis is a sort of worst-case analysis. It has (rightly) been criticized as being overly pessimistic as often the adversary is simply too powerful and allows only insignificant competitiveness results.

In comparative analysis the class of algorithms where the offline algorithm comparative is chosen from is restricted. This concept has been introduced in the context analysis of the paging problem.

Another approach to strengthen the position of an online algorithm is the concept of resource augmentation. Here, the online algorithm is given more resources (e.g., more or faster machines in scheduling) to serve requests than the offline adversary.

The diffuse adversary model introduced in, deals with the situation where the input is chosen by an adversary according to some probability distribution. Although the online algorithm is not aware of the distribution itself, it is provided the information that this distribution belongs to a specific class of distributions.

All of the extensions and alternatives to competitive analysis have been proven to be useful for some specific problem and powerful enough to obtain significant results. However, competitive analysis could not be replaced by any of these approaches and is still, the standard tool in the theoretical analysis of online algorithms.

References

- Weiss, Mark A. (2005). Data Structures and Algorithm Analysis in C++. Addison-Wesley. p. 480. ISBN 0321375319

- What-is-a-computer-algorithm-design-examples-optimization: study.com, Retrieved 19 June 2018

- Bodlaender, Hans L.; Downey, Rod G.; Fellows, Michael R.; Hermelin, Danny (2009), "On problems without polynomial kernels", Journal of Computer and System Sciences, 75(8): 423–434, doi:10.1016/j.jcss.2009.04.001

- The-elements-of-pseudocode, software-engineering-basics: vikingcodeschool.com, Retrieved 09 March 2018

- Flum, Jörg; Grohe, Martin (2006), Parameterized Complexity Theory, Springer, ISBN 978-3-540-29952-3, retrieved 2010-03-05

- What-is-a-flowchart-tutorial: lucidchart.com, Retrieved 10 March 2018

- Chen, Jianer; Kanj, Iyad A.; Jia, Weijia (2001), "Vertex cover: Further observations and further improvements", Journal of Algorithms, 41 (2): 280–301, doi:10.1006/jagm.2001.1186

- Randomized-algorithms-overview: brilliant.org, Retrieved 19 July 2018

- Downey, R. G.; Fellows, M. R. (1999), Parameterized Complexity, Monographs in Computer Science, Springer, doi:10.1007/978-1-4612-0515-9, ISBN 0-387-94883-X, MR 1656112

- Reservoir-sampling: geeksforgeeks.org, Retrieved 25 June 2018

- Lampis, Michael (2011), "A kernel of order 2k – c log k for vertex cover", Information Processing Letters, 111 (23–24): 1089–1091, doi:10.1016/j.ipl.2011.09.003

- Nondeterministic-algorithm-24618: techopedia.com, Retrieved 17 May 2018

- Niedermeier, Rolf (2006), Invitation to Fixed-Parameter Algorithms, Oxford University Press, ISBN 0-19-856607-7, archived from the original on 2008-09-24, retrieved 2017-06-01

Computational Complexity of an Algorithm

The computational complexity of an algorithm is a measure of the amount of resources that is needed for running it. Complexity may be classified into various types, such as worst-case complexity, average-case complexity, time complexity and space complexity. This chapter has been carefully written to provide an easy understanding of computational complexity of an algorithm through the elucidation of the chief aspects of computational complexity theory, Big O notation, asymptotic computational complexity, analysis of algorithms, etc.

Computational Complexity

The term "computational complexity" has two usages which must be distinguished. On the one hand, it refers to an *algorithm* for solving instances of a *problem*: broadly stated, the computational complexity of an algorithm is a measure of how many steps the algorithm will require in the worst case for an instance or input of a given size. The number of steps is measured as a function of that size.

The term's second, more important use is in reference to a problem itself. The theory of computational complexity involves classifying problems according to their inherent tractability or intractability — that is, whether they are "easy" or "hard" to solve. This classification scheme includes the well-known classes P and NP; the terms "NP-complete" and "NP-hard" are related to the class NP.

Algorithms and Complexity

To understand what is meant by the complexity of an algorithm, we must define algorithms, problems, and problem instances. Moreover, we must understand how one measures the size of a problem instance and what constitutes a "step" in an algorithm. A problem is an abstract description coupled with a question requiring an answer; for example, the Traveling Salesman Problem (TSP) is: "Given a graph with nodes and edges and costs associated with the edges, what is a least-cost closed walk (or tour) containing each of the nodes exactly once?" An instance of a problem, on the other hand, includes an exact specification of the data: for example, "The graph contains nodes 1, 2, 3, 4, 5, and 6, and edges (1, 2) with cost 10, (1, 3) with cost 14,... "and so on. Stated more mathematically, a problem can be thought of as a function p that maps an instance x to an output $p(x)$.

An algorithm for a problem is a set of instructions guaranteed to find the correct solution to any instance in a finite number of steps. In other words, for a problem p, an algorithm is a finite procedure for computing $p(x)$ for any given input x. Computer scientists model algorithms by a mathematical construct called a Turing machine, but we will consider a more concrete model here. In a simple model of a computing device, a "step" consists of one of the following operations: addition, subtraction, multiplication, finite-precision division, and comparison of two numbers. Thus if an algorithm requires one hundred additions and 220 comparisons for some instance, we say that the algorithm requires 320 steps on that instance. In order to make this number meaningful, we would like to express it as a function of the size of the corresponding instance, but determining the exact function would be impractical. Instead, since we are really concerned with how long the algorithm takes (in the worst case) asymptotically as the size of an instance gets large, we formulate a simple function of the input size that is a reasonably tight upper bound on the actual number of steps. Such a function is called the complexity or running time of the algorithm.

Technically, the size of an instance is the number of bits required to encode it. It is measured in terms of the inherent dimensions of the instance (such as the number of nodes and edges in a graph), plus the number of bits required to encode the numerical information in the instance (such as the edge costs). Since numerical data are encoded in binary, an integer C requires about $log_2|C|$ bits to encode and so contributes logarithmically to the size of the instance. The running time of the algorithm is then expressed as a function of these parameters, rather than the precise input size. For example, for the TSP, an algorithm's running time might be expressed as a function of the number of nodes, the number of edges, and the maximum number of bits required to encode any edge cost. The complexity of an algorithm is only a rough estimate of the number of steps that will be required on an instance. In general — and particularly in analyzing the inherent tractability of a problem — we are interested in an asymptotic analysis: how does the running time grow as the size of the instance gets very large? For these reasons, it is useful to introduce *Big-O* notation. For two functions $f(t)$ and $g(t)$ of a nonnegative parameter t, we say that $f(t) = O(g(t))$ if there is a constant $c > 0$ such that, for all sufficiently large t, $f(t) \leq cg(t)$. The function $cg(t)$ is thus an asymptotic upper bound on f. For example, $100(t^2 + t) = O(t^2)$, since by taking $c = 101$ the relation follows for $t \geq 100$; however, $0.0001 \ t^3$ is not $O(t^2)$. Notice that it is possible for $f(t) = O(g(t))$ and $g(t) = O(f(t))$ simultaneously.

We say that an algorithm runs in polynomial time (is a polynomial-time algorithm) if the running time $f(t) = O(P(t))$, where $P(t)$ is a polynomial function of the input size. Polynomial-time algorithms are generally (and formally) considered efficient, and problems for which polynomial time algorithms exist are considered "easy." In the text that follows, when we use the term "polynomial," we mean as a function of the input size.

The Classes P and NP

In order to establish a formal setting for discussing the relative tractability of problems, computer scientists first define a large class of problems called *recognition* (or decision) *problems*. This class comprises precisely those problems whose associated question requires the answer "yes" or "no." For example, consider the problem of determining whether an undirected graph is connected (that is, whether there a path between every pair of nodes in the graph). This problem's input is a graph G consisting of nodes and edges, and its question is, "Is G connected?" Notice that most optimization problems are not recognition problems, but most have recognition counterparts. For example, a recognition version of the TSP has as input both a graph G, with costs on the edges, *and* a number K. The associated question is, "Does G contain a traveling salesman tour of length less than or equal to K?" In general, an optimization problem is not much harder to solve than its recognition counterpart. One can usually embed the recognition algorithm in a binary search over the possible objective function values to solve the optimization problem with a polynomial number of calls to the embedded algorithm.

The class P is defined as the set of recognition problems for which there exists a polynomial-time algorithm, where "*P*" stands for "polynomial time." Thus, *P* comprises those problems that are formally considered "easy." The larger problem class *NP* contains the class *P*. The term "*NP*" stands for "nondeterministic polynomial" and refers to a different, hypothetical model of computation, which can solve the problems in *NP* in polynomial time.

The class *NP* consists of all recognition problems with the following property: for any "yes"-instance of the problem there exists a polynomial-length "certificate" or proof of this fact that can be verified in polynomial time. The easiest way to understand this idea is by considering the position of an omniscient being (say, the wizard Merlin) who is trying to convince a mere mortal that some instance is a yes-instance. Suppose the problem is the recognition version of the TSP, and the instance is a graph *G* and the number $K = 100$. Merlin knows that the instance does contain a tour with length at most 100. To convince the mortal of this fact, he simply hands her a list of the edges of this tour. This list is the certificate: it is polynomial in length, and the mortal can easily verify, in polynomial time, that the edges do in fact form a tour with length at most 100.

There is an inherent asymmetry between "yes" and "no" in the definition of *NP*. For example, there is no obvious, succinct way for Merlin to convince a mortal that a particular instance does NOT contain a tour with length at most 100. In fact, by reversing the roles played by "yes" and "no" we obtain a problem class known as *Co-NP*. In particular, for every recognition problem in *NP* there is an associated recognition problem in *Co-NP* obtained by framing the *NP* question in the negative (e.g., "Do *all* traveling salesman tours in *G* have length *greater* than *K*?"). Many recognition problems are believed to lie outside both of the classes *NP* and *Co-NP*, because they seem to possess no appropriate "certificate." An example would be the problem consisting of a graph *G* and two numbers *K* and *L*, with the question, "Is the number of distinct traveling salesman tours in *G* with length at most *K* exactly equal to *L*?"

Time Complexity

Time complexity of an algorithm signifies the total time required by the program to run till its completion.

The time complexity of algorithms is most commonly expressed using the big O notation. It's an asymptotic notation to represent the time complexity.

Time Complexity is most commonly estimated by counting the number of elementary steps performed by any algorithm to finish execution. Like in the example above, for the first code the loop will run n number of times, so the time complexity will be n atleast and as the value of n will increase the time taken will also increase. While for the second code, time complexity is constant, because it will never be dependent on the value of n, it will always give the result in 1 step.

And since the algorithm's performance may vary with different types of input data, hence for an algorithm we usually use the worst-case Time complexity of an algorithm because that is the maximum time taken for any input size.

Calculating Time Complexity

Now lets tap onto the next big topic related to Time complexity, which is How to Calculate Time Complexity. It becomes very confusing some times, but we will try to explain it in the simplest way.

Now the most common metric for calculating time complexity is Big O notation. This removes all constant factors so that the running time can be estimated in relation to N, as N approaches infinity. In general you can think of it like this:

```
statement;
```

Above we have a single statement. Its Time Complexity will be Constant. The running time of the statement will not change in relation to N.

```
for(i=0; i < N; i++)

{

    statement;

}
```

The time complexity for the above algorithm will be Linear. The running time of the loop is directly proportional to N. When N doubles, so does the running time.

```
for(i=0; i < N; i++)

{

    for(j=0; j < N;j++)

    {

    statement;

    }

}
```

This time, the time complexity for the above code will be Quadratic. The running time of the two loops is proportional to the square of N. When N doubles, the running time increases by N * N.

```
while(low <= high)

{

    mid = (low + high) / 2;

    if (target < list[mid])

        high = mid - 1;

    else if (target > list[mid])

        low = mid + 1;

    else break;

}
```

This is an algorithm to break a set of numbers into halves, to search a particular field. Now, this algorithm will have a Logarithmic Time Complexity. The running time of the algorithm is proportional to the number of times N can be divided by 2(N is high-low here). This is because the algorithm divides the working area in half with each iteration.

```
void quicksort(int list[], int left, int right)

{

    int pivot = partition(list, left, right);

    quicksort(list, left, pivot - 1);

    quicksort(list, pivot + 1, right);

}
```

Taking the previous algorithm forward, above we have a small logic of Quick Sort. Now in Quick Sort, we divide the list into halves every time, but we repeat the iteration N times(where N is the size of list). Hence time complexity will be N*log(N). The running time consists of N loops (iterative or recursive) that are logarithmic, thus the algorithm is a combination of linear and logarithmic.

In general, doing something with every item in one dimension is linear, doing something with every item in two dimensions is quadratic, and dividing the working area in half is logarithmic.

Types of Notations for Time Complexity

Now we will discuss and understand the various notations used for Time Complexity.

1. Big Oh denotes "fewer than or the same as" <expression> iterations.

2. Big Omega denotes "more than or the same as" <expression> iterations.

3. Big Theta denotes "the same as" <expression> iterations.

4. Little Oh denotes "fewer than" <expression> iterations.

5. Little Omega denotes "more than" <expression> iterations.

Understanding Notations of Time Complexity with Example

O(expression) is the set of functions that grow slower than or at the same rate as expression. It indicates the maximum required by an algorithm for all input values. It represents the worst case of an algorithm's time complexity.

Omega(expression) is the set of functions that grow faster than or at the same rate as expression. It indicates the minimum time required by an algorithm for all input values. It represents the best case of an algorithm's time complexity.

Theta(expression) consist of all the functions that lie in both O(expression) and Omega(expression). It indicates the average bound of an algorithm. It represents the average case of an algorithm's time complexity.

Suppose you've calculated that an algorithm takes f(n) operations, where,

```
f(n) = 3*n^2 + 2*n + 4.    // n^2 means square of n
```

Since this polynomial grows at the same rate as n², then you could say that the function lies in the set Theta(n²). (It also lies in the sets O(n²) and Omega(n²) for the same reason.)

The simplest explanation is, because Theta denotes the same as the expression. Hence, as f(n) grows by a factor of n2, the time complexity can be best represented as Theta(n²).

Parameterized Complexity

In computer science, parameterized complexity is a measure of complexity of problems with multiple input parameters. The theory of parameterized complexity was developed in the 1990s by Rod Downey and Michael Fellows.

The theory of parameterized complexity is motivated, among other things, by the observation that there exist several hard problems that (most likely) require exponential runtime when complexity is measured in terms of the input size only, but that are computable in a time that is polynomial in the input size and exponential in a (small) parameter k. Hence, if k is fixed at a small value, such problems can still be considered 'tractable' despite their traditional classification as 'intractable'.

The existence of efficient, exact, and deterministic solving algorithms for NP-complete, or otherwise NP-hard, problems is considered unlikely, if input parameters are not fixed; all known solving algorithms for these problems require time that is exponential in the total size of the input. However, some problems can be solved by algorithms that are exponential only in the size of a fixed parameter while polynomial in the size of the input size. Such an algorithm is called a fixed-parameter tractable (fpt-) algorithm, because the problem can be solved efficiently for small values of the fixed parameter.

Problems in which some parameter k is fixed are called parameterized problems. A parameterized problem that allows for such an fpt-algorithm is said to be a fixed-parameter tractable problem and belongs to the class FPT, and the early name of the theory of parameterized complexity was fixed-parameter tractability.

Many problems have the following form: given an object x and a nonnegative integer k, does x have some property that depends on k? For instance, for the vertex cover problem, the parameter can be the number of vertices in the cover. In many applications, for example when modelling error correction, one can assume the parameter to be "small" compared to the total input size. Then it is interesting to see whether we can find an algorithm which is exponential only in k, and not in the input size.

In this way, parameterized complexity can be seen as two-dimensional complexity theory. This concept is formalized as follows:

A parameterized problem is a language $L \subseteq \Sigma^* \times \backslash N$, where Σ is a finite alphabet. The second component is called the parameter of the problem.

A parameterized problem L is fixed-parameter tractable if the question "$(x,k) \in L$?" can be decided in running time $f(k) \cdot |x|^{O(1)}$, where f is an arbitrary function depending only on k. The corresponding complexity class is called FPT.

For example, there is an algorithm which solves the vertex cover problem in $O(kn + 1.274^k)$ time, where n is the number of vertices and k is the size of the vertex cover. This proves that vertex cover is fixed-parameter tractable with respect to this parameter.

Complexity Classes

FPT

FPT contains the *fixed parameter tractable* problems, which are those that can be solved in time $f(k) \cdot |x|^{O(1)}$ for some computable function f. Typically, this function is thought of as single exponential, such as $2^{O(k)}$ but the definition admits functions that grow even faster. This is essential for a large part of the early history of this class. The crucial part of the definition is to exclude functions of the form $f(n,k)$, such as n^k. The class FPL (fixed parameter linear) is the class of problems solvable in time $f(k) \cdot |x|$ for some computable function f Grohe (1999). FPL is thus a subclass of FPT.

An example is the satisfiability problem, parameterised by the number of variables. A given formula of size m with k variables can be checked by brute force in time $O(2^k m)$. A vertex cover of size k in a graph of order n can be found in time $O(2^k n)$, so this problem is also in FPT.

An example of a problem that is thought not to be in FPT is graph coloring parameterised by the number of colors. It is known that 3-coloring is NP-hard, and an algorithm for graph k-colouring in time $f(k)n^{O(1)}$ for $k = 3$ would run in polynomial time in the size of the input. Thus, if graph coloring parameterised by the number of colors were in FPT, then P = NP.

There are a number of alternative definitions of FPT. For example, the running time requirement can be replaced by $f(k) + |x|^{O(1)}$. Also, a parameterised problem is in FPT if it has a so-called kernel. Kernelization is a preprocessing technique that reduces the original instance to its "hard kernel", a possibly much smaller instance that is equivalent to the original instance but has a size that is bounded by a function in the parameter.

FPT is closed under a parameterised reduction called *fpt-reduction*, which simultaneously preserves the instance size and the parameter.

Obviously, FPT contains all polynomial-time computable problems. Moreover, it contains all optimisation problems in NP that allow a Fully polynomial-time approximation scheme.

W hierarchy

The *W* hierarchy is a collection of computational complexity classes. A parameterised problem is in the class *W[i]*, if every instance (x,k) can be transformed (in fpt-time) to a combinatorial circuit that has weft at most i, such that $(x,k) \in L$ if and only if there is a satisfying assignment to the inputs, which assigns 1 to at most k inputs. The weft is the largest number of logical units with unbounded fan-in on any path from an input to the output. The total number of logical units on the paths (known as depth) must be limited by a constant that holds for all instances of the problem.

FPT $= W[0]$ and $W[i] \subseteq W[j]$ for all $i \leq j$. The classes in the W hierarchy are also closed under fpt-reduction.

Many natural computational problems occupy the lower levels, $W[1]$ and $W[2]$.

$W[1]$

Examples of $W[1]$-complete problems include

- deciding if a given graph contains a clique of size k
- deciding if a given graph contains an independent set of size k
- deciding if a given nondeterministic single-tape Turing machine accepts within k steps ("short Turing machine acceptance" problem)

$W[2]$

Examples of $W[2]$-complete problems include

- deciding if a given graph contains a dominating set of size k
- deciding if a given nondeterministic multi-tape Turing machine accepts within k steps ("short multi-tape Turing machine acceptance" problem)

$W[t]$

$W[t]$ can be defined using the family of Weighted Weft-t-Depth-d SAT problems for $d \geq t$: $W[t,d]$ is the class of parameterized problems that fpt-reduce to this problem, and $W[t] = \bigcup_{d \geq t} W[t,d]$.

Here, Weighted Weft-t-Depth-d SAT is the following problem:

- Input: A Boolean formula of depth at most d and weft at most t, and a number k. The *depth* is the maximal number of gates on any path from the root to a leaf, and the *weft* is the maximal number of gates *of fan-in at least three* on any path from the root to a leaf.
- Question: Does the formula have a satisfying assignment of Hamming weight at most k?

It can be shown that the problem Weighted t-Normalize SAT is complete for $W[t]$ under fpt-reductions. Here, Weighted t-Normalize SAT is the following problem:

- Input: A Boolean formula of depth at most t with an AND-gate on top, and a number k.
- Question: Does the formula have a satisfying assignment of Hamming weight at most k?

$W[P]$

$W[P]$ is the class of problems that can be decided by a nondeterministic $h(k) \cdot |x|^{O(1)}$-time Turing-machine that makes at most $O(f(k) \cdot \log n)$ nondeterministic choices in the computation on (x,k) (a k-restricted Turing-machine).

It is known that FPT is contained in W[P], and the inclusion is believed to be strict. However, resolving this issue would imply a solution to the P versus NP problem.

Other connections to unparameterised computational complexity are that FPT equals $W[P]$ if and only if circuit satisfiability can be decided in time $\exp(o(n))m^{O(1)}$, or if and only if there is a computable, nondecreasing, unbounded function f such that all languages recognised by a nondeterministic polynomial-time Turing machine using f(n)log n nondeterministic choices are in P.

$W[P]$ can be loosely thought of as the class of problems where we have a set S of n items, and we want to find a subset $T \subset S$ of size k such that a certain property holds. We can encode a choice as a list of k integers, stored in binary. Since the highest any of these numbers can be is n, $\lceil \log_2 n \rceil$ bits are needed for each number. Therefore $k \cdot \lceil \log_2 n \rceil$ total bits are needed to encode a choice. Therefore we can select a subset $T \subset S$ with $O(k \cdot \log n)$ nondeterministic choices.

XP

XP is the class of parameterized problems that can be solved in time $n^{f(k)}$ for some computable function f.

A Hierarchy

The A hierarchy is a collection of computational complexity classes similar to the W hierarchy. However, while the W hierarchy is a hierarchy contained in NP, the A hierarchy more closely mimics the polynomial-time hierarchy from classical complexity. It is known that A[1] = W[1] holds.

Space Complexity

Space complexity is the amount of memory used by the algorithm (including the input values to the algorithm) to execute and produce the result.

Sometime Auxiliary Space is confused with Space Complexity. But Auxiliary Space is the extra space or the temporary space used by the algorithm during it's execution.

Space Complexity = Auxiliary Space + Input space

Memory Usage while Execution

While executing, algorithm uses memory space for three reasons:

Instruction Space

It's the amount of memory used to save the compiled version of instructions.

Environmental Stack

Sometimes an algorithm (function) may be called inside another algorithm (function). In such a situation, the current variables are pushed onto the system stack, where they wait for further execution and then the call to the inside algorithm (function) is made.

For example, If a function A() calls function B() inside it, then all the variables of the function A() will get stored on the system stack temporarily, while the function B() is called and executed inside the funciton A().

Data Space

Amount of space used by the variables and constants.

But while calculating the Space Complexity of any algorithm, we usually consider only Data Space and we neglect the Instruction Space and Environmental Stack.

Calculating the Space Complexity

For calculating the space complexity, we need to know the value of memory used by different type of datatype variables, which generally varies for different operating systems, but the method for calculating the space complexity remains the same.

Type	Size
bool, char, unsigned char, signed char, __int8	1 byte
__int16, short, unsigned short, wchar_t, __wchar_t	2 bytes
float, __int32, int, unsigned int, long, unsigned long	4 bytes
double, __int64, long double, long long	8 bytes

Now let's learn how to compute space complexity by taking a few examples:

```
{
    int z = a + b + c;

    return(z);

}
```

In the above expression, variables a, b, c and z are all integer types, hence they will take up 2 bytes each, so total memory requirement will be (8 + 2) = 10 bytes, this additional 2 bytes is for return value. And because this space requirement is fixed for the above example, hence it is called Constant Space Complexity.

Let's have another example, this time a bit complex one,

```
// n is the length of array a[]

int sum(int a[], int n)

{
        int x = 0;                  // 2 bytes for x

        for(int i = 0; i < n; i++)    // 2 bytes for i

        {

            x  = x + a[i];
```

```
      }

   return(x);

}
```

- In the above code, 2*n bytes of space is required for the array a[] elements.

- 2 bytes each for x, n, i and the return value.

Hence the total memory requirement will be (2n + 8), which is increasing linearly with the increase in the input value n, hence it is called as Linear Space Complexity.

Similarly, we can have quadratic and other complex space complexity as well, as the complexity of an algorithm increases.

Computational Complexity Theory

Computational complexity theory is a subfield of theoretical computer science one of whose primary goals is to classify and compare the practical difficulty of solving problems about finite combinatorial objects – e.g. given two natural numbers nn and mm, are they relatively prime? Given a propositional formula ϕ, does it have a satisfying assignment? If we were to play chess on a board of size n × n does white have a winning strategy from a given initial position? These problems are equally difficult from the standpoint of classical computability theory in the sense that they are all effectively decidable. Yet they still appear to differ significantly in practical difficulty. For having been supplied with a pair of numbers $m > n > 0$, it is possible to determine their relative primality by a method (Euclid's algorithm) which requires a number of steps proportional to $log(n)$. On the other hand, all known methods for solving the latter two problems require a 'brute force' search through a large class of cases which increase at least exponentially in the size of the problem instance.

Complexity theory attempts to make such distinctions precise by proposing a formal criterion for what it means for a mathematical problem to be *feasibly decidable* – i.e. that it can be solved by a conventional Turing machine in a number of steps which is proportional to a polynomial function of the size of its input. The class of problems with this property is known as P – or *polynomial time*– and includes the first of the three problems described above. P can be formally shown to be distinct from certain other classes such as EXP – or *exponential time*– which includes the third problem from above. The second problem from above belongs to a complexity class known as NP – or *non-deterministic polynomial time* – consisting of those problems which can be correctly decided by some computation of a non-deterministic Turing machine in a number of steps which is a polynomial function of the size of its input. A famous conjecture – often regarded as the most fundamental in all of theoretical computer science – states that P is also properly contained in NP – *i.e.*$P \subsetneq NP$.

Demonstrating the non-coincidence of these and other complexity classes remain important open problems in complexity theory.

Central to the development of computational complexity theory is the notion of a *decision problem*. Such a problem corresponds to a set X in which we wish to decide membership. For instance the problem PRIMESPRIMES corresponds to the subset of the natural numbers which are prime – i.e. $\{n \in N \mid n \text{ is prime}\}$. Decision problems are typically specified in the form of questions about a class of mathematical objects whose positive instances determine the set in question – e.g.

SAT Given a formula ϕ of propositional logic, does there exist a satisfying assignment for ϕ ?

Traveling salesman (TSP): Given a list of cities V, the integer distance $d(u,v)$ between each pair of cities $u,v \in V$, and a budget $b \in \mathbb{N}$, is there a tour visiting each city exactly once and returning to the starting city of total distance $\leq b$?

Integer programming integer programming: Given an $n \times m$ integer matrix A and an n-dimensional vector of integers $\vec{b}$, does there exist an m-dimensional vector $\vec{x}$ of integers such that $A\vec{x} = b$?

Perfect matching: perfect matching: Given a finite bipartite graph G, does there exist a perfect matching in G? (G is *bipartite* just in case its vertices can be partitioned into two disjoints sets U and V such that all of its edges E connect a vertex in U to one in V. A *matching* is a subset of edges $M \subseteq E$ no two members of which share a common vertex. M is *perfect* if it matches all vertices.)

These problems are typical of those studied in complexity theory in two fundamental respects. First, they are all *effectively decidable*. This is to say that they may all be decided in the 'in principle' sense studied in computability theory– i.e. by an effective procedure which halts in finitely many steps for all inputs. Second, they arise in contexts in which we are interested in solving not only isolated instances of the problem in question, but rather in developing methods which allow it to be efficiently solved on a mass scale – i.e. for all instances in which we might be practically concerned. Such interest often arises in virtue of the relationship of computational problems to practical tasks which we seek to analyze using the methods of discrete mathematics. For example, instances of SATSAT arise when we wish to check the consistency of a set of specifications (e.g. those which might arise in scheduling the sessions of a conference or designing a circuit board), instances of TSPTSP and INTEGER PROGRAMMING arise in many logistical and planning applications, instances of PERFECT MATCHING arise when we wish to find an optimal means of pairing candidates with jobs, etc.

The resources involved in carrying out an algorithm to decide an instance of a problems can typically be measured in terms of the number of processor cycles (i.e. elementary computational steps) and the amount of memory space (i.e. storage for auxiliary calculations) which are required to return a solution. The methods of complexity theory can be useful not only in deciding how we can most efficiently expend such resources, but also in helping us to distinguish which effectively decidable problems possess efficient decision methods in the first place. In this regard, it is traditional to distinguish pre-theoretically between the class of *feasibly decidable problems* – i.e. those which can be solved in practice by an efficient algorithm – and the class of *intractable problems* – i.e. those which lack such algorithms and may thus be regarded as intrinsically difficult to decide (despite possibly being decidable in principle).

Computational Problems

A traveling salesman tour through Germany's 15 largest cities

Problem Instances

A computational problem can be viewed as an infinite collection of *instances* together with a *solution* for every instance. The input string for a computational problem is referred to as a problem instance, and should not be confused with the problem itself. In computational complexity theory, a problem refers to the abstract question to be solved. In contrast, an instance of this problem is a rather concrete utterance, which can serve as the input for a decision problem. For example, consider the problem of primality testing. The instance is a number (e.g., 15) and the solution is "yes" if the number is prime and "no" otherwise (in this case, 15 is not prime and the answer is "no"). Stated another way, the *instance* is a particular input to the problem, and the *solution* is the output corresponding to the given input.

To further highlight the difference between a problem and an instance, consider the following instance of the decision version of the traveling salesman problem: Is there a route of at most 2000 kilometres passing through all of Germany's 15 largest cities? The quantitative answer to this particular problem instance is of little use for solving other instances of the problem, such as asking for a round trip through all sites in Milan whose total length is at most 10 km. For this reason, complexity theory addresses computational problems and not particular problem instances.

Representing Problem Instances

When considering computational problems, a problem instance is a string over an alphabet. Usually, the alphabet is taken to be the binary alphabet (i.e., the set {0,1}), and thus the strings are bitstrings. As in a real-world computer, mathematical objects other than bitstrings must be suitably encoded. For example, integers can be represented in binary notation, and graphs can be encoded directly via their adjacency matrices, or by encoding their adjacency lists in binary.

Even though some proofs of complexity-theoretic theorems regularly assume some concrete choice of input encoding, one tries to keep the discussion abstract enough to be independent of the choice of encoding. This can be achieved by ensuring that different representations can be transformed into each other efficiently.

Decision Problems as Formal Languages

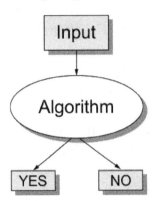

A decision problem has only two possible outputs, *yes* or *no* (or alternately 1 or 0) on any input.

Decision problems are one of the central objects of study in computational complexity theory. A decision problem is a special type of computational problem whose answer is either *yes* or *no*, or alternately either 1 or 0. A decision problem can be viewed as a formal language, where the members of the language are instances whose output is yes, and the non-members are those instances whose output is no. The objective is to decide, with the aid of an algorithm, whether a given input string is a member of the formal language under consideration. If the algorithm deciding this problem returns the answer *yes*, the algorithm is said to accept the input string, otherwise it is said to reject the input.

An example of a decision problem is the following. The input is an arbitrary graph. The problem consists in deciding whether the given graph is connected, or not. The formal language associated with this decision problem is then the set of all connected graphs — to obtain a precise definition of this language, one has to decide how graphs are encoded as binary strings.

Function Problems

A function problem is a computational problem where a single output (of a total function) is expected for every input, but the output is more complex than that of a decision problem—that is, the output isn't just yes or no. Notable examples include the traveling salesman problem and the integer factorization problem.

It is tempting to think that the notion of function problems is much richer than the notion of decision problems. However, this is not really the case, since function problems can be recast as decision problems. For example, the multiplication of two integers can be expressed as the set of triples (a, b, c) such that the relation $a \times b = c$ holds. Deciding whether a given triple is a member of this set corresponds to solving the problem of multiplying two numbers.

Measuring the Size of an Instance

To measure the difficulty of solving a computational problem, one may wish to see how much time the best algorithm requires to solve the problem. However, the running time may, in general, depend on the instance. In particular, larger instances will require more time to solve. Thus the time required to solve a problem (or the space required, or any measure of complexity) is calculated as a function of the size of the instance. This is usually taken to be the size of the input in bits. Complexity theory is interested in how algorithms scale with an increase in the input size. For instance, in the problem of finding whether a graph is connected, how much more time does it take to solve a problem for a graph with $2n$ vertices compared to the time taken for a graph with n vertices?

If the input size is n, the time taken can be expressed as a function of n. Since the time taken on different inputs of the same size can be different, the worst-case time complexity $T(n)$ is defined to be the maximum time taken over all inputs of size n. If $T(n)$ is a polynomial in n, then the algorithm is said to be a polynomial time algorithm. Cobham's thesis argues that a problem can be solved with a feasible amount of resources if it admits a polynomial time algorithm.

Machine Models and Complexity Measures

Turing Machine

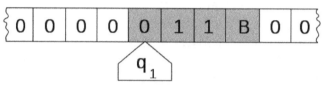

Turing machine

A Turing machine is a mathematical model of a general computing machine. It is a theoretical device that manipulates symbols contained on a strip of tape. Turing machines are not intended as a practical computing technology, but rather as a general model of a computing machine—anything from an advanced supercomputer to a mathematician with a pencil and paper. It is believed that if a problem can be solved by an algorithm, there exists a Turing machine that solves the problem. Indeed, this is the statement of the Church–Turing thesis. Furthermore, it is known that everything that can be computed on other models of computation known to us today, such as a RAM machine, Conway's Game of Life, cellular automata or any programming language can be computed on a Turing machine. Since Turing machines are easy to analyze mathematically, and are believed to be as powerful as any other model of computation, the Turing machine is the most commonly used model in complexity theory.

Many types of Turing machines are used to define complexity classes, such as deterministic Turing machines, probabilistic Turing machines, non-deterministic Turing machines, quantum Turing machines, symmetric Turing machines and alternating Turing machines. They are all equally powerful in principle, but when resources (such as time or space) are bounded, some of these may be more powerful than others.

A deterministic Turing machine is the most basic Turing machine, which uses a fixed set of rules to determine its future actions. A probabilistic Turing machine is a deterministic Turing machine with an extra supply of random bits. The ability to make probabilistic decisions often helps algorithms solve problems more efficiently. Algorithms that use random bits are called randomized algorithms. A non-deterministic Turing machine is a deterministic Turing machine with an added feature of non-determinism, which allows a Turing machine to have multiple possible future actions from a given state. One way to view non-determinism is that the Turing machine branches into many possible computational paths at each step, and if it solves the problem in any of these branches, it is said to have solved the problem. Clearly, this model is not meant to be a physically realizable model, it is just a theoretically interesting abstract machine that gives rise to particularly interesting complexity classes.

Other Machine Models

Many machine models different from the standard multi-tape Turing machines have been proposed in the literature, for example random access machines. Perhaps surprisingly, each of these models can be converted to another without providing any extra computational power. The time and memory consumption of these alternate models may vary. What all these models have in common is that the machines operate deterministically.

However, some computational problems are easier to analyze in terms of more unusual resources. For example, a non-deterministic Turing machine is a computational model that is allowed to branch out to check many different possibilities at once. The non-deterministic Turing machine has very little to do with how we physically want to compute algorithms, but its branching exactly captures many of the mathematical models we want to analyze, so that non-deterministic time is a very important resource in analyzing computational problems.

Complexity Measures

For a precise definition of what it means to solve a problem using a given amount of time and space, a computational model such as the deterministic Turing machine is used. The *time required* by a deterministic Turing machine M on input x is the total number of state transitions, or steps, the machine makes before it halts and outputs the answer ("yes" or "no"). A Turing machine M is said to operate within time $f(n)$, if the time required by M on each input of length n is at most $f(n)$. A decision problem A can be solved in time $f(n)$ if there exists a Turing machine operating in time $f(n)$ that solves the problem. Since complexity theory is interested in classifying problems based on their difficulty, one defines sets of problems based on some criteria. For instance, the set of problems solvable within time $f(n)$ on a deterministic Turing machine is then denoted by DTIME($f(n)$).

Analogous definitions can be made for space requirements. Although time and space are the most well-known complexity resources, any complexity measure can be viewed as a computational resource. Complexity measures are very generally defined by the Blum complexity axioms. Other complexity measures used in complexity theory include communication complexity, circuit complexity, and decision tree complexity.

The complexity of an algorithm is often expressed using big O notation.

Best, Worst and Average Case Complexity

The best, worst and average case complexity refer to three different ways of measuring the time complexity (or any other complexity measure) of different inputs of the same size. Since some inputs of size n may be faster to solve than others, we define the following complexities:

- Best-case complexity: This is the complexity of solving the problem for the best input of size n.

- Worst-case complexity: This is the complexity of solving the problem for the worst input of size n.

- Average-case complexity: This is the complexity of solving the problem on an average. This complexity is only defined with respect to a probability distribution over the inputs. For instance, if all inputs of the same size are assumed to be equally likely to appear, the average case complexity can be defined with respect to the uniform distribution over all inputs of size n.

For example, consider the deterministic sorting algorithm quicksort. This solves the problem of sorting a list of integers that is given as the input. The worst-case is when the input is sorted or sorted in reverse order, and the algorithm takes time $O(n^2)$ for this case. If we assume that all possible permutations of the input list are equally likely, the average time taken for sorting is $O(n \log n)$. The best case occurs when each pivoting divides the list in half, also needing $O(n \log n)$ time.

Upper and Lower Bounds on the Complexity of Problems

To classify the computation time (or similar resources, such as space consumption), one is interested in proving upper and lower bounds on the maximum amount of time required by the most efficient algorithm solving a given problem. The complexity of an algorithm is usually taken to be its worst-case complexity, unless specified otherwise. Analyzing a particular algorithm falls under the field of analysis of algorithms. To show an upper bound $T(n)$ on the time complexity of a problem, one needs to show only that there is a particular algorithm with running time at most $T(n)$. However, proving lower bounds is much more difficult, since lower bounds make a statement about all possible algorithms that solve a given problem. The phrase "all possible algorithms" includes not just the algorithms known today, but any algorithm that might be discovered in the future. To show a lower bound of $T(n)$ for a problem requires showing that no algorithm can have time complexity lower than $T(n)$.

Upper and lower bounds are usually stated using the big O notation, which hides constant factors and smaller terms. This makes the bounds independent of the specific details of the computational model used. For instance, if $T(n) = 7n^2 + 15n + 40$, in big O notation one would write $T(n) = O(n^2)$.

Complexity Classes

Defining Complexity Classes

A complexity class is a set of problems of related complexity. Simpler complexity classes are defined by the following factors:

- The type of computational problem: The most commonly used problems are decision problems. However, complexity classes can be defined based on function problems, counting problems, optimization problems, promise problems, etc.

- The model of computation: The most common model of computation is the deterministic Turing machine, but many complexity classes are based on non-deterministic Turing machines, Boolean circuits, quantum Turing machines, monotone circuits, etc.

- The resource (or resources) that are being bounded and the bounds: These two properties are usually stated together, such as "polynomial time", "logarithmic space", "constant depth", etc.

Some complexity classes have complicated definitions that do not fit into this framework. Thus, a typical complexity class has a definition like the following:

The set of decision problems solvable by a deterministic Turing machine within time $f(n)$. (This complexity class is known as DTIME($f(n)$).)

But bounding the computation time above by some concrete function $f(n)$ often yields complexity classes that depend on the chosen machine model. For instance, the language $\{xx \mid x$ is any binary string$\}$ can be solved in linear time on a multi-tape Turing machine, but necessarily requires quadratic time in the model of single-tape Turing machines. If we allow polynomial variations in running time, Cobham-Edmonds thesis states that "the time complexities in any two reasonable and general models of computation are polynomially related". This forms the basis for the complexity class P, which is the set of decision problems solvable by a deterministic Turing machine within polynomial time. The corresponding set of function problems is FP.

Important Complexity Classes

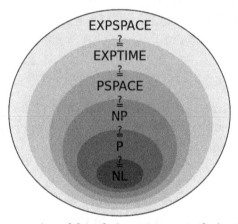

A representation of the relation among complexity classes

Many important complexity classes can be defined by bounding the time or space used by the algorithm. Some important complexity classes of decision problems defined in this manner are the following:

Complexity class	Model of computation	Resource constraint
Deterministic time		
DTIME($f(n)$)	Deterministic Turing machine	Time $f(n)$
P	Deterministic Turing machine	Time poly(n)
EXPTIME	Deterministic Turing machine	Time $2^{\text{poly}(n)}$
Non-deterministic time		
NTIME($f(n)$)	Non-deterministic Turing machine	Time $f(n)$
NP	Non-deterministic Turing machine	Time poly(n)
NEXPTIME	Non-deterministic Turing machine	Time $2^{\text{poly}(n)}$

Complexity class	Model of computation	Resource constraint
Deterministic space		
DSPACE($f(n)$)	Deterministic Turing machine	Space $f(n)$
L	Deterministic Turing machine	Space $O(\log n)$
PSPACE	Deterministic Turing machine	Space poly(n)
EXPSPACE	Deterministic Turing machine	Space $2^{\text{poly}(n)}$
Non-deterministic space		
NSPACE($f(n)$)	Non-deterministic Turing machine	Space $f(n)$
NL	Non-deterministic Turing machine	Space $O(\log n)$
NPSPACE	Non-deterministic Turing machine	Space poly(n)
NEXPSPACE	Non-deterministic Turing machine	Space $2^{\text{poly}(n)}$

The logarithmic-space classes (necessarily) do not take into account the space needed to represent the problem.

It turns out that PSPACE = NPSPACE and EXPSPACE = NEXPSPACE by Savitch's theorem.

Other important complexity classes include BPP, ZPP and RP, which are defined using probabilistic Turing machines; AC and NC, which are defined using Boolean circuits; and BQP and QMA, which are defined using quantum Turing machines. #P is an important complexity class of counting problems (not decision problems). Classes like IP and AM are defined using Interactive proof systems. ALL is the class of all decision problems.

Hierarchy Theorems

For the complexity classes defined in this way, it is desirable to prove that relaxing the requirements on (say) computation time indeed defines a bigger set of problems. In particular, although DTIME(n) is contained in DTIME(n^2), it would be interesting to know if the inclusion is strict. For time and space requirements, the answer to such questions is given by the time and space hierarchy theorems respectively. They are called hierarchy theorems because they induce a proper hierarchy on the classes defined by constraining the respective resources. Thus there are pairs of complexity classes such that one is properly included in the other. Having deduced such proper set inclusions, we can proceed to make quantitative statements about how much more additional time or space is needed in order to increase the number of problems that can be solved.

More precisely, the time hierarchy theorem states that

$$\text{DTIME}\big(f(n)\big) \subsetneq \text{DTIME}\big(f(n) \cdot \log^2(f(n))\big).$$

The space hierarchy theorem states that

$$\text{DSPACE}\big(f(n)\big) \subsetneq \text{DSPACE}\big(f(n) \cdot \log(f(n))\big).$$

The time and space hierarchy theorems form the basis for most separation results of complexity classes. For instance, the time hierarchy theorem tells us that P is strictly contained in EXPTIME, and the space hierarchy theorem tells us that L is strictly contained in PSPACE.

Reduction

Many complexity classes are defined using the concept of a reduction. A reduction is a transformation of one problem into another problem. It captures the informal notion of a problem being at most as difficult as another problem. For instance, if a problem X can be solved using an algorithm for Y, X is no more difficult than Y, and we say that X *reduces* to Y. There are many different types of reductions, based on the method of reduction, such as Cook reductions, Karp reductions and Levin reductions, and the bound on the complexity of reductions, such as polynomial-time reductions or log-space reductions.

The most commonly used reduction is a polynomial-time reduction. This means that the reduction process takes polynomial time. For example, the problem of squaring an integer can be reduced to the problem of multiplying two integers. This means an algorithm for multiplying two integers can be used to square an integer. Indeed, this can be done by giving the same input to both inputs of the multiplication algorithm. Thus we see that squaring is not more difficult than multiplication, since squaring can be reduced to multiplication.

This motivates the concept of a problem being hard for a complexity class. A problem X is *hard* for a class of problems C if every problem in C can be reduced to X. Thus no problem in C is harder than X, since an algorithm for X allows us to solve any problem in C. The notion of hard problems depends on the type of reduction being used. For complexity classes larger than P, polynomial-time reductions are commonly used. In particular, the set of problems that are hard for NP is the set of NP-hard problems.

If a problem X is in C and hard for C, then X is said to be *complete* for C. This means that X is the hardest problem in C. (Since many problems could be equally hard, one might say that X is one of the hardest problems in C.) Thus the class of NP-complete problems contains the most difficult problems in NP, in the sense that they are the ones most likely not to be in P. Because the problem P = NP is not solved, being able to reduce a known NP-complete problem, Π_2, to another problem, Π_1, would indicate that there is no known polynomial-time solution for Π_1. This is because a polynomial-time solution to Π_1 would yield a polynomial-time solution to Π_2. Similarly, because all NP problems can be reduced to the set, finding an NP-complete problem that can be solved in polynomial time would mean that P = NP.

Important Open Problems

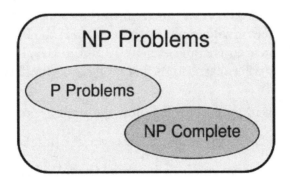

P Versus NP Problem

The complexity class P is often seen as a mathematical abstraction modeling those computational tasks that admit an efficient algorithm. This hypothesis is called the Cobham–Edmonds thesis. The complexity class NP, on the other hand, contains many problems that people would like to solve efficiently, but for which no efficient algorithm is known, such as the Boolean satisfiability problem, the Hamiltonian path problem and the vertex cover problem. Since deterministic Turing machines are special non-deterministic Turing machines, it is easily observed that each problem in P is also member of the class NP.

The question of whether P equals NP is one of the most important open questions in theoretical computer science because of the wide implications of a solution. If the answer is yes, many important problems can be shown to have more efficient solutions. These include various types of integer programming problems in operations research, many problems in logistics, protein structure prediction in biology, and the ability to find formal proofs of pure mathematics theorems.

Problems in NP not known to be in P or NP-complete

It was shown by Ladner that if P ≠ NP then there exist problems in NP that are neither in P nor NP-complete. Such problems are called NP-intermediate problems. The graph isomorphism problem, the discrete logarithm problem and the integer factorization problem are examples of problems believed to be NP-intermediate. They are some of the very few NP problems not known to be in P or to be NP-complete.

The graph isomorphism problem is the computational problem of determining whether two finite graphs are isomorphic. An important unsolved problem in complexity theory is whether the graph isomorphism problem is in P, NP-complete, or NP-intermediate. The answer is not known, but it is believed that the problem is at least not NP-complete. If graph isomorphism is NP-complete, the polynomial time hierarchy collapses to its second level. Since it is widely believed that the polynomial hierarchy does not collapse to any finite level, it is believed that graph isomorphism is not NP-complete. The best algorithm for this problem, due to László Babai and Eugene Luks has run time $O(2^{\sqrt{n \log n}})$ for graphs with n vertices, although some recent work by Babai offers some potentially new perspectives on this.

The integer factorization problem is the computational problem of determining the prime factorization of a given integer. Phrased as a decision problem, it is the problem of deciding whether the input has a prime factor less than k. No efficient integer factorization algorithm is known, and this fact forms the basis of several modern cryptographic systems, such as the RSA algorithm. The integer factorization problem is in NP and in co-NP (and even in UP and co-UP). If the problem is NP-complete, the polynomial time hierarchy will collapse to its first level (i.e., NP will equal co-NP).

The best known algorithm for integer factorization is the general number field sieve, which takes time $O(e^{\left(\frac{64}{9}\right)^{1/3} (\log n)^{1/3} (\log \log n)^{2/3}})$ to factor an integer n. However, the best known quantum algorithm for this problem, Shor's algorithm, does run in polynomial time. Unfortunately, this fact doesn't say much about where the problem lies with respect to non-quantum complexity classes.

Separations between other Complexity Classes

Many known complexity classes are suspected to be unequal, but this has not been proved. For instance $P \subseteq NP \subseteq PP \subseteq PSPACE$, but it is possible that P = PSPACE. If P is not equal to NP, then P is not equal to PSPACE either. Since there are many known complexity classes between P and PSPACE, such as RP, BPP, PP, BQP, MA, PH, etc., it is possible that all these complexity classes collapse to one class. Proving that any of these classes are unequal would be a major breakthrough in complexity theory.

Along the same lines, co-NP is the class containing the complement problems (i.e. problems with the *yes/no* answers reversed) of NP problems. It is believed that NP is not equal to co-NP; however, it has not yet been proven. It is clear that if these two complexity classes are not equal then P is not equal to NP, since if P=NP we would also have P=co-NP, since problems in NP are dual to those in co-NP.

Similarly, it is not known if L (the set of all problems that can be solved in logarithmic space) is strictly contained in P or equal to P. Again, there are many complexity classes between the two, such as NL and NC, and it is not known if they are distinct or equal classes.

It is suspected that P and BPP are equal. However, it is currently open if BPP = NEXP.

Intractability

A problem that can be solved in theory (e.g. given large but finite resources, especially time), but for which in practice *any* solution takes too many resources to be useful, is known as an intractable problem. Conversely, a problem that can be solved in practice is called a tractable problem, literally "a problem that can be handled". The term *infeasible* (literally "cannot be done") is sometimes used interchangeably with *intractable*, though this risks confusion with a feasible solution in mathematical optimization.

Tractable problems are frequently identified with problems that have polynomial-time solutions (P, PTIME); this is known as the Cobham–Edmonds thesis. Problems that are known to be intractable in this sense include those that are EXPTIME-hard. If NP is not the same as P, then NP-hard problems are also intractable in this sense.

However, this identification is inexact: a polynomial-time solution with large exponent or large constant term grows quickly, and may be impractical for practical size problems; conversely, an exponential-time solution that grows slowly may be practical on realistic input, or a solution that takes a long time in the worst case may take a short time in most cases or the average case, and thus still be practical. Saying that a problem is not in P does not imply that all large cases of the problem are hard or even that most of them are. For example, the decision problem in Presburger arithmetic has been shown not to be in P, yet algorithms have been written that solve the problem in reasonable times in most cases. Similarly, algorithms can solve the NP-complete knapsack problem over a wide range of sizes in less than quadratic time and SAT solvers routinely handle large instances of the NP-complete Boolean satisfiability problem.

To see why exponential-time algorithms are generally unusable in practice, consider a program that makes 2^n operations before halting. For small n, say 100, and assuming for the sake of example that the computer does 10^{12} operations each second, the program would run for about 4×10^{10} years, which is the same order of magnitude as the age of the universe. Even with a much faster computer, the program would only be useful for very small instances and in that sense the intractability of a problem is somewhat independent of technological progress. However, an exponential-time algorithm that takes 1.0001^n operations is practical until n gets relatively large.

Similarly, a polynomial time algorithm is not always practical. If its running time is, say, n^{15}, it is unreasonable to consider it efficient and it is still useless except on small instances. Indeed, in practice even n^3 or n^2 algorithms are often impractical on realistic sizes of problems.

Asymptotic Computational Complexity

Asymptotic computational complexity is the limiting behavior of the execution time of an algorithm when the size of the problem goes to infinity. This is usually denoted in big-O notation.

Asymptotic Analysis

When analyzing the running time or space usage of programs, we usually try to estimate the time or space as function of the input size. For example, when analyzing the worst case running time of a function that sorts a list of numbers, we will be concerned with how long it takes as a function of the length of the input list. For example, we say the standard insertion sort takes time $T(n)$ where $T(n) = c*n^2 + k$ for some constants c and k. In contrast, merge sort takes time $T'(n) = c'*n*log_2(n) + k'$.

The asymptotic behavior of a function $f(n)$ (such as $f(n) = c*n$ or $f(n) = c*n^2$, etc.) refers to the growth of $f(n)$ as n gets large. We typically ignore small values of n, since we are usually interested in estimating how slow the program will be on large inputs. A good rule of thumb is: the slower the asymptotic growth rate, the better the algorithm (although this is often not the whole story).

By this measure, a linear algorithm (i.e., $f(n) = d*n + k$) is always asymptotically better than a quadratic one (e.g., $f(n) = c*n^2 + q$). That is because for any given (positive) c,k,d, and q there is always some n at which the magnitude of $c*n^2 + q$ overtakes $d*n + k$. For moderate values of n, the quadratic algorithm could very well take less time than the linear one, for example if c is significantly smaller than d and/or k is significantly smaller than q. However, the linear algorithm will always be better for sufficiently large inputs.

Worst-Case and Average-Case Analysis

When we say that an algorithm runs in time $T(n)$, we mean that $T(n)$ is an upper bound on the running time that holds for all inputs of size n. This is called *worst-case analysis*. The algorithm may very well take less time on some inputs of size n, but it doesn't matter. If an algorithm takes $T(n) = c*n^2 + k$ steps on only a single input of each size n and only n steps on the rest, we still say that it is a quadratic algorithm.

A popular alternative to worst-case analysis is *average-case analysis*. Here we do not bound the worst case running time, but try to calculate the expected time spent on a randomly chosen input. This kind of analysis is generally harder, since it involves probabilistic arguments and often requires assumptions about the distribution of inputs that may be difficult to justify. On the other hand, it can be more useful because sometimes the worst-case behavior of an algorithm is misleadingly bad. A good example of this is the popular quicksort algorithm, whose worst-case running time on an input sequence of length n is proportional to n^2 but whose expected running time is proportional to $n \log n$.

Order of Growth and Big-O Notation

In estimating the running time of insert_sort (or any other program) we don't know what the constants c or k are. We know that it is a constant of moderate size, but other than that it is not important; we have enough evidence from the asymptotic analysis to know that amerge_sort is faster than the quadratic insert_sort, even though the constants may differ somewhat. (This does not always hold; the constants can sometimes make a difference, but in general it is a very good rule of thumb.)

We may not even be able to measure the constant c directly. For example, we may know that a given expression of the language, such as if, takes a constant number of machine instructions, but we may not know exactly how many. Moreover, the same sequence of instructions executed on a Pentium IV will take less time than on a Pentium II (although the difference will be roughly a constant factor). So these estimates are usually only accurate up to a constant factor anyway. For these reasons, we usually ignore constant factors in comparing asymptotic running times.

Computer scientists have developed a convenient notation for hiding the constant factor. We write $O(n)$ instead of "cn for some constant c." Thus an algorithm is said to be $O(n)$ or *linear time* if there is a fixed constant c such that for all sufficiently large n, the algorithm takes time at most cn on inputs of size n. An algorithm is said to be $O(n^2)$ or *quadratic time* if there is a fixed constant c such that for all sufficiently large n, the algorithm takes time at most cn^2 on inputs of size n. $O(1)$ means *constant time*.

Polynomial time means $n^{O(1)}$, or n^c for some constant c. Thus any constant, linear, quadratic, or cubic $(O(n^3))$ time algorithm is a polynomial-time algorithm.

This is called *big-O notation*. It concisely captures the important differences in the asymptotic growth rates of functions.

One important advantage of big-O notation is that it makes algorithms much easier to analyze, since we can conveniently ignore low-order terms. For example, an algorithm that runs in time

$$10n^3 + 24n^2 + 3n \log n + 144$$
is still a cubic algorithm, since
$$10n^3 + 24n^2 + 3n \log n + 144$$
$$<= 10n^3 + 24n^3 + 3n^3 + 144n^3$$
$$<= (10 + 24 + 3 + 144)n^3$$
$$= O(n^3).$$

Of course, since we are ignoring constant factors, any two linear algorithms will be considered equally good by this measure. There may even be some situations in which the constant is so huge in a linear algorithm that even an exponential algorithm with a small constant may be preferable in practice. This is a valid criticism of asymptotic analysis and big-O notation. However, as a rule of thumb it has served us well. Just be aware that it is only a rule of thumb--the asymptotically optimal algorithm is not necessarily the best one.

Some common orders of growth seen often in complexity analysis are

$O(1)$ constant
$O(log\ n)$ logarithmic
$O(n)$ linear
$O(n\ log\ n)$ "n log n"
$O(n^2)$ quadratic
$O(n^3)$ cubic

Here log means log_2 or the logarithm base 2, although the logarithm base doesn't really matter since logarithms with different bases differ by a constant factor. Also, $2^{O(n)}$ and $O(2^n)$ are not the same.

Comparing Orders of Growth

O

Let f and g be functions from positive integers to positive integers. We say f is $O(g(n))$ if g is an upper bound on f : there exists a fixed constant c and a fixed n_0 such that for all $n \geq n_0$,

$$f(n) \leq cg(n).$$

Equivalently, f is $O(g(n))$ if the function $f(n)/g(n)$ is bounded above by some constant.

o

We say f is $O(g(n))$ if for all arbitrarily small real $c > 0$, for all but perhaps finitely many n,

$$f(n) \leq cg(n).$$

Equivalently, f is $o(g)$ if the function $f(n)/g(n)$ tends to 0 as n tends to infinity. That is, f is small compared to g. If f is $o(g)$ then f is also $O(g)$

Ω

We say that f is $\Omega(g(n))$ if g is a lower bound on f for large n. Formally, f is $\Omega(g)$ if there is a fixed constant c and a fixed no such that for all n>no,

$$cg(n) \leq f(n)$$

For example, any polynomial whose highest exponent is n^k is $\Omega(n^k)$. If $f(n)$ is $\Omega(g(n))$ then $g(n)$ is $O(f(n))$. If $f(n)$ is $o(g(n))$ then $f(n)$ is *not* $\Omega(g(n))$.

Θ

We say that f is $\Theta(g(n))$ if g is an accurate characterization of f for large n: it can be scaled so it is both an upper and a lower bound of f. That is, f is both $\Theta(g(n))$ and $\Omega(g(n))$. Expanding out the definitions of Ω and O, f is $\Theta(g(n))$ if there are fixed constants c_1 and c_2 and a fixed n_0 such that for all $n > n_0$,

$$c_1 g(n) \le f(n) \le c_2 g(n)$$

For example, any polynomial whose highest exponent is n^k is $\Theta(n^k)$. If f is $\Theta(g)$, then it is $O(g)$ but not $o(g)$. Sometimes people use $\Theta(g(n))$; a bit informally to mean the stronger property $\Theta(g(n))$; however, the two are different.

Here are some examples:

- $n + \log n$ is $O(n)$ and $\Theta(n)$, because for all $n > 1, n < n + \log n < 2n$.
- n^{1000} is $o(2^n)$, because $n^{1000}/2^n$ tends to 0 as n tends to infinity.
- For any fixed but arbitrarily small real number c, $n \log n$ is $o(n^{1+c})$, since $n \log n / n^{1+c}$ tends to 0. To see this, take the logarithm

$$\log\left(n \log n / n^{1+c}\right)$$
$$= \log(n \log n) - \log\left(n^{1+c}\right)$$
$$= \log n + \log \log n - (1+c)\log n$$
$$= \log \log n - c \log n$$

and observe that it tends to negative infinity.

The meaning of an expression like $O(n^2)$ is really a set of functions: all the functions that are $O(n^2)$. When we say that $f(n)$ is $O(n^2)$, we mean that $f(n)$ is a member of this set. It is also common to write this as $f(n) = O(g(n))$ although it is not really an equality.

We now introduce some convenient rules for manipulating expressions involving order notation. These rules, which we state without proof, are useful for working with orders of growth. They are really statements about sets of functions. For example, we can read #2 as saying that the product of any two functions in $O(f(n))$ and $O(g(n))$ is in $O(f(n)g(n))$.

1. $cn^m = O(n^k)$ *for any constant* c *and any* $m \le k$.
2. $O(f(n)) + O(g(n)) = O(f(n) + g(n))$.
3. $O(f(n))O(g(n)) = O(f(n)g(n))$.
4. $O(cf(n)) = O(f(n))$ *for any constant* c.

5. c *is* $O(1)$ *for any constant* c.

6. $log_b n = O(log\ n)$ *for any base* b.

All of these rules (except #1) also hold for Θ as well.

Big O Notation

Big O notation is a particular tool for assessing algorithm efficiency. Big O notation is often used to show how programs need resources relative to their input size.

Big O notation is also known as Bachmann–Landau notation after its discoverers, or asymptotic notation.

The size of a program's input is given to the computer, and then the running time and space requirements are determined. Engineers can get a visual graph that shows needs relative to different input sizes.

Big O notation is also used in other kinds of measurements in other fields. It is an example of a fundamental equation with a lot of parameters and variables. A full notation of the big O notation equation can be found online.

In a Simple way, Big O notation is the language we use for talking about how long an algorithm takes to run. It's how we compare the efficiency of different approaches to a problem.

It's like math except it's an awesome, not-boring kind of math where you get to wave your hands through the details and just focus on what's *basically* happening.

With big O notation we express the runtime in terms of—brace yourself—*how quickly it grows relative to the input, as the input gets arbitrarily large.*

Let's break that down:

1. How quickly the runtime grows: It's hard to pin down the *exact runtime* of an algorithm. It depends on the speed of the processor, what else the computer is running, etc. So instead of talking about the runtime directly, we use big O notation to talk about *how quickly the runtime grows.*

2. Relative to the input: If we were measuring our runtime directly, we could express our speed in seconds. Since we're measuring *how quickly our runtime grows*, we need to express our speed in terms of something else. With Big O notation, we use the size of the input, which we call "n." So we can say things like the runtime grows "on the order of the size of the input" $(O(n))$ or "on the order of the square of the size of the input" $(O(n^2))$.

3. As the input gets arbitrarily large: Our algorithm may have steps that seem expensive when n is small but are eclipsed eventually by other steps as n gets huge. For big O analysis, we

care most about the stuff that grows fastest as the input grows, because everything else is quickly eclipsed as n gets very large.

If this seems abstract so far, that's because it is. Let's look at some examples.

Some Examples

```
public static void printFirstItem(int[] items) {

    System.out.println(items[0]);

}
```

This method runs in $O(1)$ time (or "constant time") relative to its input. The input array could be 1 item or 1,000 items, but this method would still just require one "step."

```
public static void printAllItems(int[] items) {

    for (int item : items) {

        System.out.println(item);

    }

}
```

This method runs in $O(n)$ time (or "linear time"), where n is the number of items in the array. If the array has 10 items, we have to print 10 times. If it has 1,000 items, we have to print 1,000 times.

```
public static void printAllPossibleOrderedPairs(int[] items) {

    for (int firstItem : items) {

        for (int secondItem : items) {

            System.out.println(firstItem + ", " + secondItem);

        }

    }

}
```

Here we're nesting two loops. If our array has nn items, our outer loop runs nn times and our inner loop runs n *times for each iteration of the outer loop*, giving us n^2 total prints. Thus this method runs in $O(n^2)$ time (or "quadratic time"). If the array has 10 items, we have to print 100 times. If it has 1,000 items, we have to print 1,000,000 times.

N could be the Actual Input, or the size of the Input

Both of these methods have $O(n)$ runtime, even though one takes an integer as its input and the other takes an array:

```
public static void sayHiNTimes(int n) {
```

```java
for (int i = 0; i < n; i++) {

    System.out.println("hi");

}

}
```

```java
public static void printAllItems(int[] items) {

    for (int item : items) {

        System.out.println(item);

    }

}
```

So sometimes *n* is an *actual number* that's an input to our method, and other times *n* is the *number of items* in an input array (or an input map, or an input object, etc.).

Drop the Constants

This is why big O notation *rules*. When you're calculating the big O complexity of something, you just throw out the constants. So like:

```java
public static void printAllItemsTwice(int[] items) {

    for (int item : items) {

        System.out.println(item);

    }


    // once more, with feeling
    for (int item : items) {

        System.out.println(item);

    }

}
```

This is $O(2n)$, which we just call $O(n)$.

```java
public static void printFirstItemThenFirstHalfThenSayHi100Times(int[] items) {
    System.out.println(items[0]);

    int middleIndex = items.length / 2;

    int index = 0;
```

```
    while (index < middleIndex) {

        System.out.println(items[index]);

        index++;

    }


    for (int i = 0; i < 100; i++) {

        System.out.println("hi");

    }

}
```

This is $O(1 + n/2 + 100)$ which we just call $O(n)$.

Why can we get away with this? Remember, for big O notation we're looking at what happens as n gets arbitrarily large. As n gets really big, adding 100 or dividing by 2 has a decreasingly significant effect.

Drop the less significant terms

For example:

```
    public static void printAllNumbersThenAllPairSums(int[] numbers) {

        System.out.println("these are the numbers:");

        for (int number : numbers) {

            System.out.println(number);

        }


        System.out.println("and these are their sums:");

        for (int firstNumber : numbers) {

            for (int secondNumber : numbers) {

                System.out.println(firstNumber + secondNumber);

            }

        }

    }
```

Here our runtime is $O(n + n^2)$, which we just call $O(n^2)$. Even if it was $O(n^2/2 + 100n)$, it would still be $O(n^2)$.

Similarly:

- $O(n^3 + 50n^2 + 10000) \, is \, O(n^3)$
- $O((n + 30) * (n + 5)) \, is \, O(n^2)$

Again, we can get away with this because the less significant terms quickly become, well, less significant as n gets big.

We're Usually Talking About the "Worst Case"

Often this "worst case" stipulation is implied.

Sometimes the worst case runtime is significantly worse than the best case runtime:

```java
public static boolean contains(int[] haystack, int needle) {


    // does the haystack contain the needle?
    for (int n : haystack) {

        if (n == needle) {

            return true;

        }

    }


    return false;

}
```

Here we might have 100 items in our haystack, but the first item might be the needle, in which case we would return in just 1 iteration of our loop.

In general we'd say this is $O(n)$ runtime and the "worst case" part would be implied. But to be more specific we could say this is worst case $O(n)$ and best case $O(1)$ runtime. For some algorithms we can also make rigorous statements about the "average case" runtime.

Space Complexity: the Final Frontier

Sometimes we want to optimize for using less memory instead of (or in addition to) using less time. Talking about memory cost (or "space complexity") is very similar to talking about time cost. We simply look at the total size (relative to the size of the input) of any new variables we're allocating.

This method takes $O(1)$ space (we use a fixed number of variables):

```java
public static void sayHiNTimes(int n) {

    for (int i = 0; i < n; i++) {
```

```
    System.out.println("hi");

  }

}
```

This method takes $O(n)$ space (the size of hiArray scales with the size of the input):

```
  public static String[] arrayOfHiNTimes(int n) {

    String[] hiArray = new String[n];

    for (int i = 0; i < n; i++) {

      hiArray[i] = "hi";

    }

    return hiArray;

}
```

Usually when we talk about space complexity, we're talking about additional space, so we don't include space taken up by the inputs. For example, this method takes constant space even though the input has n items:

```
public static int getLargestItem(int[] items) {

    int largest = Integer.MIN_VALUE;

    for (int item : items) {

        if (item > largest) {

            largest = item;

        }

    }

    return largest;

}
```

Sometimes there's a tradeoff between saving time and saving space, so you have to decide which one you're optimizing for.

Analysis of Algorithms

Analysis of algorithms is a branch of computer science that studies the performance of algorithms, especially their run time and space requirements.

Algorithm analysis is an important part of a broader computational complexity theory, which provides theoretical estimates for the resources needed by any algorithm which solves a given computational problem. These estimates provide an insight into reasonable directions of search for efficient algorithms. In theoretical analysis of algorithms it is common to estimate their complexity in the asymptotic sense, i.e., to estimate the complexity function for arbitrarily large input. Big O notation, Big-omega notation and Big-theta notation are used to this end.

- Rule of thumb: Simple programs can be analyzed by counting the nested loops of the program. A single loop over n items yields $f(n) = n$. A loop within a loop yields $f(n) = n^2$. A loop within a loop within a loop yields $f(n) = n^3$.

- Rule of thumb: Given a series of for loops that are sequential, the slowest of them determines the asymptotic behavior of the program. Two nested loops followed by a single loop is asymptotically the same as the nested loops alone, because the nested loops dominate the simple loop.

The practical goal of algorithm analysis is to predict the performance of different algorithms in order to guide design decisions.

The goal of algorithm analysis is to make meaningful comparisons between algorithms, but there are some problems:

- The relative performance of the algorithms might depend on characteristics of the hardware, so one algorithm might be faster on Machine A, another on Machine B. The general solution to this problem is to specify a machine model and analyze the number of steps, or operations, an algorithm requires under a given model.

- Relative performance might depend on the details of the dataset. For example, some sorting algorithms run faster if the data are already partially sorted; other algorithms run slower in this case. A common way to avoid this problem is to analyze the worst case scenario. It is sometimes useful to analyze average case performance, but that's usually harder, and it might not be obvious what set of cases to average over.

- Relative performance also depends on the size of the problem. A sorting algorithm that is fast for small lists might be slow for long lists. The usual solution to this problem is to express run time (or number of operations) as a function of problem size, and to compare the functions asymptotically as the problem size increases.

Analysis Types

The algorithm complexity can be best, average or worst case analysis. The algorithm analysis can be expressed using Big O notation. Best, worst, and average cases of a given algorithm express what the resource usage is at least, at most and on average, respectively. The big o notation simplifies the comparison of algorithms.

Best Case

Best case performance used in computer science to describe an algorithm's behavior under optimal conditions. An example of best case performance would be trying to sort a list that is already sorted using some sorting algorithm. E.G. [1,2,3] --> [1,2,3]

Average Case

Average case performance measured using the average optimal conditions to solve the problem. For example a list that is neither best case nor, worst case order that you want to be sorted in a certain order. E.G. [2,1,5,3] --> [1,2,3,5] OR [2,1,5,3] --> [5,3,2,1]

Worst Case

Worst case performance used to analyze the algorithm's behavior under worst case input and least possible to solve the problem. It determines when the algorithm will perform worst for the given inputs. An example of the worst case performance would be a list of names already sorted in ascending order that you want to sort in descending order.

Cost Models

Time efficiency estimates depend on what we define to be a step. For the analysis to correspond usefully to the actual execution time, the time required to perform a step must be guaranteed to be bounded above by a constant. One must be careful here; for instance, some analyses count an addition of two numbers as one step. This assumption may not be warranted in certain contexts. For example, if the numbers involved in a computation may be arbitrarily large, the time required by a single addition can no longer be assumed to be constant.

Two cost models are generally used:

- the uniform cost model, also called uniform-cost measurement (and similar variations), assigns a constant cost to every machine operation, regardless of the size of the numbers involved

- the logarithmic cost model, also called logarithmic-cost measurement (and similar variations), assigns a cost to every machine operation proportional to the number of bits involved

The latter is more cumbersome to use, so it's only employed when necessary, for example in the analysis of arbitrary-precision arithmetic algorithms, like those used in cryptography.

A key point which is often overlooked is that published lower bounds for problems are often given for a model of computation that is more restricted than the set of operations that you could use in practice and therefore there are algorithms that are faster than what would naively be thought possible.

Run-time Analysis

Run-time analysis is a theoretical classification that estimates and anticipates the increase in *running time* (or run-time) of an algorithm as its *input size* (usually denoted as n) increases. Run-time efficiency is a topic of great interest in computer science: A program can take seconds, hours, or even years to finish executing, depending on which algorithm it implements. While software profiling techniques can be used to measure an algorithm's run-time in practice, they cannot provide timing data for all infinitely many possible inputs; the latter can only be achieved by the theoretical methods of run-time analysis.

Shortcomings of Empirical Metrics

Since algorithms are platform-independent (i.e. a given algorithm can be implemented in an arbitrary programming language on an arbitrary computer running an arbitrary operating system), there are additional significant drawbacks to using an empirical approach to gauge the comparative performance of a given set of algorithms.

Take as an example a program that looks up a specific entry in a sorted list of size n. Suppose this program were implemented on Computer A, a state-of-the-art machine, using a linear search algorithm, and on Computer B, a much slower machine, using a binary search algorithm. Benchmark testing on the two computers running their respective programs might look something like the following:

n (list size)	Computer A run-time (in nanoseconds)	Computer B run-time (in nanoseconds)
16	8	100,000
63	32	150,000
250	125	200,000
1,000	500	250,000

Based on these metrics, it would be easy to jump to the conclusion that *Computer A* is running an algorithm that is far superior in efficiency to that of *Computer B*. However, if the size of the input-list is increased to a sufficient number, that conclusion is dramatically demonstrated to be in error:

n (list size)	Computer A run-time (in nanoseconds)	Computer B run-time (in nanoseconds)
16	8	100,000
63	32	150,000
250	125	200,000
1,000	500	250,000
...	...	...
1,000,000	500,000	500,000
4,000,000	2,000,000	550,000
16,000,000	8,000,000	600,000
...	...	...
$63,072 \times 10^{12}$	$31,536 \times 10^{12}$ ns, or 1 year	1,375,000 ns, or 1.375 milliseconds

Computer A, running the linear search program, exhibits a linear growth rate. The program's run-time is directly proportional to its input size. Doubling the input size doubles the run time, quadrupling the input size quadruples the run-time, and so forth. On the other hand, Computer B, running the binary search program, exhibits a logarithmic growth rate. Quadrupling the input size only increases the run time by a constant amount (in this example, 50,000 ns). Even though Computer A is ostensibly a faster machine, Computer B will inevitably surpass Computer A in run-time because it's running an algorithm with a much slower growth rate.

Orders of Growth

Informally, an algorithm can be said to exhibit a growth rate on the order of a mathematical function if beyond a certain input size n, the function $f(n)$ times a positive constant provides an upper bound or limit for the run-time of that algorithm. In other words, for a given input size n greater than some n_0 and a constant c, the running time of that algorithm will never be larger than $c \times f(n)$. This concept is frequently expressed using Big O notation. For example, since the run-time of insertion sort grows quadratically as its input size increases, insertion sort can be said to be of order $O(n^2)$.

Big O notation is a convenient way to express the worst-case scenario for a given algorithm, although it can also be used to express the average-case — for example, the worst-case scenario for quicksort is $O(n^2)$, but the average-case run-time is $O(n \log n)$.

Empirical Orders of Growth

Assuming the execution time follows power rule, $t \approx k\,n^a$. the coefficient a can be found by taking empirical measurements of run time $\{n_1, n_2\}$, at some problem-size points $\{n_1, n_2\}$, and calculating $t_2 / t_1 = (n_2 / n_1)^a$ so that $a = \log(t_2 / t_1) / \log(n_2 / n_1)$. In other words, this measures the slope of the empirical line on the log–log plot of execution time vs. problem size, at some size point. If the order of growth indeed follows the power rule (and so the line on log–log plot is indeed a straight line), the empirical value of a will stay constant at different ranges, and if not, it will change (and the line is a curved line) - but still could serve for comparison of any two given algorithms as to their *empirical local orders of growth* behaviour. This is applied to the table below:

n (list size)	Computer A run-time (in nanoseconds)	Local order of growth (n^_)	Computer B run-time (in nanoseconds)	Local order of growth (n^_)
15	7		100,000	
65	32	1.04	150,000	0.28
250	125	1.01	200,000	0.21
1,000	500	1.00	250,000	0.16
...	...		...	
1,000,000	500,000	1.00	500,000	0.10
4,000,000	2,000,000	1.00	550,000	0.07
16,000,000	8,000,000	1.00	600,000	0.06
...	...		...	

It is clearly seen that the first algorithm exhibits a linear order of growth indeed following the power rule. The empirical values for the second one are diminishing rapidly, suggesting it follows another rule of growth and in any case has much lower local orders of growth (and improving further still), empirically, than the first one.

Evaluating Run-time Complexity

The run-time complexity for the worst-case scenario of a given algorithm can sometimes be evaluated by examining the structure of the algorithm and making some simplifying assumptions. Consider the following pseudocode:

```
1       get a positive integer from input

2       if n > 10

3           print "This might take a while..."

4       for i = 1 to n

5           for j = 1 to i

6               print i * j

7       print "Done."
```

A given computer will take a discrete amount of time to execute each of the instructions involved with carrying out this algorithm. The specific amount of time to carry out a given instruction will vary depending on which instruction is being executed and which computer is executing it, but on a conventional computer, this amount will be deterministic. Say that the actions carried out in step 1 are considered to consume time T_1, step 2 uses time T_2, and so forth.

In the algorithm above, steps 1, 2 and 7 will only be run once. For a worst-case evaluation, it should be assumed that step 3 will be run as well. Thus the total amount of time to run steps 1-3 and step 7 is:

$$T_1 + T_2 + T_3 + T_7.$$

The loops in steps 4, 5 and 6 are trickier to evaluate. The outer loop test in step 4 will execute (n + 1) times (note that an extra step is required to terminate the for loop, hence n + 1 and not n execu-tions), which will consume T_4(n + 1) time. The inner loop, on the other hand, is governed by the value of j, which iterates from 1 to i. On the first pass through the outer loop, j iterates from 1 to 1: The inner loop makes one pass, so running the inner loop body (step 6) consumes T_6 time, and the inner loop test (step 5) consumes $2T_5$ time. During the next pass through the outer loop, j iterates from 1 to 2: the inner loop makes two passes, so running the inner loop body (step 6) consumes $2T_6$ time, and the inner loop test (step 5) consumes $3T_5$ time.

Altogether, the total time required to run the inner loop body can be expressed as an arithmetic progression:

$$T_6 + 2T_6 + 3T_6 + \cdots + (n-1)T_6 + nT_6$$

which can be factored as

$$T_6[1 + 2 + 3 + \cdots + (n-1) + n] = T_6\left[\frac{1}{2}(n^2 + n)\right]$$

The total time required to run the outer loop test can be evaluated similarly:

$$2T_5 + 3T_5 + 4T_5 + \cdots + (n-1)T_5 + nT_5 + (n+1)T_5$$
$$= T_5 + 2T_5 + 3T_5 + 4T_5 + \cdots + (n-1)T_5 + nT_5 + (n+1)T_5 - T_5$$

which can be factored as

$$T_5\left[1+2+3+\cdots+(n-1)+n+(n+1)\right]-T_5$$

$$=\left[\frac{1}{2}(n^2+n)\right]T_5+(n+1)T_5-T_5$$

$$=T_5\left[\frac{1}{2}(n^2+n)\right]+nT_5$$

$$=\left[\frac{1}{2}(n^2+3n)\right]T_5$$

Therefore, the total running time for this algorithm is:

$$f(n)=T_1+T_2+T_3+T_7+(n+1)T_4+\left[\frac{1}{2}(n^2+n)\right]T_6+\left[\frac{1}{2}(n^2+3n)\right]T_5$$

which reduces to

$$f(n)=\left[\frac{1}{2}(n^2+n)\right]T_6+\left[\frac{1}{2}(n^2+3n)\right]T_5+(n+1)T_4+T_1+T_2+T_3+T_7$$

As a rule-of-thumb, one can assume that the highest-order term in any given function dominates its rate of growth and thus defines its run-time order. In this example, n^2 is the highest-order term, so one can conclude that $f(n) = O(n^2)$. Formally this can be proven as follows:

Prove that $\left[\frac{1}{2}(n^2+n)\right]T_6+\left[\frac{1}{2}(n^2+3n)\right]T_5+(n+1)T_4+T_1+T_2+T_3+T_7\le cn^2, n\ge n_0$

$$\left[\frac{1}{2}(n^2+n)\right]T_6+\left[\frac{1}{2}(n^2+3n)\right]T_5+(n+1)T_4+T_1+T_2+T_3+T_7$$

$$\le(n^2+n)T_6+(n^2+3n)T_5+(n+1)T_4+T_1+T_2+T_3+T_7 \text{ (for } n\ge0)$$

Let k be a constant greater than or equal to $[T_1..T_7]$

$$T_6(n^2+n)+T_5(n^2+3n)+(n+1)T_4+T_1+T_2+T_3+T_7\le k(n^2+n)+k(n^2+3n)+kn+5k$$
$$=2kn^2+5kn+5k\le 2kn^2+5kn^2+5kn^2 \text{ (for } n\ge1)=12kn^2$$

Therefore $\left[\frac{1}{2}(n^2+n)\right]T_6+\left[\frac{1}{2}(n^2+3n)\right]T_5+(n+1)T_4+T_1+T_2+T_3+T_7\le cn^2, n\ge n_0$ for $c=12k, n_0=1$

A more elegant approach to analyzing this algorithm would be to declare that $[T_1..T_7]$ are all equal to one unit of time, in a system of units chosen so that one unit is greater than or equal to the actual times for these steps. This would mean that the algorithm's running time breaks down as follows:

$$4+\sum_{i=1}^{n}i\le 4+\sum_{i=1}^{n}n=4+n^2\le 5n^2 \text{ (for } n\ge1)=O(n^2).$$

Growth Rate Analysis of Other Resources

The methodology of run-time analysis can also be utilized for predicting other growth rates, such as consumption of memory space. As an example, consider the following pseudocode which manages and reallocates memory usage by a program based on the size of a file which that program manages:

```
while (file still open)

    let n = size of file

    for every 100,000 kilobytes of increase in file size

        double the amount of memory reserved
```

In this instance, as the file size n increases, memory will be consumed at an exponential growth rate, which is order $O(2^n)$. This is an extremely rapid and most likely unmanageable growth rate for consumption of memory resources.

Relevance

Algorithm analysis is important in practice because the accidental or unintentional use of an inefficient algorithm can significantly impact system performance. In time-sensitive applications, an algorithm taking too long to run can render its results outdated or useless. An inefficient algorithm can also end up requiring an uneconomical amount of computing power or storage in order to run, again rendering it practically useless.

Constant Factors

Analysis of algorithms typically focuses on the asymptotic performance, particularly at the elementary level, but in practical applications constant factors are important, and real-world data is in practice always limited in size. The limit is typically the size of addressable memory, so on 32-bit machines $2^{32} = 4$ GiB (greater if segmented memory is used) and on 64-bit machines $2^{64} = 16$ EiB. Thus given a limited size, an order of growth (time or space) can be replaced by a constant factor, and in this sense all practical algorithms are $O(1)$ for a large enough constant, or for small enough data.

This interpretation is primarily useful for functions that grow extremely slowly: (binary) iterated logarithm ($\log^*$) is less than 5 for all practical data (2^{65536} bits); (binary) log-log ($\log \log n$) is less than 6 for virtually all practical data (2^{64} bits); and binary log ($\log n$) is less than 64 for virtually all practical data (2^{64} bits). An algorithm with non-constant complexity may nonetheless be more efficient than an algorithm with constant complexity on practical data if the overhead of the constant time algorithm results in a larger constant factor, e.g., one may have $K > k \log \log n$ so long as $K / k > 6$ and $n < 2^{2^6} = 2^{64}$.

For large data linear or quadratic factors cannot be ignored, but for small data an asymptotically inefficient algorithm may be more efficient. This is particularly used in hybrid algorithms, like Timsort, which use an asymptotically efficient algorithm (here merge sort, with time complexity $n \log n$), but switch to an asymptotically inefficient algorithm (here insertion sort, with time complexity n^2) for small data, as the simpler algorithm is faster on small data.

Empirical Algorithmics

Methods from empirical algorithmics complement theoretical methods for the analysis of algorithms. Through the principled application of empirical methods, particularly from statistics, it is often possible to obtain insights into the behavior of algorithms such as high-performance heuristic algorithms for hard combinatorial problems that are (currently) inaccessible to theoretical analysis Empirical methods can also be used to achieve substantial improvements in algorithmic efficiency

In the absence of empirical algorithmics, analyzing the complexity of an algorithm can involve various theoretical methods applicable to various situations in which the algorithm may be used. Memory and cache considerations are often significant factors to be considered in the theoretical choice of a complex algorithm, or the approach to its optimization, for a given purpose. Performance profiling is a dynamic program analysis technique typically used for finding and analyzing bottlenecks in an entire application's code or for analyzing an entire application to identify poorly performing code. A profiler can reveal the code most relevant to an application's performance issues.

A profiler may help to determine when to choose one algorithm over another in a particular situation. When an individual algorithm is profiled, as with complexity analysis, memory and cache considerations are often more significant than instruction counts or clock cycles; however, the profiler's findings can be considered in light of how the algorithm accesses data rather than the number of instructions it uses.

Profiling may provide intuitive insight into an algorithm's behavior by revealing performance findings as a visual representation. Performance profiling has been applied, for example, during the development of algorithms for matching wildcards. Early algorithms for matching wildcards, such as Rich Salz' wildmat algorithm, typically relied on recursion, a technique criticized on grounds of performance. The Krauss matching wildcards algorithm was developed based on an attempt to formulate a non-recursive alternative using test cases followed by optimizations suggested via performance profiling, resulting in a new algorithmic strategy conceived in light of the profiling along with other considerations. Profilers that collect data at the level of basic blocks or that rely on hardware assistance provide results that can be accurate enough to assist software developers in optimizing algorithms for a particular computer or situation. Performance profiling can aid developer understanding of the characteristics of complex algorithms applied in complex situations, such as coevolutionary algorithms applied to arbitrary test-based problems, and may help lead to design improvements.

Empirical Analysis of Algorithms

- In practice, we will often need to resort to empirical rather than theoretical analysis to compare algorithms.

  o We may want to know something about performance of the algorithm "on average" for real instances.

  o Our model of computation may not capture important effects of the hardware architecture that arise in practice.

- o There may be implementational details that affect constant factors and are not captured by asymptotic analysis.
- For this purpose, we need a methodology for comparing algorithms based on real-world performance.

Issues to Consider

- Empirical analysis introduces many more factors that need to be controlled for in some way.
  - o Test platform (hardware, language, compiler)
  - o Measures of performance (what to compare)
  - o Benchmark test set (what instances to test on)
  - o Algorithmic parameters
  - o Implementational details
- It is much less obvious how to perform a rigorous analysis in the presence of so many factors.
- Practical considerations prevent complete testing.

Measures of Performance

- For the time being, we focus on sequential algorithms.
- What is the goal?
  - o Compare two algorithms.
  - o Improve the implementation of a single algorithm.
- Possible measures
  - o Empirical running time (CPU time, wall clock)
  - o Representative operation counts

Measuring Time

- There are three relevant measures of time taken by a process.
  - o User time measures the amount of time (number of cycles taken by a process in "user mode."
  - o System time the time taken by the kernel executing on behalf of the process.
  - o Wall clock time is the total "real" time taken to execute the process.
- Generally speaking, user time is the most relevant, though it ignores some important operations (I/O, etc.).

- Wallclock time should be used cautiously/sparingly, but may be necessary for assessment of parallel codes,

Representative Operation Counts

- In some cases, we may want to count operations, rather than time

  - Identify bottlenecks

  - Counterpart to theoretical analysis

- What operations should we count?

  - Profilers can count function calls and executions of individual lines of code to identify bottlenecks.

  - We may know a priori what operations we want to measure (example: comparisons and swaps in sorting).

Test Sets

- It is crucial to choose your test set well.

- The instances must be chosen carefully in order to allow proper conclusions to be drawn.

- We must pay close attention to their size, inherent difficulty, and other important structural properties.

- This is especially important if we are trying to distinguish among multiple algorithms.

- Example: Sorting

Comparing Algorithms

- Given a performance measure and a test set, the question still arises how to decide which algorithm is "better."

- We can do the comparison using some sort of summary statistic.

  - Arithmetic mean

  - Geometric mean

  - Variance

- These statistics hide information useful for comparison.

Accounting for Stochasticity

- In empirical analysis, we must take account of the fact that running times are inherently stochastic.

- If we are measuring wallclock time, this may vary substantially for seemingly identical executions.

- In the case of parallel processing, stochasticity may also arise due to asynchronism (order of operations).

- In such case, multiple identical runs may be used to estimate the affect of this randomness.

- If necessary, statistical analysis may be used to analyze the results, but this is beyond the scope of this course.

Performance Profiles

- Performance profiles allow comparison of algorithms across an entire test set without loss of information.

- They provide a visual summary of how algorithms compare on a performance measure across a test set.

Example Performance Profile

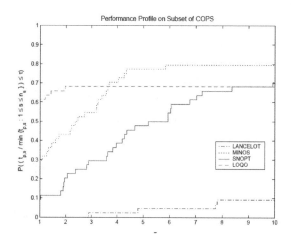

Empirical Versus Theoretical Analysis

- For sequential algorithms, asymptotic analysis is often good enough for choosing between algorithms.

- It is less ideal with respect to tuning of implementational details.

- For parallel algorithms, asymptotic analysis is far more problematic.

- The details not captured by the model of computation can matter much more.

- There is an additional dimension on which we must compare algorithms: scalability

Amortized Analysis

Amortized analysis is applied on data structures that support many operations. The sequence of operations and the multiplicity of each operation is application specific or the associated algorithm specific. Classical asymptotic analysis gives worst case analysis of each operation without taking the effect of one operation on the other, whereas amortized analysis focuses on a sequence of operations, an interplay between operations, and thus yielding an analysis which is precise and depicts a micro-level analysis. Since many operations are involved as part of the analysis, the objective is to perform efficiently as many operations as possible, leaving very few costly operations (the time complexity is relatively more for these operations). To calculate the cost of an operation or the amortized cost of an operation, we take the average over all operations. In particular, worst case time of each operation is taken into account to calculate the average cost in the worst case. Some of the highlights of amortized analysis include;

- Amortized Analysis is applied to algorithms where an occasional operation is very slow, but most of the other operations are faster.

- In Amortized Analysis, we analyze a sequence of operations and guarantee a worst case average time which is lower than the worst case time of a particular expensive operation.

- Amortized analysis is an upper bound: it is the average performance of each operation in the worst case. Amortized analysis is concerned with the over all cost of a sequence of operations. It does not say anything about the cost of a specific operation in that sequence.

- Amortized analysis can be understood to take advantage of the fact that some expensive operations may pay for future operations by somehow limiting the number or cost of expensive operations that can happen in the near future.

- Amortized analysis may consist of a collection of cheap, less expensive and expensive operations, however, amortized analysis (due to its averaging argument) will show that average cost of an operation is cheap.

- This is different from average case analysis, wherein averaging argument is given over all inputs for a specific operation. Inputs are modeled using a suitable probability distribution. In amortized analysis, no probability is involved.

Approaches to Amortized Analysis

It is important to note that these approaches are for analysis purpose only. The underlying algorithm design is unaltered and the purpose of these micro-level analysis is to get a good insight into the operations being performed.

- Aggregate Analysis: Aggregate analysis is a simple method that involves computing the total cost $T(n)$ for a sequence of n operations, then dividing $T(n)$ by the number n of operations to obtain the amortized cost or the average cost in the worst case. For all operations the same amortized cost $T(n)/n$ is assigned, even if they are of different types. The other two methods may allow for assigning different amortized costs to different types of operations in the same sequence.

- Accounting Method: As part of accounting method we maintain an account with the underlying data structure. Initially, the account contains 'o' credits (charges). When we perform an operation, we charge the operation, and if we over charge an operation, the excess charge will be deposited to the account as credit. For some operation, we may charge nothing, in such a case, we make use of charges available at credit. Such operations are referred to as free operations. Analysis ensures that the account is never at debit (negative balance). This technique is good, if for example, there are two operations O1 and O2 which are tightly coupled, then O1 can be over charged and O2 is free. Typically, the charge denotes the actual cost of that operation. The excess charge will be stored at objects (elements) of a data structure. In the accounting method, the amount charged for each operation type is the amortized cost for that type. As long as the charges are set so that it is impossible to go into debt, the amortized cost will be an upper bound on the actual cost for any sequence of operations. Therefore, the trick to successful amortized analysis with the accounting method is to pick appropriate charges and show that these charges are sufficient to allow payment for any sequence of operations.

- Potential Function Method: Here, the analysis is done by focusing on structural parameters such as the number of elements, the height, the number of property violations of a data structure. For an operation, after performing the operation, the change in a structural parameter is captured as a function which is stored at a data structure. The function that captures the change is known as a potential function. As part of the analysis, we work with non-negative potential functions. If the change in potential is positive, then that operation is over charged and similar to accounting method, the excess potential will be stored at the data structure. If the change in potential is negative, then that operation is under charged which would be compensated by excess potential available at the data structure.

Formally, let c_i denote the actual cost of the ith operation and $\hat{c}_i$ denote the amortized cost of the ith operation. If $\hat{c}_i > c_i$, then the ith operation leaves some positive amount of credit, the credits $\hat{c}_i > c_i$ can be used up by future operations. And as long as

$$\sum_{i=1}^{n} \hat{c}_i \geq \sum_{i=1}^{n} c_i$$

the total available credit will always be non negative, and the sum of amortized costs will be an upper bound on the actual cost. The potential function method defines a function that maps a data structure onto a real valued non-negative number. In the potential method, the amortized cost of operation i is equal to the actual cost plus the increase in potential due to that operation:

$$\hat{c}_i = c_i + \phi_i - \phi_{i-1}$$

From equation 1 and 2:

$$\sum_{i=1}^{n} \hat{c}_i = \sum_{i=1}^{n} \left(c_i + \phi_i - \phi_{i-1} \right)$$

$$\sum_{i=1}^{n} \hat{c}_i = \left\langle \sum_{i=1}^{n} c_i \right\rangle + \phi_n - \phi_0$$

Case Studies

We shall present three case studies to explain each analysis technique in detail.

Stack

Our stack implementation consists of three operations, namely push(), pop() and multi-pop(). The operation multi-pop(k) fetches top k elements of the stack if stack contains at least k elements. If stack contains less than k elements, then output the entire stack.

Let us analyze stack from the perspective of amortized analysis by assuming there are n of the above operations which are performed in some order. In classical world, the actual cost in worst case for push and pop is O(1) and multi-pop is O(n). We now show that the amortized cost of all three operations is O(1).

Aggregate Analysis

Let us assume that in a sequence of n operations, there are l multi-pop operations and the rest are push and pop operations. Clearly, l multi-pop operations perform at most n pops and therefore, the cost is O(n). The cost for the other n − l operations is O(n). The amortized cost is O(n) + O(n) divided by n which is O(1). Since aggregate analysis assigns the same cost to all operations, push, pop and multi-pop incur O(1) amortized cost.

Accounting Method

As part of accounting method, we need to assign credits to objects of stack S. Whenever we push an element x into S, we charge '2' credits. One credit will be used for pushing the element which is the actual cost for pushing x into S and the other credit is stored at x which would be used later. For pop operation, we charge nothing, i.e., pop operation is free. Although, the actual cost is '1', in our analysis we charge '0'. The excess credit '1' available at the element will be used when we perform a pop operation. Since pop is peformed on a non-empty stack, the account will always be at credit. Similarly, we charge nothing for multi-pop as sufficient credits are available for all k elements at elements themselves. Thus, the amortised cost of push is 2 = O(1), pop is 0 = O(1) and multi-pop is 0 = O(1).

Potential Function Method

The first thing in this method is to define a potential function capturing some structural parameter. A natural structural parameter of interest for stack is the number of elements. Keeping the number of elements as the potential function, we now analyze all three operations.

Push

$$\hat{c}_{push} = c_{push} + + \phi_i - \phi_i - 1$$

=1 + x + 1 − x, where x denotes the number of elements in S before push operation.

=2

Pop

$$\hat{c}_{push} = c_{push} + + \phi_i - \phi_i - 1$$

$$= 1 + x - 1 - x$$

$$= 0$$

Multi-pop(k)

$$\hat{c}_{push} = c_{push} + +\phi_i - \phi_i - 1$$

$$= k + n - k - n, \text{ where } n = |S|.$$

$$= 0$$

Thus, the amortized cost of all three operations is O(1). Note the similarity between this method and the accounting method. The potential function, in particular, the change in potential helps us to fix the excess value to be stored at each element of S. Also, note that potential functions such as $2 \cdot |S|$ or $c \cdot |S|$, where c is a constant will also work fine and still yields O(1) amortized cost. The excess potential will be simply stored at the data structure as credits. Similarly, in accounting method, if we charge, say 4 credits for push, then excess credits will be stored at elements.

Suppose, we introduce another operation, namely, multi-push(k) which pushes k elements into S. Let us analyze the cost of multi-push in all three techniques.

- Aggregate Analysis: In any sequence of n operations consisting of push, pop, multi-pop and multi-push, we may find l_1 multi-pop, l_2 multi-push and the rest are push and pop operations. In the worst case scenario, l_2 = O(1) and each multi-push pushes O(n) elements. For example, three multi-push with each push inserts n/3 elements. Therefore, the total cost is O(n) and the amortized cost is O(n)/O(1) which is O(n). Thus, for all operations, the amortized cost is O(n).

- Accounting Method: As before, we use '2' credits for push and '0' for pop. With this credit scheme, the cost of push, pop and multi-pop is O(1) amortized, whereas, multi-push is $2 \cdot$ O(n)/O(1) which is O(n). Therefore, the amortized cost of multi-push is O(n).

- Potential Function Method: For multi-push(k);

$$\hat{c}_{push} = c_{push} + +\phi_i - \phi_i - 1$$

$$= k + n - k - n, \text{ where } n = |S|.$$

$$= 2 \cdot k = O(n).$$

Binary Counter

Consider a binary counter on k bits which is intially set to all 0's. The primitive operations are Increment, Decrement and Reset. Increment on a counter adds a bit '1' to the current value of the counter. Similarly, decrement on a counter subtracts a bit '1' from the current value of the counter. For example, if counter contains '001101', on increment, the content of the counter is '001110' and on decrement, the result is '001100'. The reset operation makes the counter bits all 0's. The objectives here are to analyze amortized costs of (i) a sequence of n increment operations, (ii) a sequence of n increment and decrement operations, (iii) a sequence of n increment, decrement and reset operations.

Sequence of n Increment Operations

Given a binary counter on k-bits, we shall now analyze the amortized cost of a sequence of n increment operations. A trivial analysis shows O(k) for each increment and for n increment operation, the total cost is O(nk) and the average cost is O(k). We now present a micro-level analysis using which we show that the amortized cost is O(1). Note that not all bits in the counter flip in each increment operation.

The 0th bit flips in each increment and there are $\lfloor n \rfloor$ flips. The 1st bit is flipped alternately and thus $\left\lfloor \dfrac{n}{2} \right\rfloor$ flips in total.

The ith bit is flipped $\left\lfloor \dfrac{n}{2^i} \right\rfloor$ times in total. It is important to note that, for $i > \lfloor \log n \rfloor$, bit $A[i]$ never flips at all. The total number of flips in a sequence of n increments is thus

$$\sum_{i=0}^{\lfloor \log n \rfloor} \left\lfloor \frac{n}{2^i} \right\rfloor \quad < n \sum_{i=0}^{\infty} \frac{1}{2^i} = 2n$$

The worst-case time for a sequence of n increment operations on an initially zero counter is therefore O(n). The average cost of each operation, and therefore the amortized cost per operation, is O(n)/n = O(1). This completes the argument for aggregate analysis.

As part of accounting method, we assign '2' credits with each bit when it is flipped from 0 to 1. '1' credit will be used for the actual flip and the other '1' credit will be stored at the bit itself. When a bit is flipped from 1 to 0 in subsequent increments, it is done for free. The credit '1' stored at the bit (1) will actually pay for

Counter value	A[7]	A[6]	A[5]	A[4]	A[3]	A[2]	A[1]	A[0]	Total cost
0	0	0	0	0	0	0	0	0	0
1	0	0	0	0	0	0	0	1	1
2	0	0	0	0	0	0	1	0	3
3	0	0	0	0	0	0	1	1	4
4	0	0	0	0	0	1	0	0	7
5	0	0	0	0	0	1	0	1	8
6	0	0	0	0	0	1	1	0	10
7	0	0	0	0	0	1	1	1	11
8	0	0	0	0	1	0	0	0	15
9	0	0	0	0	1	0	0	1	16
10	0	0	0	0	1	0	1	0	18
11	0	0	0	0	1	0	1	1	19
12	0	0	0	0	1	1	0	0	22
13	0	0	0	0	1	1	0	1	23
14	0	0	0	0	1	1	1	0	25
15	0	0	0	0	1	1	1	1	26
16	0	0	0	1	0	0	0	0	31

An 8-bit binary counter where the value goes from 0 to 16 by a sequence of 16 increment operations. Bits that flip to achieve the next value are shaded.

this operation. At the end of each increment, the number of 1's in the counter is the credit accumulated at the counter. The primitive operations are flipping a bit from 1 to 0 and 0 to 1. The former charges 2 credits which $O(1)$ and the latter charges 0 credits which is also $O(1)$. Thus, the amortized cost of increment is $O(1)$.

For potential function method, the structural parameter of interest is the number of 1's in the counter. During i^{th} iteration all ones after the last zero is set to zero and the last zero is set to 1. For example, when increment is called on a counter with its contents being '11001111', the result is '11010000'. Let x denotes the total number of 1's before the ith operation and t denote the number of ones after the last zero. At the end of i th operation there will be $x - t + 1$ ones, t ones are changed to 0 and the last zero is changed to 1. Thus, the actual cost for the increment is $1 + t$. Therefore, the amortized cost is

$$\hat{c}_i = c_i + \phi_i - \phi_i - 1$$
$$= 1 + t + (x - t + 1) - x$$
$$= 2$$
$$= O(1)$$

Amortized analysis for a sequence of n decrement operations is similar to the analysis presented above and hence, a sequence of n decrements incur $O(1)$ amortized.

Sequence of n Increment and Decrement Operations

Consider a sequence having $\frac{n}{2}$ increments followed by $\frac{n}{2}$ increments and decrements happen alternately. As far as aggregate analysis is concerned, the actual cost for the first half of the operations is $O(n)$, whereas the second half incurs $\frac{n}{2} \cdot O(k)$. Thus, the amortized cost is $O(k)$. In general, there are l increments in a row followed by alternating increment and decrement operations. This is an example of worst case sequence for which amortized cost is $O(k)$. Therefore, both increment and decrement incur $O(k)$ amortized cost.

As part of accounting method, we assign k credits for both increment and decrement operations. Therefore, the amortized cost for both operations is $O(k)$ amortized.

For potential function method, the function refers to the number of 1's in the counter. For increment operation let x and t denote the number of 1's in the counter and the number of 1's after the last zero. Thus, the amortised cost of increment is

$$\hat{c}_i = c_i + \phi_i - \phi_i - 1$$
$$= 1 + t + (x - t + 1) - x$$
$$= 2$$
$$= O(1)$$

For decrement, let x and t denote the number of 1's in the counter and the number of 0's after the last one. Thus, the amortised cost of $\hat{c}_i = c_i + \phi_i - \phi_i - 1$

$$= 1 + t + (x + t - 1) - x$$
$$= 2t$$
$$= O(k)$$

Thus, the amortized cost of increment is O(1) and that of decrement is O(k).

Amortized analysis: a sequence of n increment, decrement and reset operations

Consider a sequence having $\frac{n}{2}$ increments followed by one reset operation. The total cost is O(n) + O(k). Thus, aggregate analysis for the $\frac{n}{2}$ 2 increments is O(1) amortized and that of reset is O(k) amortized. Therefore, the amortized cost for this sequence is O(k) amortized.

We shall now analyze amortized analysis of reset operation using potential function method. The actual cost of reset is O(k) and assume that there are x 1's in the current configuration of the counter.

$$\hat{c}_i = c_i + \phi_i - \phi_i - 1$$
$$= k + 0 - x$$
$$= O(k) \text{ if } x = O(1)$$

Thus, the amortized cost of reset is O(k). The analysis of increment and decrement are O(1) amortized and O(k) amortized, respectively.

Accounting Method

The accounting method, or the "banker's view," assigns charges to operations as if the computer were coinoperated. One can think of each operation always being accompanied by inserting one or more coins into the computer to pay for the operation, according to a predetermined charge for that operation type (e.g., a stack push might have one charge, and a pop of several items from the stack might have another charge). The charge does not necessarily correspond to the actual time required for the particular operation; it is possible that the operation will complete in less time than the time charged, in which case some positive accumulation of credit is left after the time required for the operation to finish is subtracted from the operation payment. Or, it is possible that the operation will need more time than the time charged, in which case the operation can be paid for by previously accumulated credit.

In the accounting method, the amount charged for each operation type is the amortized cost for that type. As long as the charges are set so that it is impossible to go into debt (i.e., one can show that there will never be an operation whose actual cost is greater than the sum of its charge plus the previously accumulated credit), the amortized cost will be an upper bound on the actual cost for any sequence of operations. Therefore, the trick to successful amortized analysis with the accounting method is to pick appropriate charges and show that these charges are sufficient to allow payment for any sequence of operations.

More formally, denote the actual cost of the ith operation by c_i and the amortized cost (charge) of the operation by $\hat{c}_i$. If $\hat{c}_i > c_i$, the ith operation leaves some positive amount of credit, $credit_i = \hat{c}_i - c_i$ that can be used up by future operations. And as long as

$$\sum_{i=1}^{n} \hat{c}_i \geq \sum_{i=1}^{n} c_i$$

the total available credit will always be nonnegative, and the sum of amortized costs will be an upper bound on the actual cost.

It is common to keep track of stored credit by assigning it to a particular location in the data structure, for example some part of the structure that will be altered later by some expensive operation that was (partially) made possible by the operation that provided the credit. This location could be a node in a tree, a position in a stack, or something else. Different types of operations that provide credit might store their credit in different structures, but a single operation type will have a single, well defined location to store its credit. Reasoning about when credit is produced, where it is stored, and how it is used up is key to showing that equation above holds for all operation sequences. Finally, remember that amortization is an analytical device only. The credits "stored" in the data structure are imaginary tools we use to reason about the behavior of an algorithm or data structure, not something that is explicit or accessible in a data structure abstraction or its implementation code.

Example

This first example supplies a trivial illustration of the accounting method, adapted from Tarjan and Cormen. Suppose you have a simple stack of items, where you can push an item onto the stack or pop an item from the stack in constant time. The stack is constrained to naturally contain 0 or more items at all times. Suppose there is only one operation type defined for this stack, called OP, which involves applying zero or more pops followed by one push:

```
OP(n)  {}

//requires at least n items are on the stack pop n items from stack

push 1 item onto stack
```

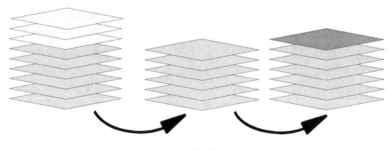

OP(3) applied to a stack

Also suppose that m such operations have been performed. The worst case running time for an OP operation in the sequence is $O(m)$, which occurs if operations 1 through $m - 1$ have each been OP(0) (each popping no items and pushing one), and the mth operation is OP(m 1) (popping *all* items from the stack, then pushing one). A simple worst case analysis would consider m operations with a worst case peroperation cost of $O(m)$ to have an upper bound of $O(m^2)$.

It should be intuitively obvious that not every single OP operation can have a cost of m, since previous operations have to push items onto the stack before they can be popped. Amortized analysis captures this intuition. Consider assigning each OP a charge of 2. The first OP must be OP(0), popping nothing from the empty stack and pushing one item. The actual cost of this operation is 1, and the amortized cost is 2, so the credit remaining is $2 - 1 = 1$. This credit of 1 is stored with the new item in the stack. If this item is popped from the stack in the future, the pop will be paid for by this stored 1 credit. In this way, any sequence of OPs maintains the invariant that there is one credit stored per stacked item. The algorithm will never run out of credit, because each pop is already prepaid, and each push only uses up 1 of the two credits paid the OP. The amortized cost of each OP is 2, so the amortized cost of any sequence of m OPs is $2m$, which is $O(m)$. This is quite an improvement over the $O(m^2)$ analysis.

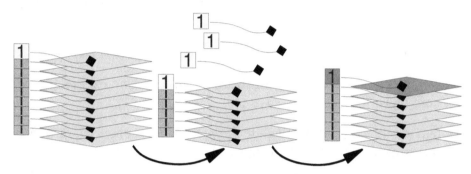

In the accounting method, one credit is stored with each stack item. OP(3) pays for 3 pops using the popped items' credits, pays for the push with one of OP's own 2 payments, and stores the other of its 2 payments as a credit tied to the new item.

If a data structure possesses little or no stored credit, this is an indication that the "badness" resulting from a subsequent particular operation having actual cost that exceeds its amortized cost is limited, as the stored credit cannot fall below 0. On the other hand, if a data structure possesses much stored credit, it might be possible that a subsequent operation may have actual cost that far outweighs its amortized cost, as it may eat up the prepayments of the previous operations.

Master Theorem

In the analysis of algorithms, the master theorem provides a cookbook solution in asymptotic terms (using Big O notation) for recurrence relations of types that occur in the analysis of many divide and conquer algorithms. Not all recurrence relations can be solved with the use of the master theorem; its generalizations include the Akra–Bazzi method.

Consider a problem that can be solved using a recursive algorithm such as the following:

```
procedure T( n : size of problem ) defined as:

  if n < 1 then exit

  Do work of amount f(n)

  T(n/b)
```

```
  T(n/b)

  ...repeat for a total of a times... T(n/b)

 end procedure
```

In the above algorithm we are dividing the problem into a number of subproblems recursively, each subproblem being of size n/b. This can be visualized as building a call tree with each node of the tree as an instance of one recursive call and its child nodes being instances of subsequent calls. In the above example, each node would have a number of child nodes. Each node does an amount of work that corresponds to the size of the sub problem n passed to that instance of the recursive call and given by $f(n)$. The total amount of work done by the entire tree is the sum of the work performed by all the nodes in the tree.

Algorithms such as above can be represented as a recurrence relation $T(n) = a\,T\left(\dfrac{n}{b}\right) + f(n)$.

This recursive relation can be successively substituted into itself and expanded to obtain expression for total amount of work done.

The Master theorem allows us to easily calculate the running time of such a recursive algorithm in Θ-notation without doing an expansion of the recursive relation above.

Generic Form

The master theorem concerns recurrence relations of the form:

$$T(n) = a\,T\left(\frac{n}{b}\right) + f(n) \text{ where } a \geq 1, b > 1$$

In the application to the analysis of a recursive algorithm, the constants and function take on the following significance:

- n is the size of the problem.

- a is the number of subproblems in the recursion.

- n/b is the size of each subproblem. (Here it is assumed that all subproblems are essentially the same size.)

- $f(n)$ is the cost of the work done outside the recursive calls, which includes the cost of dividing the problem and the cost of merging the solutions to the subproblems.

It is possible to determine an asymptotic tight bound in these three cases:

Case 1

Generic form

$$\text{If } f(n) = \Theta(n^c) \text{ where } c < \log_b a \,(\text{using Big O notation})$$

then:

$$T(n) = \Theta\left(n^{\log_b a}\right)$$

Example

$$T(n) = 8T\left(\frac{n}{2}\right) + 1000n^2$$

As one can see from the formula above:

$$a = 8, b = 2, f(n) = 1000n^2, \text{so}$$
$$f(n) = \Theta(n^c), \text{where } c = 2$$

Next, we see if we satisfy the case 1 condition:

$$\log_b a = \log_2 8 = 3 > c.$$

It follows from the first case of the master theorem that

$$T(n) = \Theta\left(n^{\log_b a}\right) = \Theta(n^3)$$

(Indeed, the exact solution of the recurrence relation is $T(n) = 1001n^3 - 1000n^2$, assuming $T(1) = 1$).

Case 2

Generic Form

If it is true, for some constant $k \geq 0$, that:

$$f(n) = \Theta(n^c \log^k n) \text{where } c = \log_b a$$

then:

$$T(n) = 2T\left(\frac{n}{2}\right) + 10n$$

As we can see in the formula above the variables get the following values:

$$a = 2, b = 2, c = 1 f(n) = 10n$$
$$f(n) = \Theta(n^c \log^k n) \text{where } c = 1, k = 0$$

Next, we see if we satisfy the case 2 condition:

log   = log 2 = 1, and therefore, yes, $c = \log_b a$

So it follows from the second case of the master theorem:

$$T(n)=\Theta\left(n^{\log_b a}\log^{k+1}n\right)\Theta\left(n^1\log^1 n\right)=\Theta\left(n\log n\right)$$

Thus the given recurrence relation *T(n)* was in Θ(n log n).

This result is confirmed by the exact solution of the recurrence relation, which is $T(n)=n+10n\log_2 n$, assuming $T(1)=1$.

Case 3

Generic Form

If it is true that:

$$f(n)=\Theta\left(n^c\right)\text{ where }c>\log_b a$$

then:

$$T(n)=\Theta\left(f(n)\right)$$

Example

$$T(n)=2T\left(\frac{n}{2}\right)+n^2$$

As we can see in the formula above the variables get the following values:

$$a=2,b=2,f(n)=n^2$$
$$f(n)=\Theta\left(n^c\right),\text{ where }c=2$$

Next, we see if we satisfy the case 3 condition:

$$\log_b a=\log_2 2=1,\text{ and therefore, yes, }c>\log_b a$$

So it follows from the third case of the master theorem:

$$T(n)=\Theta\left(f(n)\right)=\Theta\left(n^2\right).$$

Thus the given recurrence relation T(n) was in Θ(n²), that complies with the f (n) of the original formula. (This result is confirmed by the exact solution of the recurrence relation, which is $T(n)=2n^2-n$, assuming $T(1)=1$.)

Inadmissible equations

The following equations cannot be solved using the master theorem:

$$T(n)=2^n T\left(\frac{n}{2}\right)+n^n$$

a is not a constant; the number of subproblems should be fixed

$$T(n) = 2T\left(\frac{n}{2}\right) + \frac{n}{\log n}$$

non-polynomial difference between f(n) and $n^{\log_b a}$

$$T(n) = 0.5T\left(\frac{n}{2}\right) + n$$

$a < 1$ cannot have less than one sub problem

$$T(n) = 64T\left(\frac{n}{8}\right) - n^2 \log n$$

f(n) which is the combination time is not positive

$$T(n) = T\left(\frac{n}{8}\right) + n(2 - \cos n)$$

case 3 but regularity violation.

In the second inadmissible example above, the difference between $f(n)$ and $n^{\log_b a}$ can be expressed with the ratio $\dfrac{f(n)}{n^{\log_b a}} = \dfrac{\frac{n}{\log n}}{n^{\log_2 2}} = \dfrac{n}{n \log n} = \dfrac{1}{\log n}.$

It is clear that $\dfrac{1}{\log n} < n^\varepsilon$ for any constant $\varepsilon > 0$. Therefore, the difference is not polynomial and the Master Theorem does not apply.

Algorithmic Efficiency

The topic of algorithms is a topic that is central to computer science. Measuring an algorithm's efficiency is important because your choice of an algorithm for a given application often has a great impact. Word processors, ATMs, video games and life support systems all depend on efficient algorithms.

Consider two searching algorithms. What does it mean to compare the algorithms and conclude that one is better than the other?

The analysis of algorithms is the area of computer science that provides tools for contrasting the efficiency of different methods of solution. Notice the use of the term *methods of solution* rather than *programs*; it is important to emphasize that the analysis concerns itself primarily with *significant* differences in efficiency – differences that you can usually obtain only through superior methods of solution and rarely through clever tricks in coding.

Although the efficient use of both time and space is important, inexpensive memory has reduced the significance of space efficiency. Thus, we will focus primarily on time efficiency. How do you compare the time efficiency of two algorithms that solve the same problem? One possible approach is to implement the two algorithms in C++ and run the programs. There are three difficulties with this approach:

1. How are the algorithms coded? Does one algorithm run faster than another because of better programming? We should not compare implementations rather than the algorithms. Implementations are sensitive to factors such as programming style that cloud the issue.

2. What computer should you use? The only fair way would be to use the same computer for both programs. But even then, the particular operations that one algorithm uses may be faster or slower than the other – and may be just the reverse on a different computer. In short, we should compare the efficiency of the algorithms independent of a particular computer.

3. What data should the programs use? There is always a danger that we will select instances of the problem for which one of the algorithms runs uncharacteristically fast. For example, when comparing a sequential search and a binary search of a sorted array. If the test case happens to be that we are searching for an item that happens to be the smallest in the array, the sequential search will find the item more quickly than the binary search.

To overcome these difficulties, computer scientists employ mathematical techniques that analyze algorithms independently of specific implementations, computers or data. You begin this analysis by counting the number of significant operations in a particular solution.

As an example of calculating the time it takes to execute a piece of code, consider the nested for loops below:

```
for (i = 1; i <= N;

++i) for (j = 1; j <=

i; ++j)

for (k = 0; k < 5;

++k) Task T;
```

If task T requires t time units, the innermost loop on K requires 5*t time units. We will discuss how to calculate the total time, which is: $5*t*N*(N+1)/2$ time units.

This example derives an algorithm's time requirements as a function of problem size. The way to measure a problem's size depends on the application. The searches we have discussed depend on the size of the array we are searching. The most important thing to learn is how quickly the algorithm's time requirement grows as a function of the problem size. A statement such as:

Algorithm A requires time proportional to f(N) enables you to compare algorithm A with another algorithm B which requires $g(N)$ time units. Algorithm A is said to be order $f(N)$, which is denoted as $O(f(N))$; $f(N)$ is called the algorithm's growth rate function. Because the notation uses the capital letter O to denote order, it is called Big O notation. If a problem of size N requires time that is directly proportional to N, the problem is $O(N)$ – that is, order N. If the time requirement is directly proportional to N^2, the problem is $O(N^2)$, and so on.

Algorithm A is order $f(N)$ – denoted $O(f(N))$ – if constants c and No exist such that A requires no more than $c*f(N)$ time units to solve a problem of size $N >= No$. That is, $g(N)$ is $O(f(N))$ if the constants c and No exist such that $g(N) < c*f(N)$ for $N >= No$. If $g(N)$ is the time required to run Algorithm A, the A is $O(F(N))$.

The requirement $N >= No$ in the definition of $O(f(N))$ means that the time estimate is correct for sufficiently large problems.

These growth-rate functions have the following intuitive interpretations:

1   A growth-rate functions of 1 implies a problem whose time requirement is constant and, therefore, independent of the problem's size.

log2N   The time requirement for a logarithmic algorithm increases slowly as the problem size increases. The binary search algorithm has this behavior.

N   The time requirement for a linear algorithm increases directly with the size of the problem.

Nlog2N   The time requirement increases more rapidly than a linear algorithm. Such algorithms usually divide a problem into smaller problems that are each solved separately.

N^2 The time requirement for a quadratic algorithm increases rapidly with the size of the problem. Algorithms that use two nested loops are often quadratic.

N^3 The time requirement for a cubic algorithm increases more rapidly with the size of the problem than the time requirement for a quadratic algorithm. Algorithms that use three nested loops are often cubic and are practical only for small problems.

2^N As the size of a problem increases, the time requirement for an exponential algorithm usually increases too rapidly to be practical.

If algorithm A requires time that is proportional to function f and algorithm B requires time that is proportional to a slower-growing function g, it is apparent that B will always be significantly more efficient than A for large enough problems. For large problems, the proportional growth rate dominates all other factors in determining an algorithm's efficiency.

Some properties of Big O notation help to simplify the analysis of an algorithm. You should keep in mind the $O(f(N))$ means "is of order $f(N)$" or "has order $f(N)$." O is not a function.

1. You can ignore low order terms in an algorithm's growth-rate function.

2. You can ignore a multiplicative constant in the high-order term of an algorithm's growth rate function.

3. $O(f(N)) + O(g(N)) = O(f(N) + g(N))$. You can combine growth-rate functions.

These properties imply that you need only an estimate of the time requirement to obtain an algorithm's growth rate; you do not need an exact statement of an algorithm's time requirement, which is fortunate because deriving the exact time requirement is often difficult and sometimes impossible.

Worst-case analysis: A particular algorithm might require different times to solve different problems of the same size. For example, the time an algorithm requires to search N items might depend on the nature of the items. Usually you consider the maximum amount of time that an algorithm can require to solve a problem of size N – that is, the worst case. Although worst-case analysis can produce a pessimistic time estimate, such an estimate does not mean that your algorithm will always be slow. Instead, you have shown that the algorithm will never be slower than your estimate. An algorithm's worst case might happen rarely, if at all, in practice.

Tightness: We want the "tightest" big-O upper bound we can prove. If $f(N)$ is $O(N^2)$, we want to say so even though the statement $f(N)$ is $O(N^3)$ is technically true but "weaker."

Simplicity: We will generally regard $f(N)$ as "simple" if it is a single term and the coefficient of that term is 1. N^2 is simple, $2N^2$ and $N^2 + N$ are not.

References

- Cygan, Marek; Fomin, Fedor V.; Kowalik, Lukasz; Lokshtanov, Daniel; Marx, Daniel; Pilipczuk, Marcin; Pilipczuk, Michal; Saurabh, Saket (2015). Parameterized Algorithms. Springer. p. 555. ISBN 978-3-319-21274-6

- Time-complexity-of-algorithms, data-structures: studytonight.com, Retrieved 11 May 2018

- Chen, Jianer; Kanj, Iyad A.; Xia, Ge (2006). "Improved Parameterized Upper Bounds for Vertex Cover". Mfcs 2006. 4162: 238–249. doi:10.1007/11821069_21

- Computational-complexity: plato.stanford.edu, Retrieved 14 April 2018

- Moret, Bernard M. E.; Bader, David A.; Warnow, Tandy (2002). "High-Performance Algorithm Engineering for Computational Phylogenetics" (PDF). The Journal of Supercomputing. 22 (1): 99–111

- Big-o-notation-25480: techopedia.com, Retrieved 29 June 2018

- Niedermeier, Rolf (2006). Invitation to Fixed-Parameter Algorithms. Oxford University Press. ISBN 0-19-856607-7. Archived from the original on 2008-09-24

- Big-o-notation-time-and-space-complexity: interviewcake.com, Retrieved 20 March 2018

- Guzman, John Paul; Limoanco, Teresita (2017). "An Empirical Approach to Algorithm Analysis Resulting in Approximations to Big Theta Time Complexity" (PDF). Journal of Software. 12 (12)

- Amortized-Analysis-Explained-Fiebrink: cs.princeton.edu, Retrieved 16 July 2018

Sorting Algorithms

Sorting algorithm is an algorithm in computer science that arranges elements of a list in a specific numerical or lexicographical order. Sorting when done in an efficient way optimizes the efficiency of other algorithms. The diverse topics covered in this chapter on comparison sort, comb sort, insertion sort, shellsort, selection sort, etc. will help in providing a better perspective about sorting algorithm.

A sorting algorithm is a method for reorganizing a large number of items into a specific order, such as alphabetical, highest-to-lowest value or shortest-to-longest distance. Sorting algorithms take lists of items as input data, perform specific operations on those lists and deliver ordered arrays as output. The many applications of sorting algorithms include organizing items by price on a retail website and determining the order of sites on a search engine results page.

In other words, a sorted array is an array that is in a particular order. For example, $[a,b,c,d]$ is sorted alphabetically, $[1,2,3,4,5]$ is a list of integers sorted in increasing order, and $[5,4,3,2,1]$ is a list of integers sorted in decreasing order.

A sorting algorithm takes an array as input and outputs a permutation of that array that is sorted.

There are two broad types of sorting algorithms: integer sorts and comparison sorts.

Comparison Sort

Comparison sorts compare elements at each step of the algorithm to determine if one element should be to the left or right of another element.

Comparison sorts are usually more straightforward to implement than integer sorts, but comparison sorts are limited by a lower bound of $O(n\log n)$, meaning that, on average, comparison sorts cannot be faster than $O(n\log n)$, A lower bound for an algorithm is the *worst-case* running time of the *best* possible algorithm for a given problem. The "on average" part here is important: there are many algorithms that run in very fast time if the inputted list is *already* sorted, or has some very particular (and overall unlikely) property. There is only one permutation of a list that is sorted, but $n!$ possible lists, so the chances that the input is already sorted is very unlikely, and on average, the list will not be very sorted.

The running time of comparison-based sorting algorithms is bounded by $\Omega(n\log n)$.

A comparison sort can be modeled as a large binary tree called a decision tree where each node represents a single comparison. Because the sorted list is some permutation of the input list, for an input list of length n there are $n!$ possible permutations of that list. This is a decision tree because each of the $n!$ is represented by a leaf, and the path the algorithm must take to get to each leaf is the series of comparisons and outcomes that yield that particular ordering.

At each level of the tree, a comparison is made. Comparisons happen, and we keep traveling down the tree; until the algorithm reaches the leaves of the tree, there will be a leaf for each permutation, so there are $n!$ leaves.

Each comparison halves the number of future comparisons the algorithm must do (since if the algorithm selects the right edge out of a node at a given step, it will not search the nodes and paths connected to the left edge). Therefore, the algorithm performs $O(n \log n)$, comparisons. Any binary tree, with height h, has a number of leaves that is less than or equal to 2^h.

From this,

$$2^h \geq n!.$$

Taking the logarithm results in

$$h \geq \log(n!).$$

From Stirling's approximation,

$$n! > \left(\frac{n}{e}\right)^n.$$

Therefore,

$$h \geq \log\left(\frac{n}{e}\right)^n$$
$$= n \log\left(\frac{n}{e}\right)^n$$
$$= n \log n - n \log e$$
$$= \Omega(n \log n).$$

Integer Sort

Integer sorts are sometimes called counting sorts (though there is a specific integer sort algorithm called counting sort). Integer sorts do not make comparisons, so they are not bounded by $\Omega(n \log n)$. Integer sorts determine for each element x how many elements are less than x If there are 14 elements that are less than x then x will be placed in the 15th slot. This information is used to place each element into the correct slot immediately—no need to rearrange lists

Properties of Sorting Algorithms

All sorting algorithms share the goal of outputting a sorted list, but the way that each algorithm goes about this task can vary. When working with any kind of algorithm, it is important to know how fast it runs and in how much space it operates—in other words, its time complexity and space complexity. Comparison-based sorting algorithms have a time complexity of $\Omega(n \log n)$, meaning the algorithm can't be faster than $n \log n$. However, usually, the running time of algorithms is discussed in terms of big O, and not Omega. For example, if an algorithm had a worst-case running time of $\Omega(n \log n)$, then it is guaranteed that the algorithm will never be slower than $\Omega(n \log n)$, and if an algorithm has an average-case running time of $O(n^2)$, then on average, it will not be slower than $O(n^2)$.

The running time describes how many operations an algorithm must carry out before it completes. The space complexity describes how much space must be allocated to run a particular algorithm. For example, if an algorithm takes in a list of size n and for some reason makes a new list of size n for each element in n the algorithm needs n^2 space.

Additionally, for sorting algorithms, it is sometimes useful to know if a sorting algorithm is stable.

Stability

A sorting algorithm is stable if it preserves the original order of elements with equal key values (where the key is the value the algorithm sorts by). For example,

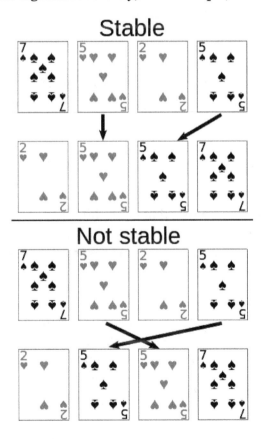

When the cards are sorted by value with a stable sort, the two 5s must remain in the same order in the sorted output that they were originally in. When they are sorted with a non-stable sort, the 5s may end up in the opposite order in the sorted output.

Common Sorting Algorithms

There are many different sorting algorithms, with various pros and cons. Here are a few examples of common sorting algorithms.

Merge Sort

Mergesort is a comparison-based algorithm that focuses on how to merge together two pre-sorted arrays such that the resulting array is also sorted.

Insertion Sort

Insertion sort is a comparison-based algorithm that builds a final sorted array one element at a time. It iterates through an input array and removes one element per iteration, finds the place the element belongs in the array, and then places it there.

Bubble Sort

Bubble sort is a comparison-based algorithm that compares each pair of elements in an array and swaps them if they are out of order until the entire array is sorted. For each element in the list, the algorithm compares every pair of elements.

Quicksort

Quicksort is a comparison-based algorithm that uses divide-and-conquer to sort an array. The algorithm picks a pivot element, $A[q]$, and then rearranges the array into two subarrays $A[p...q-1]$, such that all elements are less than $A[q]$, and $A[q+1...r]$, such that all elements are greater than or equal to $A[q]$.

Heapsort

Heapsort is a comparison-based algorithm that uses a binary heap data structure to sort elements. It divides its input into a sorted and an unsorted region, and it iteratively shrinks the unsorted region by extracting the largest element and moving that to the sorted region.

Counting Sort

Counting sort is an integer sorting algorithm that assumes that each of the n input elements in a list has a key value ranging from 0 to k for some integer k. For each element in the list, counting sort determines the number of elements that are less than it. Counting sort can use this information to place the element directly into the correct slot of the output array.

Choosing a Sorting Algorithm

To choose a sorting algorithm for a particular problem, consider the running time, space complexity, and the expected format of the input list.

Algorithm	Best-case	Worst-case	Average-case	Space Complexity	Stable?
Merge Sort	$O(n \log n)$	$O(n \log n)$	$O(n \log n)$	$O(n)$	Yes
Insertion Sort	$O(n)$	$O(n^2)$	$O(n^2)$	$O(1)$	Yes
Bubble Sort	$O(n)$	$O(n^2)$	$O(n^2)$	$O(1)$	Yes
Quicksort	$O(n \log n)$	$O(n^2)$	$O(n \log n)$	$\log n$ best, n avg	Usually not*
Heapsort	$O(n \log n)$	$O(n \log n)$	$O(n \log n)$	$O(1)$	No
Counting Sort	$O(k+n)$	$O(k+n)$	$O(k+n)$	$O(k+n)$	Yes

*Most quicksort implementations are not stable, though stable implementations do exist.

When choosing a sorting algorithm to use, weigh these factors. For example, quicksort is a very fast algorithm but can be pretty tricky to implement; bubble sort is a slow algorithm but is very easy to implement. To sort small sets of data, bubble sort may be a better option since it can be implemented quickly, but for larger datasets, the speedup from quicksort might be worth the trouble implementing the algorithm.

Comparison Sort

A Comparison Sort is a sorting algorithm where the final order is determined only by comparisons between the input elements. In this there are three sorting algorithms: merge-sort, quicksort, and heap-sort.

Each of these algorithms takes an input array a and sorts the elements of a into non-decreasing order in $O(n \log n)$ (expected) time. These algorithms are all comparison-based. Their second argument, c, is a Comparator that implements the compare(a,b) method. These algorithms don't care what type of data is being sorted; the only operation they do on the data is comparisons using the compare(a,b) method. compare(a,b) returns a negative value if $a < b$, a positive value if $a > b$, and zero if $a = b$.

Merge Sort

The merge-sort algorithm is a classic example of recursive divide and conquer: If the length of a is at most 1, then a is already sorted, so we do nothing. Otherwise, we split a into two halves, $a0 = a[0],...,a[\ /2-1]$ and $a1 = a[n/2],...,a[n-1]$. We recursively sort $a0$ and $a1$, and then we merge (the now sorted) $a0$ and $a1$ to get our fully sorted array a:

```
<T> void mergeSort(T[] a, Comparator<T> c) {

    if (a.length <= 1) return;

    T[] a0 = Arrays.copyOfRange(a, 0, a.length/2);

    T[] a1 = Arrays.copyOfRange(a, a.length/2, a.length);

    mergeSort(a0, c);

    mergeSort(a1, c);

    merge(a0, a1, a, c);

}
```

An example is shown in Figure below

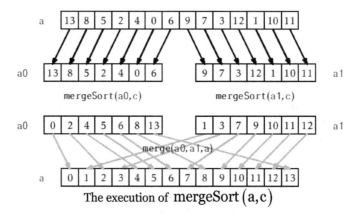

The execution of mergeSort (a,c)

Compared to sorting, merging the two sorted arrays a0 and a1 is fairly easy. We add elements to a one at a time. If a0 or a1 is empty, then we add the next elements from the other (non-empty) array. Otherwise, we take the minimum of the next element in a0 and the next element in a1 and add it to a:

```
<T> void merge(T[] a0, T[] a1, T[] a, Comparator<T> c) {


int i0 = 0, i1 = 0;

    for (int i = 0; i < a.length; i++) {

        if (i0 == a0.length)

            a[i] = a1[i1++];

        else if (i1 == a1.length)

            a[i] = a0[i0++];

        else if (compare(a0[i0], a1[i1]) < 0)

            a[i] = a0[i0++];

        else
```

```
        a[i] = a1[i1++];

    }
```

Notice that the merge$(a0, a1, a, c)$ algorithm performs at most n-1 comparisons before running out of elements in one of a0 or a1.

To understand the running-time of merge-sort, it is easiest to think of it in terms of its recursion tree. Suppose for now that n is a power of two, so that $n = 2^{\log n}$, and $\log n$ is an integer. Merge-sort turns the problem of sorting n elements into two problems, each of sorting $n/2$ elements. These two subproblem are then turned into two problems each, for a total of four subproblems, each of size $n/4$. These four subproblems become eight subproblems, each of size $n/8$, and so on. At the bottom of this process, $n/2$ subproblems, each of size two, are converted into n problems, each of size one. For each subproblem of size $n/2^i$, the time spent merging and copying data is $O(n/2^i)$. Since there are 2^i subproblems of size $n/2^i$, the total time spent working on problems of size 2^i, not counting recursive calls, is

$$2^i \times O(n/2^i) = O(n).$$

Therefore, the total amount of time taken by merge-sort is

$$\sum_{i=0}^{\log n} O(n) = O(n \log n).$$

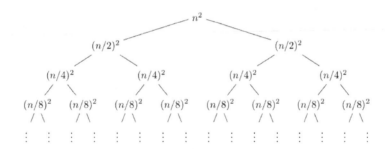

The merge-sort recursion tree.

The proof of the following theorem is based on preceding analysis, but has to be a little more careful to deal with the cases where n is not a power of 2.

Theorem: *The* mergeSort(a, c) *algorithm runs in* $O(n \log n)$ *time and performs at most* n logn *comparisons.*

Proof. The proof is by induction on n. The base case, in which $n = 1$, is trivial; when presented with an array of length 0 or 1 the algorithm simply returns without performing any comparisons.

Merging two sorted lists of total length n requires at most n−1 comparisons. Let $C(n)$ denote the maximum number of comparisons performed by mergeSort(a, c) on an array a of length n. If n is even, then we apply the inductive hypothesis to the two subproblems and obtain

$$C(n) \leq n-1+2C(n/2)$$
$$\leq n-1+2\big((n/2)\log(n/2)\big)$$
$$= n-1+n\log(n/2)$$
$$= n-1+n\log n-n$$
$$< n \log n.$$

The case where n is odd is slightly more complicated. For this case, we use two inequalities that are easy to verify:

$$\log(x+1) \leq \log(x)+1,$$

for all $x \geq 1$ and

$$\log(x+1/2)+\log(x-1/2) \leq 2\log(x),$$

for all $x \geq 1/2$. Inequality ($\log(x+1) \leq \log(x)+1$,)comes from the fact that $\log(x)+1 = \log(2x)$ while ($\log(x+1/2)+\log(x-1/2) \leq 2\log(x)$,) follows from the fact that $\log$ is a concave function. With these tools in hand we have, for odd n,

$$C(n) \leq n-1+C(\lceil n/2 \rceil)+C(\lfloor n/2 \rfloor)$$
$$\leq n-1+\lceil n/2 \rceil \log \lceil n/2 \rceil + \lfloor n/2 \rfloor \log \lfloor n/2 \rfloor$$
$$= n-1+n\log(n/2+1/2)\log(n/2+1/2)+(n/2-1/2)\log(n/2-1/2)$$
$$\leq n-1+n\log(n/2)+(1/2)\big(\log(n/2+1/2)-\log(n/2-1/2)\big)$$
$$\leq n-1+n\log(n/2)+1/2$$
$$< n+n\log(n/2)$$
$$= n+n(\log n-1)$$
$$= n \log n.$$

Quicksort

The quicksort algorithm is another classic divide and conquer algorithm. Unlike merge-sort, which does merging after solving the two subproblems, quicksort does all of its work upfront.

Quicksort is simple to describe: Pick a random pivot element, x, from a; partition a into the set of elements less than x, the set of elements equal to x, and the set of elements greater than x; and, finally, recursively sort the first and third sets in this partition.

```
<T> void quickSort(T[] a, Comparator<T> c) {

    quickSort(a, 0, a.length, c);

}
```

```
<T> void quickSort(T[] a, int i, int n, Comparator<T> c) {

    if (n <= 1) return;

    T x = a[i + rand.nextInt(n)];

    int p = i-1, j = i, q = i+n;

    // a[i..p]<x,  a[p+1..q-1]??x, a[q..i+n-1]>x

    while (j < q) {

        int comp = compare(a[j], x);

        if (comp < 0) {          // move to beginning of array

            swap(a, j++, ++p);

        } else if (comp > 0) {

            swap(a, j, --q);   // move to end of array

        } else {

            j++;                    // keep in the middle

        }

    }

    // a[i..p]<x,  a[p+1..q-1]=x, a[q..i+n-1]>x

    quickSort(a, i, p-i+1, c);

    quickSort(a, q, n-(q-i), c);
```

An example execution of quick Sort $(a, 0, 14, c)$

All of this is done in place, so that instead of making copies of subarrays being sorted, the quick Sort (a, i, n, c) method only sorts the subarray $a[i], ... a[i+n-1]$. Initially, this method is invoked with the arguments quick Sort $(a, 0, a.length, c)$.

At the heart of the quicksort algorithm is the in-place partitioning algorithm. This algorithm, without using any extra space, swaps elements in a and computes indices p and q so that

$$a[i] \begin{cases} < x & \text{if } 0 \le i \le p \\ = x & \text{if } p \le i \le q \\ > x & \text{if } q \le i \le n\text{-}1 \end{cases}$$

This partitioning, which is done by the while loop in the code, works by iteratively increasing p and decreasing q while maintaining the first and last of these conditions. At each step, the element at position j is either moved to the front, left where it is, or moved to the back. In the first two cases, j is incremented, while in the last case, j is not incremented since the new element at position j has not yet been processed.

Quicksort is very closely related to the random binary search trees. In fact, if the input to quicksort consists of n distinct elements, then the quicksort recursion tree is a random binary search tree. To see this, recall that when constructing a random binary search tree the first thing we do is pick a random element x and make it the root of the tree. After this, every element will eventually be compared to , with smaller elements going into the left subtree and larger elements into the right.

In quicksort, we select a random element x and immediately compare everything to x, putting the smaller elements at the beginning of the array and larger elements at the end of the array. Quicksort then recursively sorts the beginning of the array and the end of the array, while the random binary search tree recursively inserts smaller elements in the left subtree of the root and larger elements in the right subtree of the root.

The above correspondence between random binary search trees and quicksort means that we can translate Lemma below to a statement about quicksort:

Lemma: *When quicksort is called to sort an array containing the integers* $0,....,n-1$, *the expected number of times element* i *is compared to a pivot element is at most* H_{i+1} H_{n+1}.

A little summing up of harmonic numbers gives us the following theorem about the running time of quicksort:

Theorem: *When quicksort is called to sort an array containing* n *distinct elements, the expected number of comparisons performed is at most* $2n \ln n + O(n)$.

Proof. Let T be the number of comparisons performed by quicksort when sorting n distinct elements. Using Lemma above and linearity of expectation, we have:

$$E(T) = \sum_{i=0}^{n-1}(H_{i+1} + H_{n-1})$$

$$= 2\sum_{i=0}^{n} H_i$$

$$\le 2\sum_{i=0}^{n} H_n$$

$$\le 2n \ln n + 2n = 2n\ln n + O(n)$$

Theorem below describes the case where the elements being sorted are all distinct. When the input array, a, contains duplicate elements, the expected running time of quicksort is no worse, and can be even better; any time a duplicate element x is chosen as a pivot, all occurrences of x get grouped together and do not take part in either of the two subproblems.

Theorem: *The* quick Sort(a,c) *method runs in* $O(n \log n)$ *expected time and the expected number of comparisons it performs is at most* $2n \ln n + O(n)$.

Heapsort

The heap-sort algorithm is another in-place sorting algorithm. Heap-sort uses the binary heaps. Recall that the BinaryHeap data structure represents a heap using a single array. The heap-sort algorithm converts the input array a into a heap and then repeatedly extracts the minimum value.

More specifically, a heap stores n elements in an array, a, at array locations $a[0],...a[n-1]$ with the smallest value stored at the root, $a[0]$. After transforming a into a BinaryHeap, the heap-sort algorithm repeatedly swaps a and $a[n-1]$, decrements n, and calls trick le Down(0) so that $a[0],...a[n-2]$ once again are a valid heap representation. When this process ends (because n-0) the elements of a are stored in decreasing order, so a is reversed to obtain the final sorted order. Figure below shows an example of the execution of heap Sort(a,c).

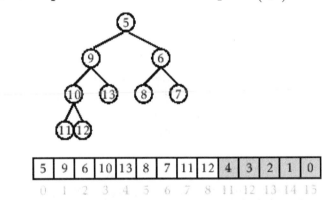

The shaded part of the array is already sorted. The unshaded part is a BinaryHeap.
During the next iteration, element 5 will be placed into array location

```
<T> void sort(T[] a, Comparator<T> c) {

        BinaryHeap<T> h = new BinaryHeap<T>(a, c);

        while (h.n > 1) {

            h.swap(--h.n, 0);

            h.trickleDown(0);

        }

        Collections.reverse(Arrays.asList(a));

}
```

A key subroutine in heap sort is the constructor for turning an unsorted array a into a heap. It would be easy to do this in $O(n \log n)$ time by repeatedly calling the BinaryHeap $add(x)$ method, but we can do better by using a bottom-up algorithm. Recall that, in a binary heap, the children of $a[i]$ are stored at positions $a[2i+1]$ and $a[2i+2]$. This implies that the elements $a[\lfloor n/2 \rfloor],\dots a[n-1]$ have no children. In other words, each of $a[\lfloor n/2 \rfloor],\dots a[n-1]$ is a sub-heap of size 1. Now, working backwards, we can call trickle Down(i) for each $i \in \{\lfloor n/2 \rfloor - 1,\dots,0\}$. This works, because by the time we call trickle Down(i), each of the two children of $a[i]$ are the root of a sub-heap, so calling trickle Down(i) makes $a[i]$ into the root of its own subheap.

```
BinaryHeap(T[] a, Comparator<T> c) {
    this.c = c;
    this.a = a;
    n = a.length;
    for (int i = n/2-1; i >= 0; i--) {
        trickleDown(i);
    }
}
```

The interesting thing about this bottom-up strategy is that it is more efficient than calling $add(x)$ n times. To see this, notice that, for $n/2$ elements, we do no work at all, for $n/4$ elements, we call trickle Down(i) on a subheap rooted at $a[i]$ and whose height is one, for $n/8$ elements, we call trickle Down(i) on a subheap whose height is two, and so on. Since the work done by trickle Down(i) is proportional to the height of the sub-heap rooted at $a[i]$, this means that the total work done is at most

$$\sum_{i=1}^{\log n} O\big((i-1)n/2^i\big) \leq \sum_{i=1}^{\infty} O(n/2^i) = O(n)\sum_{i=1}^{\infty} i/2^i = O(2n) = O(n).$$

The second-last equality follows by recognizing that the sum $\sum_{i=1}^{\infty} i/2^i$ is equal, by definition of expected value, to the expected number of times we toss a coin up to and including the first time the coin comes up as heads and applying Lemma.

The following theorem describes the performance of heap Sort(a,c).

Theorem: *The* heap Sort(a,c) *method runs in* $O(n \log n)$ *time and performs at most* $2n \log n + O(n)$ *comparisons.*

Proof. The algorithm runs in three steps: (1) transforming a into a heap, (2) repeatedly extracting the minimum element from a, and (3) reversing the elements in a. We have just argued that step 1 takes $O(n)$ time and performs $O(n)$ comparisons. Step 3 takes $O(n)$ time and performs no comparisons. Step 2 performs n calls to trickle Down(0). The i th such call operates on a heap of size $n-i$ and performs at most $2 \log (n-i)$ comparisons. Summing this over i gives

$$\sum_{i=0}^{n-i} 2\log(n-i) \le \sum_{i=0}^{n-i} 2\log n = 2n \log n$$

Adding the number of comparisons performed in each of the three steps completes the proof.

A Lower-Bound for Comparison-Based Sorting

We have now seen three comparison-based sorting algorithms that each run in $O(n \log n)$ time. By now, we should be wondering if faster algorithms exist. The short answer to this question is no. If the only operations allowed on the elements of a are comparisons, then no algorithm can avoid doing roughly n log n comparisons. This is not difficult to prove, but requires a little imagination. Ultimately, it follows from the fact that

$$\log(n!) = \log n + \log(n-1) + ... + \log(1) = n \log n - O(n).$$

We will start by focusing our attention on deterministic algorithms like merge-sort and heap-sort and on a particular fixed value of n. Imagine such an algorithm is being used to sort n distinct elements. The key to proving the lower-bound is to observe that, for a deterministic algorithm with a fixed value of n, the first pair of elements that are compared is always the same. For example, in heap Sort(a,c), when n is even, the first call to trickle Down(i) is with $i = n/2 - 1$ and the first comparison is between elements $a[n/2-1]$ and $a[n-1]$.

Since all input elements are distinct, this first comparison has only two possible outcomes. The second comparison done by the algorithm may depend on the outcome of the first comparison. The third comparison may depend on the results of the first two, and so on. In this way, any deterministic comparison-based sorting algorithm can be viewed as a rooted binary comparison tree. Each internal node, u, of this tree is labeled with a pair of indices $u.i$ and $u.j$. If $a[u.i] < a[u.j]$ the algorithm proceeds to the left subtree, otherwise it proceeds to the right subtree. Each leaf w of this tree is labeled with a permutation $w.p[0],...,w.p[n-1]$ of $0,...n-1$. This permutation represents the one that is required to sort a if the comparison tree reaches this leaf. That is,

$$a[w.p[0]] < a[w.p[1]] < ... < a[w.p[n-1]].$$

An example of a comparison tree for an array of size $n = 3$ is shown in figure below.

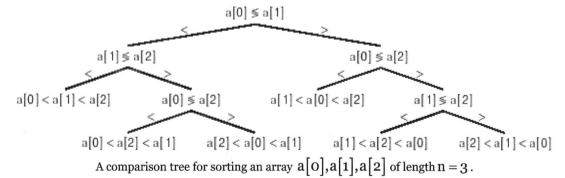

A comparison tree for sorting an array $a[0], a[1], a[2]$ of length $n = 3$.

The comparison tree for a sorting algorithm tells us everything about the algorithm. It tells us exactly the sequence of comparisons that will be performed for any input array, a, having n distinct elements and it tells us how the algorithm will reorder a in order to sort it. Consequently, the comparison tree must have at least n! leaves; if not, then there are two distinct permutations that lead to the same leaf; therefore, the algorithm does not correctly sort at least one of these permutations.

For example, the comparison tree in above figure has only $4 < 3! = 6$ leaves. Inspecting this tree, we see that the two input arrays $3,1,2$ and $3,2,1$ both lead to the rightmost leaf. On the input $3,1,2$ this leaf correctly outputs $a[1] = 1, a[2] = 2. a[0] = 3$. However, on the input $3,2,1$, this node incorrectly outputs $a[1] = 2, a[2] = 1. a[0] = 3$. This discussion leads to the primary lower-bound for comparison-based algorithms.

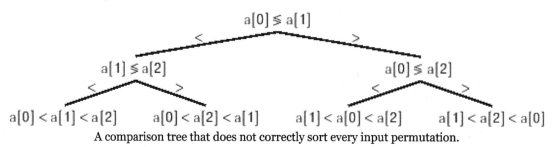

A comparison tree that does not correctly sort every input permutation.

Theorem: *For any deterministic comparison-based sorting algorithm A and any integer $n \geq 1$, there exists an input array a of length n such that A performs at least $\log(n!) = n \log n - O(n)$ comparisons when sorting a.*

Proof: By the preceding discussion, the comparison tree defined by A must have at least n! leaves. An easy inductive proof shows that any binary tree with k leaves has a height of at least $\log k$. Therefore, the comparison tree for A has a leaf, w , with a depth of at least $\log(n!)$ and there is an input array a that leads to this leaf. The input array a is an input for which A does at least $\log(n!)$ comparisons. □

Above theorem deals with deterministic algorithms like merge-sort and heap-sort, but doesn't tell us anything about randomized algorithms like quicksort. Could a randomized algorithm beat the $\log(n!)$ lower bound on the number of comparisons? The answer, again, is no. Again, the way to prove it is to think differently about what a randomized algorithm is.

In the following discussion, we will assume that our decision trees have been "cleaned up" in the following way: Any node that cannot be reached by some input array a is removed. This cleaning up implies that the tree has exactly n! leaves. It has at least n! leaves because, otherwise, it could not sort correctly. It has at most n! leaves since each of the possible n! permutation of n distinct elements follows exactly one root to leaf path in the decision tree.

We can think of a randomized sorting algorithm, R, as a deterministic algorithm that takes two inputs: The input array a that should be sorted and a long sequence $b = b_1, b_2, b_3, ..., b_m$ of random real numbers in the range $[0,1]$. The random numbers provide the randomization for the algorithm. When the algorithm wants to toss a coin or make a random choice, it does so by using some element from b . For example, to compute the index of the first pivot in quicksort, the algorithm could use the formula $\lfloor nb_1 \rfloor$.

Now, notice that if we fix b to some particular sequence $\hat{b}$ then R becomes a deterministic sorting algorithm, $R\left(\hat{b}\right)$, that has an associated comparison tree, $T\left(\hat{b}\right)$. Next, notice that if we select a to be a random permutation of $\{1,...,n\}$, then this is equivalent to selecting a random leaf, w , from the n! leaves of $T\left(\hat{b}\right)$.

If we select a random leaf from any binary tree with k leaves, then the expected depth of that leaf is at least $\log k$. Therefore, the expected number of comparisons performed by the (deterministic) algorithm $R\left(\hat{b}\right)$ when given an input array containing a random permutation of $\{1,...,n\}$ is at least $\log(n!)$. Finally, notice that this is true for every choice of $\hat{b}$, therefore it holds even for R. This completes the proof of the lower-bound for randomized algorithms.

Theorem: *For any integer $n \geq 1$ and any (deterministic or randomized) comparison-based sorting algorithm A, the expected number of comparisons done by A when sorting a random permutation of $\{1,...,n\}$ is at least $\log(n!) = n \log n - O(n)$.*

Bubble Sort

Bubble sort is a simple sorting algorithm. This sorting algorithm is comparison-based algorithm in which each pair of adjacent elements is compared and the elements are swapped if they are not in order. This algorithm is not suitable for large data sets as its average and worst case complexity are of O(n²) where n is the number of items.

Working of Bubble sort

We take an unsorted array for our example. Bubble sort takes O(n²) time so we're keeping it short and precise.

Bubble sort starts with very first two elements, comparing them to check which one is greater.

In this case, value 33 is greater than 14, so it is already in sorted locations. Next, we compare 33 with 27.

We find that 27 is smaller than 33 and these two values must be swapped.

The new array should look like this –

Next we compare 33 and 35. We find that both are in already sorted positions.

Then we move to the next two values, 35 and 10.

We know then that 10 is smaller 35. Hence they are not sorted.

We swap these values. We find that we have reached the end of the array. After one iteration, the array should look like this –

To be precise, we are now showing how an array should look like after each iteration. After the second iteration, it should look like this –

Notice that after each iteration, at least one value moves at the end.

And when there's no swap required, bubble sorts learns that an array is completely sorted.

Now we should look into some practical aspects of bubble sort.

Algorithm

We assume list is an array of n elements. We further assume that swapfunction swaps the values of the given array elements.

```
begin BubbleSort(list)

   for all elements of list
      if list[i] > list[i+1]
         swap(list[i], list[i+1])
      end if
   end for


   return list


end BubbleSort
```

Pseudocode

We observe in algorithm that Bubble Sort compares each pair of array element unless the whole array is completely sorted in an ascending order. This may cause a few complexity issues like what if the array needs no more swapping as all the elements are already ascending.

To ease-out the issue, we use one flag variable swapped which will help us see if any swap has happened or not. If no swap has occurred, i.e. the array requires no more processing to be sorted, it will come out of the loop.

Pseudocode of BubbleSort algorithm can be written as follows –

```
procedure bubbleSort( list : array of items )


   loop = list.count;


   for i = 0 to loop-1 do:
      swapped = false
```

```
        for j = 0 to loop-1 do:

            /* compare the adjacent elements */
            if list[j] > list[j+1] then
                /* swap them */
                swap( list[j], list[j+1] )
                swapped = true
            end if

        end for


        /*if no number was swapped that means
        array is sorted now, break the loop.*/

        if(not swapped) then
            break
        end if

    end for


end procedure return list
```

Implementation

One more issue we did not address in our original algorithm and its improvised pseudocode, is that, after every iteration the highest values settles down at the end of the array. Hence, the next iteration need not include already sorted elements. For this purpose, in our implementation, we restrict the inner loop to avoid already sorted values.

Comb Sort

Comb sort is a simple sorting algorithm which improves on bubble sort. The main idea for this type of algorithm is to eliminate the small values near the end of the list, as these slow down the sorting process.

How it works:

In comb sort, the main usage is of gaps. For example, in bubble sort the gap between two elements was 1 whilst here the gap starts out as a large value and shrinks until it reaches the value 1, when it practically becomes bubble sort. The shrink factor determines how much the gap is lessened. The value is crucial, so an ideal value would be 1.3.

Step by Step Example

Having the following list, let's try to use comb sort to arrange the numbers from lowest to greatest:

Unsorted list:

5	7	9	10	3	1	4	8	2	6

Iteration 1, gap = 8. The distance of 8 from the first element 5 to the next element, leads to the element of 2, these numbers are not in the right order so they have to swap. Also, the same distance is between 7 and 6 which also are not in the right order, so again a swap is required:

2	7	9	10	3	1	4	8	5	6
2	6	9	10	3	1	4	8	5	7

Iteration 2, gap =6, the elements that were compare on each line are 2 with 4, 6 with 8, 5 with 9 and 7 with 10:

2	7	9	10	3	1	4	8	5	7
2	6	9	10	3	1	4	8	5	7
2	6	5	10	3	1	4	8	9	7
2	6	5	7	2	1	4	8	9	10

Iteration 3, gap = 4:

2	7	9	10	3	1	4	8	5	10
2	1	9	10	3	6	4	8	5	10
2	1	4	10	3	6	5	8	9	10
2	1	4	7	3	6	5	8	9	10
2	1	4	7	3	6	5	8	9	10
2	1	4	7	3	6	5	8	9	10

Iteration 4, gap = 3:

2	1	4	7	3	6	5	8	9	10
2	1	4	7	3	6	5	8	9	10
2	1	4	7	3	6	5	8	9	10
2	1	4	5	3	6	7	8	9	10
2	1	4	5	3	6	5	8	9	10
2	1	4	5	3	6	5	8	9	10
2	1	4	5	3	6	7	8	9	10

Iteration 5, gap =2:

2	1	4	5	3	6	7	8	9	10
2	1	4	5	3	6	7	8	9	10
2	1	3	5	4	6	7	8	9	10
2	1	3	5	4	6	7	8	9	10
2	1	3	5	4	6	7	8	9	10
2	1	3	5	4	6	7	8	9	10
2	1	3	5	4	6	7	8	9	10
2	1	3	5	4	6	7	8	9	10

Iteration 6, gap =1:

1	2	3	5	4	6	7	8	9	10
1	2	3	5	4	6	7	8	9	10
1	2	3	4	5	6	7	8	9	10
1	2	3	4	5	6	7	8	9	10
1	2	3	4	5	6	7	8	9	10
2	2	3	4	5	6	7	8	9	10
1	2	3	4	5	6	7	8	9	10
1	2	3	4	5	6	7	8	9	10

Iteration: since the items are sorted, no swaps will be made and the algorithm ends its execution.

Sample code

```
1.  #include < iostream >

2. using namespace std;
```

```
3.  int newGap(int gap) {
4.     gap = (gap * 10) / 13;
5.     if (gap == 9 || gap == 10)
6.        gap = 11;
7.     if (gap < 1)
8.        gap = 1;
9.     return gap;
10. }
11. void combsort(int a[], int aSize) {
12.    int gap = aSize;
13.    for (;;) {
14.       gap = newGap(gap);
15.       bool swapped = false;
16.       for (int i = 0; i < aSize - gap; i++) {
17.          int j = i + gap;
18.          if (a[i] > a[j]) {
19.             std::swap(a[i], a[j]);
20.             swapped = true;
21.          }
22.       }
23.       if (gap == 1 && .swapped)
24.          break;
25.    }
26. }
27. int main ()
28. {
29.    int n;
30.    int *a;
31.    cout << "Please insert the number of elements to be sorted: ";
32.    cin >> n;      // The total number of elements
```

```cpp
33.    a = (int *)calloc(n, sizeof(int));

34.    for(int i=0;i< n;i++)

35.    {

36.

37.            cout << "Input " << i << " element: ";

38.            cin >>a[i]; // Adding the elements to the array

39.    }

40.    cout << "Unsorted list:" << endl; // Displaying the unsorted
       array

41.    for(int i=0;i< n;i++)

42.    {

43.            cout << a[i] << " ";

44.    }

45.    combsort(a,n);

46.    cout << "nSorted list:" << endl;  // Display the sorted array

47.    for(int i=0;i < n;i++)

48.    {

49.            cout << a[i] << " ";

50.    }

51.    return 0;

52. }
```

Output

Code Explanation

At first, the method newGap calculates the size of the gap, based on the number of elements to be sorted. The combsort method is the one who sorts the numbers from the array, at first with the highest gap, which is calculated by calling the newGap method, then it passes through the array and checks the proper elements if they are in the right order, and if not, the library function swap is executed. This continues until the gap reaches the value 1 and no more swaps have been executed.

Complexity

This is quite surprising. Despite being based on the idea of a Bubble Sort the time complexity is just O(n log n), and space complexity for in-place sorting is O(1).

Advantages

- is proper for data sets composed of either numbers or strings;
- time complexity very good, could be compared to quick sort;
- no recursive function-calls;
- in-place-sorting, no extra memory needed;
- no worst-case-situation like in Quicksort.

Disadvantages

- you have to resize the gap with a division by 1.3, which is a fraction;

Insertion Sort

Insertion sort is based on the idea that one element from the input elements is consumed in each iteration to find its correct position i.e, the position to which it belongs in a sorted array.

It iterates the input elements by growing the sorted array at each iteration. It compares the current element with the largest value in the sorted array. If the current element is greater, then it leaves the element in its place and moves on to the next element else it finds its correct position in the sorted array and moves it to that position. This is done by shifting all the elements, which are larger than the current element, in the sorted array to one position ahead.

Implementation

```
void insertion_sort ( int A[ ] , int n)

{

    for( int i = 0 ;i < n ; i++ ) {

    /*storing current element whose left side is checked for its

            correct position .*/
```

```
    int temp = A[ i ];

    int j = i;



    /* check whether the adjacent element in left side is greater or
        less than the current element. */



    while(  j > 0  && temp < A[ j -1]) {



        // moving the left side element to one position forward.
            A[ j ] = A[ j-1];
            j= j - 1;



        }

    // moving current element to its  correct position.
        A[ j ] = temp;

    }

}
```

Take array $A[]=[7,4,5,2]$.

Since 7 is the first element has no other element to be compared with, it remains at its position. Now when on moving towards 4, 7 is the largest element in the sorted list and greater than 4. So, move 4 to its correct position i.e. before 7. Similarly with 5, as 7 (largest element in the sorted list) is greater than 5, we will move 5 to its correct position. Finally for 2, all the elements on the left side of 2 (sorted list) are moved one position forward as all are greater than 2 and then 2 is placed in the first position. Finally, the given array will result in a sorted array.

Time Complexity

In worst case,each element is compared with all the other elements in the sorted array. For N elements, there will be N2 comparisons. Therefore, the time complexity is O(N²)

Shell Sort

The shell sort, sometimes called the "diminishing increment sort," improves on the insertion sort by breaking the original list into a number of smaller sublists, each of which is sorted using an insertion sort. The unique way that these sublists are chosen is the key to the shell sort. Instead of breaking the list into sublists of contiguous items, the shell sort uses an increment i, sometimes called the gap, to create a sublist by choosing all items that are i items apart.

This can be seen in first figure below. This list has nine items. If we use an increment of three, there are three sublists, each of which can be sorted by an insertion sort. After completing these sorts, we get the list shown in second figure below. Although this list is not completely sorted, something very interesting has happened. By sorting the sublists, we have moved the items closer to where they actually belong.

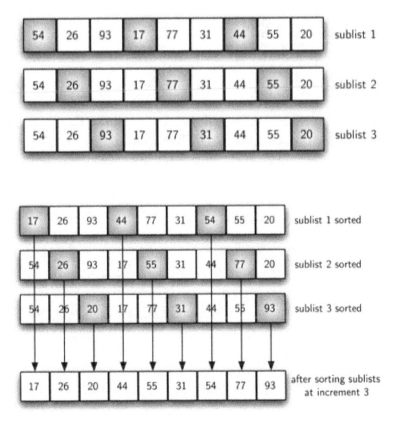

Figure above shows a final insertion sort using an increment of one; in other words, a standard insertion sort. Note that by performing the earlier sublist sorts, we have now reduced the total number of shifting operations necessary to put the list in its final order. For this case, we need only four more shifts to complete the process.

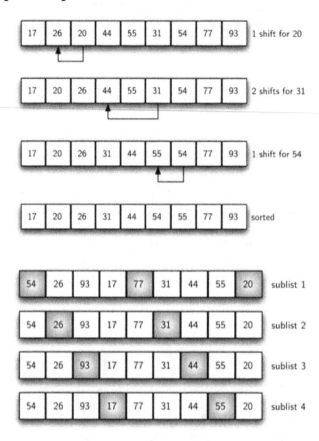

We said earlier that the way in which the increments are chosen is the unique feature of the shell sort. The function shown in ActiveCode 1 uses a different set of increments. In this case, we begin with $\frac{n}{2}$ sublists. On the next pass, $\frac{n}{4}$ sublists are sorted. Eventually, a single list is sorted with the basic insertion sort.

Following is the implementation of ShellSort.

```cpp
// C++ implementation of Shell Sort

#include <iostream>
using namespace std;


/* function to sort arr using shellSort */
int shellSort(int arr[], int n)
{
    // Start with a big gap, then reduce the gap
    for (int gap = n/2; gap > 0; gap /= 2)
```

```
    {
        // Do a gapped insertion sort for this gap size.
        // The first gap elements a[0..gap-1] are already in gapped order
        // keep adding one more element until the entire array is
        // gap sorted
        for (int i = gap; i < n; i += 1)
        {
            // add a[i] to the elements that have been gap sorted
            // save a[i] in temp and make a hole at position i
            int temp = arr[i];

            // shift earlier gap-sorted elements up until the correct
            // location for a[i] is found
            int j;
            for (j = i; j >= gap && arr[j - gap] > temp; j -= gap)
                arr[j] = arr[j - gap];

            //  put temp (the original a[i]) in its correct location
            arr[j] = temp;

        }
    }
    return 0;
}


void printArray(int arr[], int n)
{
    for (int i=0; i<n; i++)
        cout << arr[i] << " ";
}
```

```
int main()

{

    int arr[] = {12, 34, 54, 2, 3}, i;

    int n = sizeof(arr)/sizeof(arr[0]);


    cout << "Array before sorting: \n";

    printArray(arr, n);


    shellSort(arr, n);


    cout << "\nArray after sorting: \n";

    printArray(arr, n);


    return 0;

}
```

Output:

```
Array before sorting:

12 34 54 2 3

Array after sorting:

2 3 12 34 54
```

Time Complexity: Time complexity of above implementation of shellsort is O(n²). In the above implementation gap is reduce by half in every iteration. There are many other ways to reduce gap which lead to better time complexity.

Selection Sort

Selection sort is conceptually the most simplest sorting algorithm. This algorithm will first find the smallest element in the array and swap it with the element in the first position, then it will find the second smallest element and swap it with the element in the second position, and it will keep on doing this until the entire array is sorted.

It is called selection sort because it repeatedly selects the next-smallest element and swaps it into the right place.

Working of Selection Sort

Following are the steps involved in selection sort(for sorting a given array in ascending order):

1. Starting from the first element, we search the smallest element in the array, and replace it with the element in the first position.

2. We then move on to the second position, and look for smallest element present in the sub-array, starting from index 1, till the last index.

3. We replace the element at the second position in the original array, or we can say at the first position in the subarray, with the second smallest element.

4. This is repeated, until the array is completely sorted.

Let's consider an array with values {3, 6, 1, 8, 4, 5}

Below, we have a pictorial representation of how selection sort will sort the given array.

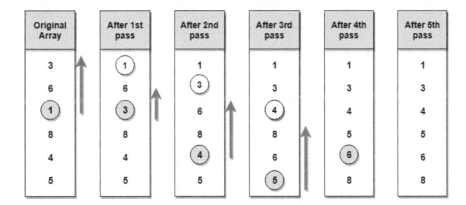

In the first pass, the smallest element will be 1, so it will be placed at the first position.

Then leaving the first element, next smallest element will be searched, from the remaining elements. We will get 3 as the smallest, so it will be then placed at the second position.

Then leaving 1 and 3(because they are at the correct position), we will search for the next smallest element from the rest of the elements and put it at third position and keep doing this until array is sorted.

Finding Smallest Element in a Subarray

In selection sort, in the first step, we look for the smallest element in the array and replace it with the element at the first position. This seems doable, isn't it?

Consider that you have an array with following values {3, 6, 1, 8, 4, 5}. Now as per selection sort, we will start from the first element and look for the smallest number in the array, which is 1 and we will find it at the index 2. Once the smallest number is found, it is swapped with the element at the first position.

Well, in the next iteration, we will have to look for the second smallest number in the array. How can we find the second smallest number? This one is tricky?

If you look closely, we already have the smallest number/element at the first position, which is the right position for it and we do not have to move it anywhere now. So we can say, that the first element is sorted, but the elements to the right, starting from index 1 are not.

So, we will now look for the smallest element in the subarray, starting from index 1, to the last index.

After we have found the second smallest element and replaced it with element on index 1(which is the second position in the array), we will have the first two positions of the array sorted.

Then we will work on the subarray, starting from index 2 now, and again looking for the smallest element in this subarray.

Implementing Selection Sort Algorithm

In the C program below, we have tried to divide the program into small functions, so that it's easier for you to understand which part is doing what.

There are many different ways to implement selection sort algorithm, here is the one that we like:

```c
// C program implementing Selection Sort

# include <stdio.h>


// function to swap elements at the given index values
void swap(int arr[], int firstIndex, int secondIndex)
{
    int temp;
    temp = arr[firstIndex];
    arr[firstIndex] = arr[secondIndex];
    arr[secondIndex] = temp;
}


// function to look for smallest element in the given subarray
int indexOfMinimum(int arr[], int startIndex, int n)
{
```

```
    int minValue = arr[startIndex];

    int minIndex = startIndex;


    for(int i = minIndex + 1; i < n; i++) {

        if(arr[i] < minValue)

        {

            minIndex = i;

            minValue = arr[i];

        }

    }

    return minIndex;

}


void selectionSort(int arr[], int n)

{

    for(int i = 0; i < n; i++)

    {

        int index = indexOfMinimum(arr, i, n);

        swap(arr, i, index);

    }


}


void printArray(int arr[], int size)

{

    int i;

    for(i = 0; i < size; i++)

    {

        printf("%d ", arr[i]);

    }
```

```
        printf("\n");
}


int main()
{
        int arr[] = {46, 52, 21, 22, 11};
        int n = sizeof(arr)/sizeof(arr[0]);
        selectionSort(arr, n);
        printf("Sorted array: \n");
        printArray(arr, n);
        return 0;
}
```

Selection sort is an unstable sort i.e it might change the occurrence of two similar elements in the list while sorting. But it can also work as a stable sort when it is implemented using linked list.

Complexity Analysis of Selection Sort

Selection Sort requires two nested for loops to complete itself, one for loop is in the function selectionSort, and inside the first loop we are making a call to another function indexOfMinimum, which has the second(inner) for loop.

Hence for a given input size of n, following will be the time and space complexity for selection sort algorithm:

Worst Case Time Complexity [Big-O]: $O(n^2)$

Best Case Time Complexity [Big-omega]: $O(n^2)$

Average Time Complexity [Big-theta]: $O(n^2)$

Space Complexity: $O(1)$

External Sorting

The problem of sorting collections of records too large to fit in main memory. Because the records must reside in peripheral or external memory, such sorting methods are called *external sorts*. This is in contrast to *internal sorts*, which assume that the records to be sorted are stored in main memory. Sorting large collections of records is central to many applications, such as processing payrolls and other large business databases. As a consequence, many external sorting algorithms have been devised. Years ago, sorting algorithm designers sought to optimize the use of specific hardware configurations, such as multiple tape or *disk drives*. Most computing today is done on personal computers and low-end workstations with relatively powerful CPUs, but only one or at most two disk drives. The techniques presented here are geared toward optimized processing on a single disk drive. This approach allows us to cover the most important issues in external sorting while skipping many less important machine-dependent details.

When a collection of records is too large to fit in *main memory*, the only practical way to sort it is to read some records from disk, do some rearranging, then write them back to disk. This process is repeated until the file is sorted, with each record read perhaps many times. Given the high cost of *disk I/O*, it should come as no surprise that the primary goal of an external sorting algorithm is to minimize the number of times information must be read from or written to disk. A certain amount of additional CPU processing can profitably be traded for reduced disk access.

Before discussing external sorting techniques, consider again the basic model for accessing information from disk. The file to be sorted is viewed by the programmer as a sequential series of fixed-size *blocks*. Assume (for simplicity) that each block contains the same number of fixed-size data records. Depending on the application, a record might be only a few bytes—composed of little or nothing more than the key—or might be hundreds of bytes with a relatively small key field. Records are assumed not to cross block boundaries. These assumptions can be relaxed for special-purpose sorting applications, but ignoring such complications makes the principles clearer.

A sector is the basic unit of I/O. In other words, all disk reads and writes are for one or more complete sectors. Sector sizes are typically a power of two, in the range 512 to 16K bytes, depending on the operating system and the size and speed of the disk drive. The block size used for external sorting algorithms should be equal to or a multiple of the sector size.

Under this model, a sorting algorithm reads a block of data into a buffer in main memory, performs some processing on it, and at some future time writes it back to disk. *Recall that* reading or writing a block from disk takes on the order of one million times longer than a memory access. Based on this fact, we can reasonably expect that the records contained in a single block can be sorted by an internal sorting algorithm such as *Quicksort* in less time than is required to read or write the block.

Under good conditions, reading from a file in sequential order is more efficient than reading blocks in random order. Given the significant impact of seek time on disk access, it might seem obvious that sequential processing is faster. However, it is important to understand precisely under what circumstances sequential file processing is actually faster than random access, because it affects our approach to designing an external sorting algorithm.

Efficient sequential access relies on seek time being kept to a minimum. The first requirement is that the blocks making up a file are in fact stored on disk in sequential order and close together, preferably filling a small number of contiguous tracks. At the very least, the number of extents making up the file should be small. Users typically do not have much control over the layout of their file on disk, but writing a file all at once in sequential order to a disk drive with a high percentage of free space increases the likelihood of such an arrangement.

The second requirement is that the disk drive's I/O head remain positioned over the file throughout sequential processing. This will not happen if there is competition of any kind for the I/O head. For example, on a multi-user time-shared computer the sorting process might compete for the I/O head with the processes of other users. Even when the sorting process has sole control of the I/O head, it is still likely that sequential processing will not be efficient. Imagine the situation where all processing is done on a single disk drive, with the typical arrangement of a single bank of read/ write heads that move together over a stack of platters. If the sorting process involves reading from an input file, alternated with writing to an output file, then the I/O head will continuously seek between the input file and the output file. Similarly, if two input files are being processed simultaneously (such as during a merge process), then the I/O head will continuously seek between these two files.

The moral is that, with a single disk drive, there often is no such thing as efficient sequential processing of a data file. Thus, a sorting algorithm might be more efficient if it performs a smaller number of non-sequential disk operations rather than a larger number of logically sequential disk operations that require a large number of seeks in practice.

As mentioned previously, the record size might be quite large compared to the size of the key. For example, payroll entries for a large business might each store hundreds of bytes of information including the name, ID, address, and job title for each employee. The sort key might be the ID number, requiring only a few bytes. The simplest sorting algorithm might be to process such records as a whole, reading the entire record whenever it is processed. However, this will greatly increase the amount of I/O required, because only a relatively few records will fit into a single disk block. Another alternative is to do a *key sort*. Under this method, the keys are all read and stored together in an *index file*, where each key is stored along with a pointer indicating the position of the corresponding record in the original data file. The key and pointer combination should be substantially smaller than the size of the original record; thus, the index file will be much smaller than the complete data file. The index file will then be sorted, requiring much less I/O because the index records are smaller than the complete records.

Once the index file is sorted, it is possible to reorder the records in the original database file. This is typically not done for two reasons. First, reading the records in sorted order from the record file requires a random access for each record. This can take a substantial amount of time and is only of value if the complete collection of records needs to be viewed or processed in sorted order (as opposed to a search for selected records). Second, database systems typically allow searches to be done on multiple keys. For example, today's processing might be done in order of ID numbers. Tomorrow, the boss might want information sorted by salary. Thus, there might be no single "sorted" order for the full record. Instead, multiple index files are often maintained, one for each sort key.

Simple Approaches to External Sorting

If your operating system supports virtual memory, the simplest "external" sort is to read the entire file into virtual memory and run an internal sorting method such as Quicksort. This approach allows the virtual memory manager to use its normal buffer pool mechanism to control disk accesses. Unfortunately, this might not always be a viable option. One potential drawback is that the size of virtual memory is usually limited to something much smaller than the disk space available.

Thus, your input file might not fit into virtual memory. Limited virtual memory can be overcome by adapting an internal sorting method to make use of your own buffer pool.

A more general problem with adapting an internal sorting algorithm to external sorting is that it is not likely to be as efficient as designing a new algorithm with the specific goal of minimizing disk I/O. Consider the simple adaptation of Quicksort to use a buffer pool. Quicksort begins by processing the entire array of records, with the first partition step moving indices inward from the two ends. This can be implemented efficiently using a buffer pool. However, the next step is to process each of the subarrays, followed by processing of sub-subarrays, and so on. As the subarrays get smaller, processing quickly approaches random access to the disk drive. Even with maximum use of the buffer pool, Quicksort still must read and write each record logn times on average. We can do much better. Finally, even if the virtual memory manager can give good performance using a standard Quicksort, this will come at the cost of using a lot of the system's working memory, which will mean that the system cannot use this space for other work. Better methods can save time while also using less memory.

Our approach to external sorting is derived from the Mergesort algorithm. The simplest form of external Mergesort performs a series of sequential passes over the records, merging larger and larger sublists on each pass. The first pass merges sublists of size 1 into sublists of size 2; the second pass merges the sublists of size 2 into sublists of size 4; and so on. A sorted sublist is called a *run*. Thus, each pass is merging pairs of runs to form longer runs. Each pass copies the contents of the file to another file. Here is a sketch of the algorithm.

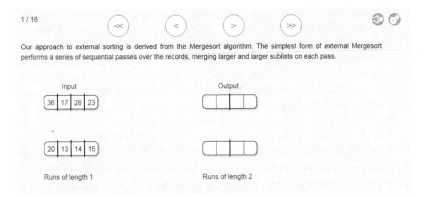

1. Split the original file into two equal-sized *run files*.

2. Read one block from each run file into input buffers.

3. Take the first record from each input buffer, and write a run of length two to an output buffer in sorted order.

4. Take the next record from each input buffer, and write a run of length two to a second output buffer in sorted order.

5. Repeat until finished, alternating output between the two output run buffers. Whenever the end of an input block is reached, read the next block from the appropriate input file. When an output buffer is full, write it to the appropriate output file.

6. Repeat steps 2 through 5, using the original output files as input files. On the second pass, the first two records of each input run file are already in sorted order. Thus, these two runs may be merged and output as a single run of four elements.

7. Each pass through the run files provides larger and larger runs until only one run remains.

This algorithm can easily take advantage of double buffering. Note that the various passes read the input run files sequentially and write the output run files sequentially. For sequential processing and double buffering to be effective, however, it is necessary that there be a separate I/O head available for each file. This typically means that each of the input and output files must be on separate disk drives, requiring a total of four disk drives for maximum efficiency.

Improving Performance

The external Mergesort algorithm just described requires that log n passes be made to sort a file of n records. Thus, each record must be read from disk and written to disk logn times. The number of passes can be significantly reduced by observing that it is not necessary to use Mergesort on small runs. A simple modification is to read in a block of data, sort it in memory (perhaps using Quicksort), and then output it as a single sorted run.

1 / 9   <<   <   >   >>

Assume that each record has four bytes of data and a 4-byte key, for a total of eight bytes per record:

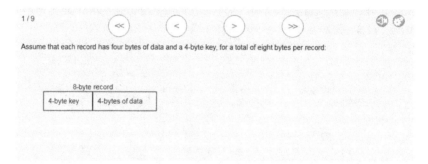

We can extend this concept to improve performance even further. Available main memory is usually much more than one block in size. If we process larger initial runs, then the number of passes required by Mergesort is further reduced. For example, most modern computers can provide tens or even hundreds of megabytes of RAM to the sorting program. If all of this memory (excepting a small amount for buffers and local variables) is devoted to building initial runs as large as possible, then quite large files can be processed in few passes.

Another way to reduce the number of passes required is to increase the number of runs that are merged together during each pass. While the standard Mergesort algorithm merges two runs at a time, there is no reason why merging needs to be limited in this way.

Over the years, many variants on external sorting have been presented, but all are based on the following two steps:

1. Break the file into large initial runs.

2. Merge the runs together to form a single sorted file.

Replacement Selection

Here we treat the problem of creating initial runs as large as possible from a disk file, assuming a fixed amount of RAM is available for processing. As mentioned previously, a simple approach is to allocate as much RAM as possible to a large array, fill this array from disk, and sort the array using Quicksort. Thus, if the size of memory available for the array is M records, then the input file can be broken into initial runs of length M. A better approach is to use an algorithm called replacement selection that, on average, creates runs of 2M records in length. Replacement selection is actually a slight variation on the Heapsort algorithm. The fact that Heapsort is slower than Quicksort is irrelevant in this context because I/O time will dominate the total running time of any reasonable external sorting algorithm. Building longer initial runs will reduce the total I/O time required.

Replacement selection views RAM as consisting of an array of size M in addition to an input buffer and an output buffer. (Additional I/O buffers might be desirable if the operating system supports double buffering, because replacement selection does sequential processing on both its input and its output.) Imagine that the input and output files are streams of records. Replacement selection takes the next record in sequential order from the input stream when needed, and outputs runs one record at a time to the output stream. Buffering is used so that disk I/O is performed one block at a time. A block of records is initially read and held in the input buffer. Replacement selection removes records from the input buffer one at a time until the buffer is empty. At this point the next block of records is read in. Output to a buffer is similar: Once the buffer fills up it is written to disk as a unit. This process is illustrated by figure below.

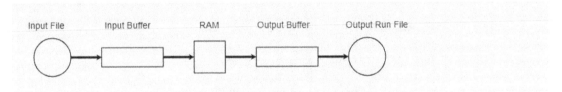

Overview of replacement selection.

Input records are processed sequentially. Initially RAM is filled with M records. As records are processed, they are written to an output buffer. When this buffer becomes full, it is written to disk. Meanwhile, as replacement selection needs records, it reads them from the input buffer. Whenever this buffer becomes empty, the next block of records is read from disk.

Replacement selection works as follows. Assume that the main processing is done in an array of size M records.

1. Fill the array from disk. Set LAST = M-1.

2. Build a min-heap. (Recall that a min-heap is defined such that the record at each node has a key value less than the key values of its children.)

3. Repeat until the array is empty:

a) Send the record with the minimum key value (the root) to the output buffer.

b) Let R be the next record in the input buffer. If R's key value is greater than the key value just output

   i.   Then place R at the root.

   ii.   Else replace the root with the record in array position LAST, and place R at position LAST. Set LAST = LAST - 1.

c) Sift down the root to reorder the heap.

When the test at step 3(b) is successful, a new record is added to the heap, eventually to be output as part of the run. As long as records coming from the input file have key values greater than the last key value output to the run, they can be safely added to the heap. Records with smaller key values cannot be output as part of the current run because they would not be in sorted order. Such values must be stored somewhere for future processing as part of another run. However, because the heap will shrink by one element in this case, there is now a free space where the last element of the heap used to be. Thus, replacement selection will slowly shrink the heap and at the same time use the discarded heap space to store records for the next run. Once the first run is complete (i.e., the heap becomes empty), the array will be filled with records ready to be processed for the second run. Here is a visualization to show a run being created by replacement selection.

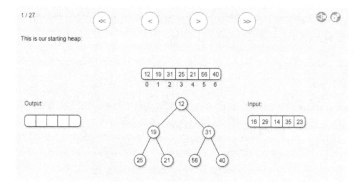

It should be clear that the minimum length of a run will be M records if the size of the heap is M, because at least those records originally in the heap will be part of the run. Under good conditions (e.g., if the input is sorted), then an arbitrarily long run is possible. In fact, the entire file could be processed as one run. If conditions are bad (e.g., if the input is reverse sorted), then runs of only size M result.

What is the expected length of a run generated by replacement selection? It can be deduced from an analogy called the snowplow argument. Imagine that a snowplow is going around a circular track during a heavy, but steady, snowstorm. After the plow has been around at least once, snow on the track must be as follows. Immediately behind the plow, the track is empty because it was just plowed. The greatest level of snow on the track is immediately in front of the plow, because this is the place least recently plowed. At any instant, there is a certain amount of snow S on the track. Snow is constantly falling throughout the track at a steady rate, with some snow falling "in front" of the plow and some "behind" the plow. During the next revolution of the plow, all snow S on the track is removed, plus half of what falls. Because everything is assumed to be in steady state, after one revolution S snow is still on the track, so 2S snow must fall during a revolution, and 2S snow is removed during a revolution (leaving S snow behind).

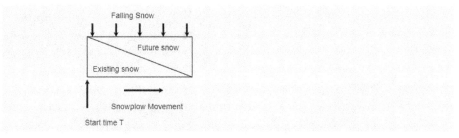

The snowplow analogy showing the action during one revolution of the snowplow.

A circular track is laid out straight for purposes of illustration, and is shown in cross section. At any time T, the most snow is directly in front of the snowplow. As the plow moves around the track, the same amount of snow is always in front of the plow. As the plow moves forward, less of this is snow that was in the track at time T; more is snow that has fallen since.

At the beginning of replacement selection, nearly all values coming from the input file are greater (i.e., "in front of the plow") than the latest key value output for this run, because the run's initial key values should be small. As the run progresses, the latest key value output becomes greater and so new key values coming from the input file are more likely to be too small (i.e., "after the plow"); such records go to the bottom of the array. The total length of the run is expected to be twice the size of the array. Of course, this assumes that incoming key values are evenly distributed within the key range (in terms of the snowplow analogy, we assume that snow falls evenly throughout the track). Sorted and reverse sorted inputs do not meet this expectation and so change the length of the run.

Multiway Merging

The second stage of a typical external sorting algorithm merges the runs created by the first stage. Assume that we have R runs to merge. If a simple two-way merge is used, then R runs (regardless of their sizes) will require log R passes through the file. While R should be much less than the total number of records (because the initial runs should each contain many records), we would like to reduce still further the number of passes required to merge the runs together. Note that two-way merging does not make good use of available memory. Because merging is a sequential process on the two runs, only one block of records per run need be in memory at a time. Keeping more than one block of a run in memory at any time will not reduce the disk I/O required by the merge process (though if several blocks are read from a file at once time, at least they take advantage of sequential access). Thus, most of the space just used by the heap for replacement selection (typically many blocks in length) is not being used by the merge process.

We can make better use of this space and at the same time greatly reduce the number of passes needed to merge the runs if we merge several runs at a time. Multiway merging is similar to two-way merging. If we have B runs to merge, with a block from each run available in memory, then the B-way merge algorithm simply looks at B values (the front-most value for each input run) and selects the smallest one to output. This value is removed from its run, and the process is repeated. When the current block for any run is exhausted, the next block from that run is read from disk.

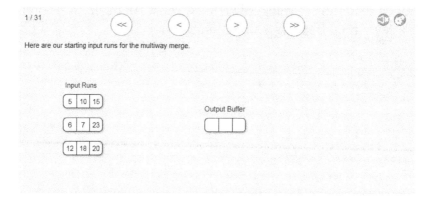

1 / 31

Here are our starting input runs for the multiway merge.

Conceptually, multiway merge assumes that each run is stored in a separate file. However, this is not necessary in practice. We only need to know the position of each run within a single file, and use seek to move to the appropriate block whenever we need new data from a particular run. Naturally, this approach destroys the ability to do sequential processing on the input file. However, if all runs were stored on a single disk drive, then processing would not be truly sequential anyway because the I/O head would be alternating between the runs. Thus, multiway merging replaces several (potentially) sequential passes with a single random access pass. If the processing would not be sequential anyway (such as when all processing is on a single disk drive), no time is lost by doing so.

Multiway merging can greatly reduce the number of passes required. If there is room in memory to store one block for each run, then all runs can be merged in a single pass. Thus, replacement selection can build initial runs in one pass, and multiway merging can merge all runs in one pass, yielding a total cost of two passes. However, for truly large files, there might be too many runs for each to get a block in memory. If there is room to allocate B blocks for a B-way merge, and the number of runs R is greater than B, then it will be necessary to do multiple merge passes. In other words, the first B runs are merged, then the next B, and so on. These super-runs are then merged by subsequent passes, B super-runs at a time.

How big a file can be merged in one pass? Assuming B blocks were allocated to the heap for replacement selection (resulting in runs of average length 2B blocks), followed by a B-way merge, we can process on average a file of size $(2B^2)$ blocks in a single multiway merge. $2Bk^{+1}$ blocks on average can be processed in k B-way merges. To gain some appreciation for how quickly this grows, assume that we have available 0.5MB of working memory, and that a block is 4KB, yielding 128 blocks in working memory. The average run size is 1MB (twice the working memory size). In one pass, 128 runs can be merged. Thus, a file of size 128MB can, on average, be processed in two passes (one to build the runs, one to do the merge) with only 0.5MB of working memory. As another example, assume blocks are 1KB long and working memory is 1MB = 1024 blocks. Then 1024 runs of average length 2MB (which is about 2GB) can be combined in a single merge pass. A larger block size would reduce the size of the file that can be processed in one merge pass for a fixed-size working memory; a smaller block size or larger working memory would increase the file size that can be processed in one merge pass. Two merge passes allow much bigger files to be processed. With 0.5MB of working memory and 4KB blocks, a file of size 16~gigabytes could be processed in two merge passes, which is big enough for most applications. Thus, this is a very effective algorithm for single disk drive external sorting.

Table below shows a comparison of the running time to sort various-sized files for the following implementations:

(1) standard Mergesort with two input runs and two output runs,

(2) two-way Mergesort with large initial runs (limited by the size of available memory), and

(3) R-way Mergesort performed after generating large initial runs. In each case, the file was composed of a series of four-byte records (a two-byte key and a two-byte data value), or 256K records per megabyte of file size.

We can see from this table that using even a modest memory size (two blocks) to create initial runs results in a tremendous savings in time. Doing 4-way merges of the runs provides another considerable speedup, however large-scale multi-way merges for R beyond about 4 or 8 runs does not help much because a lot of time is spent determining which is the next smallest element among the R runs.

A comparison of three external sorts on a collection of small records for files of various sizes. Each entry in the table shows time in seconds and total number of blocks read and written by the program. File sizes are in Megabytes. For the third sorting algorithm, on a file size of 4MB, the time and blocks shown in the last column are for a 32-way merge (marked with an asterisk). 32 is used instead of 16 because 32 is a root of the number of blocks in the file (while 16 is not), thus allowing the same number of runs to be merged at every pass.

File Size (Mb)	Sort 1	Sort 2 Memory size (in blocks)				Sort 3 Memory size (in blocks)		
		2	4	16	256	2	4	16
1	0.61 4,864	0.27 2,048	0.24 1,792	0.19 1,280	0.10 256	0.21 2,048	0.15 1,024	0.13 512
4	2.56 21,504	1.30 10,240	1.19 9,216	0.96 7,168	0.61 3,072	1.15 10,240	0.68 5,120	0.66* 2,048
16	11.28 94,208	6.12 49,152	5.63 45,056	4.78 36,864	3.36 20,480	5.42 49,152	3.19 24,516	3.10 12,288
256	220.39 1,769 k	132.47 1,048K	123.68 983K	110.01 852K	86.66 589K	115.73 1,049K	69.31 524K	68.71 262K

We see from this experiment that building large initial runs reduces the running time to slightly more than one third that of standard Mergesort, depending on file and memory sizes. Using a multi-way merge further cuts the time nearly in half.

Distribution Sorts

Any sort algorithm where items are distributed from the input to multiple intermediate structures, which are then gathered and placed on the output.

Bucket Sort

Bucket sort is a comparison sort algorithm that operates on elements by dividing them into different buckets and then sorting these buckets individually. Each bucket is sorted individually using a separate sorting algorithm or by applying the bucket sort algorithm recursively. Bucket sort is mainly useful when the input is uniformly distributed over a range.

Assume one has the following problem in front of them:

One has been given a large array of floating point integers lying uniformly between the lower and upper bound. This array now needs to be sorted. A simple way to solve this problem would be to use another sorting algorithm such as Merge sort, Heap Sort or Quick Sort. However, these algorithms guarantee a best case time complexity of $O(NlogN)$. However, using bucket sort, the above task can be completed in $O(N)$ time. Let's have a closer look at it.

Consider one needs to create an array of lists, i.e of buckets. Elements now need to be inserted into these buckets on the basis of their properties. Each of these buckets can then be sorted individually using Insertion Sort. Consider the pseudo code to do so:

```
void bucketSort(float[] a,int n)

{

    for(each floating integer 'x' in n)

    {

        insert x into bucket[n*x];

    }

    for(each bucket)

    {

        sort(bucket);

    }

}
```

Time Complexity

If one assumes that insertion in a bucket takes $O(1)$ time, then steps 1 and 2 of the above algorithm clearly take $O(n)$ time.

Steps on How it Works

1. Create an empty array.

2. Loop through the original array and put each object in a "bucket".

3. Sort each of the non-empty buckets

4. Check the buckets in order and then put all objects back into the original array.

Below is an image of an array, which needs to be sorted. We will use the Bucket Sort Algorithm, to sort this array:

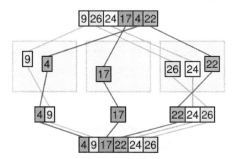

Bucket sort moves elements to buckets, then sorts the buckets.

And here is another image:

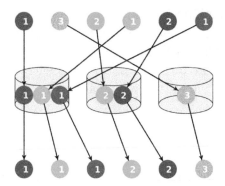

Bucket Sort: An Example

Here is an example of writing the Bucket Sort Algorithm based on the steps we provided earlier. Below, there is a function, which accepts the following parameter: an array and a key. The function returns the sorted array.

```javascript
function bucketSort(array, key) {
    key = key || function(x) { return x };
    var buckets = [],
        i, j, b, d = 0;
    for (; d < 32; d += 4) {
        for (i = 16; i--;)
            buckets[i] = [];
        for (i = array.length; i--;)
            buckets[(key(array[i]) >> d) & 15].push(array[i]);
        for (b = 0; b < 16; b++)
            for (j = buckets[b].length; j--;)
                array[++i] = buckets[b][j];
    }
    return a;
}
```

Characteristics of Bucket Sort

•   Bucket sort assumes that the input is drawn from a uniform distribution.

•   The computational complexity estimates involve the number of buckets.

- Bucket sort can be exceptionally fast because of the way elements are assigned to buckets, typically using an array where the index is the value.

- This means that more auxiliary memory is required for the buckets at the cost of running time than more comparison sorts.

- The average time complexity for Bucket Sort is $O(n + k)$. The worst time complexity is $O(n^2)$.

- The space complexity for Bucket Sort is $O(n+k)$.

Variants

Generic Bucket Sort

The most common variant of bucket sort operates on a list of n numeric inputs between zero and some maximum value M and divides the value range into n buckets each of size M/n. If each bucket is sorted using insertion sort, the sort can be shown to run in expected linear time (where the average is taken over all possible inputs). However, the performance of this sort degrades with clustering; if many values occur close together, they will all fall into a single bucket and be sorted slowly. This performance degradation is avoided in the original bucket sort algorithm by assuming that the input is generated by a random process that distributes elements uniformly over the interval $[0,1)$. Since there are n uniformly distributed elements sorted in to n buckets the probable number of inputs in each bucket follows a binomial distribution with $E(n_i) = 1$ and hence the entire bucket sort will be $O(n)$ despite the repeated use of $O(n^2)$ insertion sort.

ProxmapSort

Similar to generic bucket sort as described above, ProxmapSort works by dividing an array of keys into subarrays via the use of a "map key" function that preserves a partial ordering on the keys; as each key is added to its subarray, insertion sort is used to keep that subarray sorted, resulting in the entire array being in sorted order when ProxmapSort completes. ProxmapSort differs from bucket sorts in its use of the map key to place the data approximately where it belongs in sorted order, producing a "proxmap" a proximity mapping of the keys.

Histogram Sort

Another variant of bucket sort known as histogram sort or counting sort adds an initial pass that counts the number of elements that will fall into each bucket using a count array. Using this information, the array values can be arranged into a sequence of buckets in-place by a sequence of exchanges, leaving no space overhead for bucket storage.

Postman's Sort

The Postman's sort is a variant of bucket sort that takes advantage of a hierarchical structure of elements, typically described by a set of attributes. This is the algorithm used by letter-sorting machines in post offices: mail is sorted first between domestic and international; then by state, province or territory; then by destination post office; then by routes, etc. Since keys are not compared against each other, sorting time is O(cn), where c depends on the size of the key and number of buckets. This is similar to a radix sort that works "top down," or "most significant digit first."

Shuffle Sort

The shuffle sort is a variant of bucket sort that begins by removing the first 1/8 of the n items to be sorted, sorts them recursively, and puts them in an array. This creates $n/8$ "buckets" to which the remaining 7/8 of the items are distributed. Each "bucket" is then sorted, and the "buckets" are concatenated into a sorted array.

Comparison with other Sorting Algorithms

Bucket sort can be seen as a generalization of counting sort; in fact, if each bucket has size 1 then bucket sort degenerates to counting sort. The variable bucket size of bucket sort allows it to use O(n) memory instead of O(M) memory, where M is the number of distinct values; in exchange, it gives up counting sort's O($n + M$) worst-case behavior.

Bucket sort with two buckets is effectively a version of quicksort where the pivot value is always selected to be the middle value of the value range. While this choice is effective for uniformly distributed inputs, other means of choosing the pivot in quicksort such as randomly selected pivots make it more resistant to clustering in the input distribution.

The n-way mergesort algorithm also begins by distributing the list into n sublists and sorting each one; however, the sublists created by mergesort have overlapping value ranges and so cannot be recombined by simple concatenation as in bucket sort. Instead, they must be interleaved by a merge algorithm. However, this added expense is counterbalanced by the simpler scatter phase and the ability to ensure that each sublist is the same size, providing a good worst-case time bound.

Top-down radix sort can be seen as a special case of bucket sort where both the range of values and the number of buckets is constrained to be a power of two. Consequently, each bucket's size is also a power of two, and the procedure can be applied recursively. This approach can accelerate the scatter phase, since we only need to examine a prefix of the bit representation of each element to determine its bucket.

Counting Sort

Counting sort is an algorithm for sorting a collection of objects according to keys that are small integers; that is, it is an integer sorting algorithm. It operates by counting the number of objects that have each distinct key value, and using arithmetic on those counts to determine the positions of each key value in the output sequence. Its running time is linear in the number of items and the difference between the maximum and minimum key values, so it is only suitable for direct use in situations where the variation in keys is not significantly greater than the number of items. However, it is often used as a subroutine in another sorting algorithm, radix sort, that can handle larger keys more efficiently.

Because counting sort uses key values as indexes into an array, it is not a comparison sort, and the $\Omega(n \log n)$ lower bound for comparison sorting does not apply to it. Bucket sort may be used for many of the same tasks as counting sort, with a similar time analysis; however, compared to counting sort, bucket sort requires linked lists, dynamic arrays or a large amount of preallocated memory to hold the sets of items within each bucket, whereas counting sort instead stores a single number (the count of items) per bucket.

The Algorithm

In summary, the algorithm loops over the items, computing a histogram of the number of times each key occurs within the input collection. It then performs a prefix sum computation (a second loop, over the range of possible keys) to determine, for each key, the starting position in the output array of the items having that key. Finally, it loops over the items again, moving each item into its sorted position in the output array.

In pseudocode, this may be expressed as follows:

```
# variables:
#     input -- the array of items to be sorted;
#     key(x) -- function that returns the key for item x
#     k -- a number such that all keys are in the range 0..k-1
#     count -- an array of numbers, with indexes 0..k-1, initially all zero
#     output -- an array of items, with indexes 0..n-1
#     x -- an individual input item, used within the algorithm
#     total, oldCount, i -- numbers used within the algorithm


# calculate the histogram of key frequencies:
for x in input:
    count[key(x)] += 1


# calculate the starting index for each key:
total = 0
for i in range(k):    # i = 0, 1, ... k-1
    oldCount = count[i]
    count[i] = total
    total += oldCount


# copy to output array, preserving order of inputs with equal keys:
```

```
for x in input:

    output[count[key(x)]] = x

    count[key(x)] += 1


return output
```

After the first for loop, count[i] stores the number of items with key equal to i. After the second for loop, it instead stores the number of items with key less than i, which is the same as the first index at which an item with key i should be stored in the output array. Throughout the third loop, count[i] always stores the next position in the output array into which an item with key i should be stored, so each item is moved into its correct position in the output array. The relative order of items with equal keys is preserved here; i.e., this is a stable sort.

Complexity Analysis

Because the algorithm uses only simple for loops, without recursion or subroutine calls, it is straightforward to analyze. The initialization of the count array, and the second for loop which performs a prefix sum on the count array, each iterate at most $k + 1$ times and therefore take $O(k)$ time. The other two for loops, and the initialization of the output array, each take $O(n)$ time. Therefore, the time for the whole algorithm is the sum of the times for these steps, $O(n + k)$.

Because it uses arrays of length $k + 1$ and n, the total space usage of the algorithm is also $O(n + k)$. For problem instances in which the maximum key value is significantly smaller than the number of items, counting sort can be highly space-efficient, as the only storage it uses other than its input and output arrays is the Count array which uses space $O(k)$.

Variant Algorithms

If each item to be sorted is itself an integer, and used as key as well, then the second and third loops of counting sort can be combined; in the second loop, instead of computing the position where items with key i should be placed in the output, simply append Count[i] copies of the number i to the output.

This algorithm may also be used to eliminate duplicate keys, by replacing the Count array with a bit vector that stores a one for a key that is present in the input and a zero for a key that is not present. If additionally the items are the integer keys themselves, both second and third loops can be omitted entirely and the bit vector will itself serve as output, representing the values as offsets of the non-zero entries, added to the range's lowest value. Thus the keys are sorted and the duplicates are eliminated in this variant just by being placed into the bit array.

For data in which the maximum key size is significantly smaller than the number of data items, counting sort may be parallelized by splitting the input into subarrays of approximately equal size, processing each subarray in parallel to generate a separate count array for each subarray, and then merging the count arrays. When used as part of a parallel radix sort algorithm, the key size (base of the radix representation) should be chosen to match the size of the split subarrays. The simplicity of the counting sort algorithm and its use of the easily parallelizable prefix sum primitive also make it usable in more fine-grained parallel algorithms.

Counting sort is not an in-place algorithm; even disregarding the count array, it needs separate input and output arrays. It is possible to modify the algorithm so that it places the items into sorted order within the same array that was given to it as the input, using only the count array as auxiliary storage; however, the modified in-place version of counting sort is not stable.

Radix Sort

Radix Sort is an algorithm that sorts a list of numbers and comes under the category of distribution sort. This sorting algorithm doesn't compare the numbers but distributes them, it works as follows:

1. Sorting takes place by distributing the list of number into a bucket by passing through the individual digits of a given number one-by-one beginning with the least significant part. Here, the number of buckets are a total of ten, which bare key values starting from 0 to 9.

2. After each pass, the numbers are collected from the buckets, keeping the numbers in order.

3. Now, recursively redistribute the numbers as in the above step '1' but with a following reconsideration: take into account next most significant part of the number, which is then followed by above step '2'.

Radix Sort arranges the elements in order by comparing the digits of the numbers.

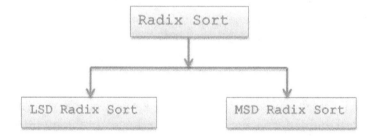

LSD Radix Sort

Least-significant-digit-first radix sort.

LSD radix sorts process the integer representations starting from the least significant digit and move the processing towards the most significant digit.

MSD Radix Sort

Most-significant-digit-first radix sort.

MSD radix sort starts processing the keys from the most significant digit, leftmost digit, to the least significant digit, rightmost digit. This sequence is opposite that of least significant digit (LSD) radix sorts.

Algorithm of Radix Sort

1. RADIX-SORT (A ,d)

2.

3. 1) for i ? 1 to d;

4.

5. 2) do use a stable sort to sort Array A on digit i // counting sort will do the job//

6.

c Fuction for radix sort

```
1.  radix_sort(int arr[], int n)

2.

3.  {

4.

5.    int bucket[10][5],buck[10],b[10];

6.

7.    int i,j,k,l,num,div,large,passes;

8.

9.

10.

11.   div=1;

12.

13.   num=0;

14.

15.   large=arr[0];

16.

17.

18.

19.   for(i=0 ; i< n ; i++)

20.

21.   {

22.
```

```
23.          if(arr[i] > large)

24.

25.          {

26.

27.                  large = arr[i];

28.

29.          }

30.

31.          while(large > 0)

32.

33.          {

34.

35.                  num++;

36.

37.                  large = large/10;

38.

39.          }

40.

41.          for(passes=0 ; passes < num ; passes++)

42.

43.          {

44.

45.                  for(k=0 ; k< 10 ; k++)

46.

47.                  {

48.

49.                          buck[k] = 0;

50.

51.                  }

52.
```

```
53.                 for(i=0 ; i< n   ;i++)

54.

55.                 {

56.

57.                         l = ((arr[i]/div)%10);

58.

59.                         bucket[l][buck[l]++] = arr[i];

60.

61.                 }

62.

63.

64.

65.             i=0;

66.

67.             for(k=0 ; k < 10 ; k++)

68.

69.             {

70.

71.                     for(j=0 ; j < buck[k] ; j++)

72.

73.                     {

74.

75.                             arr[i++] = bucket[k][j];

76.

77.                     }

78.

79.             }

80.

81.             div*=10;

82.
```

```
83.              }
84.
85.      }
86.
87. }
88.
```

Implementation of Radix Sort

```
1.      #include<stdio.h>

2.

3.      #include<conio.h>

4.

5.

6.

7.      radix_sort(int array[], int n);

8.

9.      void main()

10.

11.     {

12.

13.             int array[100],n,i;

14.

15.             clrscr();

16.

17.             printf("Enter the number of elements to be sorted: ");

18.

19.             scanf("%d",&n);

20.

21.             printf("\nEnter the elements to be sorted: \n");

22.

23.             for(i = 0 ; i < n ; i++ )
```

```
24.

25.            {

26.

27.                    scanf("%d",&array[i]);

28.

29.            }

30.

31.

32.

33.         printf("\nBefore Radix Sort:");

34.

35.         for(i = 0; i < n; i++)

36.

37.            {

38.

39.                    printf("%d\t", array[i]);

40.

41.            }

42.

43.         printf("\n");

44.

45.         radix_sort(array,n);

46.

47.         printf("\nArray After Radix Sort: ");   //Array After Radix Sort

48.

49.         for(i = 0; i < n; i++)

50.

51.            {

52.

53.                    printf("%d\t", array[i]);
```

```
54.

55.                 }

56.

57.             printf("\n");

58.

59.             getch();

60.

61.     }

62.

63.

64.

65.     radix_sort(int arr[], int n)

66.

67.     {

68.

69.             int bucket[10][5],buck[10],b[10];

70.

71.             int i,j,k,l,num,div,large,passes;

72.

73.

74.

75.             div=1;

76.

77.             num=0;

78.

79.             large=arr[0];

80.

81.

82.

83.             for(i=0 ; i < n ; i++)
```

```
84.

85.                    {

86.

87.                        if(arr[i] > large)

88.

89.                            {

90.

91.                                large = arr[i];

92.

93.                            }

94.

95.                        while(large > 0)

96.

97.                            {

98.

99.                                num++;

100.

101.                               large = large/10;

102.

103.                           }

104.

105.                       for(passes=0 ; passes < num ; passes++)

106.

107.                           {

108.

109.                               for(k=0 ; k < 10 ; k++)

110.

111.                                   {

112.

113.                                       buck[k] = 0;
```

```
114.
115.                        }
116.
117.                        for(i=0 ; i < n  ;i++)
118.
119.                        {
120.
121.                                l = ((arr[i]/div)%10);
122.
123.                                bucket[l][buck[l]++] = arr[i];
124.
125.                        }
126.
127.
128.
129.                        i=0;
130.
131.                        for(k=0 ; k< 10 ; k++)
132.
133.                        {
134.
135.                                for(j=0 ; j < buck[k] ; j++)
136.
137.                                {
138.
139.                                        arr[i++] = bucket[k][j];
140.
141.                                }
142.
143.                        }
```

144.

145.   div*=10;

146.

147.   }

148.

149.   }

150.

151.   }

OUTPUT

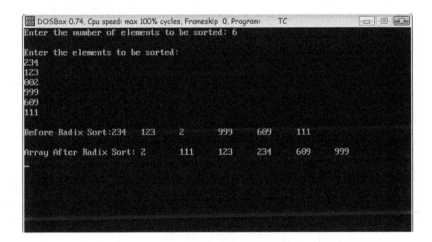

Consider a group of numbers. It is given by the list:

123, 002, 999, 609, 111

STEP1:

Sort the list of numbers according to the ascending order of least significant bit. The sorted list is given by:

111, 002, 123, 999, 609

STEP2:

Then sort the list of numbers according to the ascending order of 1st significant bit. The sorted list is given by:

609, 002, 111, 123, 999

STEP3:

Then sort the list of numbers according to the ascending order of most significant bit. The sorted list is given by:

1.　　　002, 111, 123, 609, 999

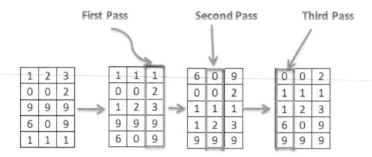

Analysis Of Radix sort	
Class	Sorting algoritdm
Data structure	Array
Worst case performance	O(K N)
Worst case space complexity	O(K N)

Hybrid Sorting Algorithm

A Hybrid Algorithm is an algorithm that combines two or more other algorithms that solve the same problem, either choosing one (depending on the data), or switching between them over the course of the algorithm. This is generally done to combine desired features of each, so that the overall algorithm is better than the individual components.

Quicksort is one of the fastest sorting algorithms for sorting large data. When implemented well, it can be about two or three times faster than its main competitors,

Tail Recursion

To make sure at most O(log n) space is used, recurse rst into the smaller side of the partition, then use a tail call to recurse into the other. As such, we successfully sort the array in a way that it minimizes the recursive depth.

Hybrid with Insertion Sort

When the number of elements is below some threshold (perhaps 10 elements), switch to a non-recursive sorting algorithm such as insertion sort that performs fewer swaps, comparisons or other operations on such small arrays.

Instead of "many small sorts" optimization, when the number of elements is less than some threshold k, we can simply stop. Later when the whole array has been processed, each element will be at most k positions away from its nal sorted position. Now if we perform insertion sort on it, it will take O(kn) time to nish the sort, which is linear as k is a constant.

Timsort

Timsort is a stable algorithm and beats every other sorting algorithm in time. It has O(nlogn) time complexity for worst case unlike quick sort and O(n) for best case scenarios unlike merge sort and heap sort.

In real-world scenarios, most of the times input array is naturally ordered array hence merge sort and quick sort aren't the efficient choices. Timsort shines when data is ordered and of course when data is random.

Timsort is a hybrid algorithm which uses Binary insertion sort and improved merge sort by using galloping in a combination. Binary insertion sort is the best method to sort when data is already or partially sorted and merge sort is best when the input is large.

Binary insertion sort uses Binary search to insert a new value in a sorted array. Binary search reduces the number of comparisons thus more efficient than linear search.

In above example, Binary insertion sort requires 2 iterations to find a location to insert 8 whereas a linear search would find a location in 4th iteration.

N: Number of elements inside the input array.

If N <= 64 then Timsort uses binary insertion sort to sort the elements and doesn't go in fancy details.

What if N is large

An input array is divided into different sub-arrays, count of elements inside a sub-array is defined as a *RUN*, the minimum value of such runs is a MIN_RUN.

A RUN can be either ascending or strictly descending. If elements are decreasing then in place swapping converts them into ascending order, elements that have equal values aren't swapped to maintain stability A run smaller than min run is extended to make count equal to min run. Now, this new run is sorted using binary insertion sort which has a best run time on partially ordered data. Ultimately, every run should be greater or equal to the min run and it shouldn't be less than 2.

Why Compute MIN_RUN

MIN_RUN ensures that the input array is split in such a way that when the merge happens, it happens in a perfectly balanced manner.

Let's understand it with an example below-:

In the left figure above, we have 4 sub-arrays of size 2 which perform perfectly balanced merge at each step. In the right figure, we have 5 sub-arrays of size 2 which doesn't allow the perfect balanced merge to happen.

Perfectly balanced merge allows one on one comparisons between items. An unbalanced merge can cause extra comparisons and impacts performance.

Ideally, Timsort wants the value of min run to be such that N / MIN_RUN equals to the power of 2 or close to it so that when the merge happens it gets a perfectly balanced merge for example When an input array has 256 elements Timsort would like to divide the array into equal sized sub-arrays. 256 / 32 will give us 8 equal sized sub-arrays that perform the perfectly balanced merge.

Merging

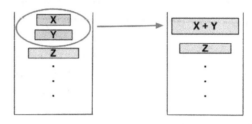

The runs are inserted in a stack. If $|Z| \leq |Y| + |X|$, then X and Y are merged and replaced on the stack. In this way, merging is continued until all runs satisfy i. $|Z| > |Y| + |X|$ and ii. $|Y| > |X|$.

Concurrently with the search for runs, the runs are merged with merge sort. Except where Timsort tries to optimise for merging disjoint runs in galloping mode, runs are repeatedly merged two at a time, with the only concerns being to maintain stability and merge balance.

Stability requires non-consecutive runs are not merged, as elements could be transferred across equal elements in the intervening run, violating stability. Further, it would be impossible to recover the order of the equal elements at a later point.

In pursuit of balanced merges, Timsort considers three runs on the top of the stack, X, Y, Z, and maintains the invariants:

   i. $|Z| > |Y| + |X|$

   ii. $|Y| > |X|$

If the invariants are violated, Y is merged with the smaller of X or Z and the invariants are checked again. Once the invariants hold, the next run is formed.

Somewhat inappreciably, the invariants maintain merges as being approximately balanced while maintaining a compromise between delaying merging for balance, and exploiting fresh occurrence of runs in cache memory, and also making merge decisions relatively simple.

On reaching the end of the data, Timsort repeatedly merges the two runs on the top of the stack, until only one run of the entire data remains.

Individual Merges

Timsort performs an almost in-place merge sort, as actual in-place merge sort implementations have a high overhead. First Timsort performs a binary search to find the location in the first run of the first element in the second run, and the location in the second run of the last element in the first run. Elements before and after these locations are already in their correct place, and may be removed from further consideration. This not only optimises element movements and running time, but also allows the use of less temporary memory. Then the smaller of the remaining runs is copied into temporary memory, and elements are merged with the larger run, into the now free space. If the first run is smaller, the merge starts at the beginning; if the second is smaller, the merge starts at the end.

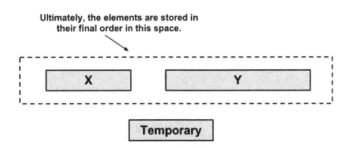

To merge, Timsort copies the elements of the smaller array (X in this illustration) to temporary memory, then sorts and fills elements in final order into the combined space of X and Y.

Say, for example, two runs A and B are to be merged, with A being the smaller run. In this case a binary search examines A to find the first element a' larger than the first element of B. Note that A and B are already sorted individually. When a' is found, the algorithm can ignore elements before that position when merging. Similarly, the algorithm also looks for the first element b' in B greater than the last element of A. The elements after b' can also be ignored when merging. This preliminary searching is not efficient for highly random data, but is efficient in other situations and is hence included.

Galloping Mode

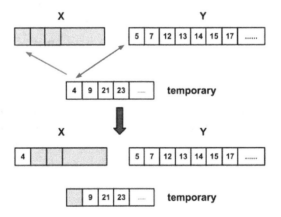

Elements (pointed to by blue arrow) are compared and the smaller element is moved to its final position (pointed to by red arrow).

An individual merge keeps a count of consecutive elements selected from the same input set. The algorithm switches to galloping mode when this reaches the *minimum galloping threshold* (*min_gallop*) in an attempt to capitalise on sub-runs in the data. The success or failure of galloping is used to adjust *min_gallop*, as an indication of whether the data does or does not contain sufficient sub-runs.

In galloping mode, the algorithm searches for the first element of one array in the other. This is done by comparing that initial element with the $(2^k - 1)$th element of the other array (first, third, seventh, and so on) so as to get a range of elements between which the initial element will lie. This shortens the range for binary searching, thus increasing efficiency. In cases where galloping is found to be less efficient than binary search, galloping mode is exited.

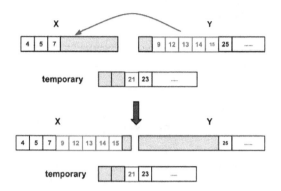

All red elements are smaller than blue (here, 21). Thus they can be moved in a chunk to the final array.

Galloping is beneficial only when the initial element of one run is not one of the first seven elements of the other run. This implies an initial threshold of 7. To avoid the drawbacks of galloping mode, the merging functions adjust the threshold value. If the selected element is from the same array that returned an element previously, *min_gallop* is reduced by one. Otherwise, the value is incremented by one, thus discouraging a return to galloping mode. In the case of random data, the value of *min_gallop* becomes so large that galloping mode never recurs.

When merging is done right-to-left, galloping starts from the right end of the data, that is, the last element. Galloping from the beginning also gives the required results, but makes more comparisons. Thus, the galloping algorithm uses a variable that gives the index at which galloping should begin. Timsort can enter galloping mode at any index and continue checking at the next index which is offset by 1, 3, 7, ..., $(2^k - 1)$... and so on from the current index. In the case of right-to-left merging, the offsets to the index will be −1, −3, −7, ...

Galloping is not always efficient. In some cases galloping mode requires more comparisons than a simple linear search. While for the first few cases both modes may require the same number of comparisons, over time galloping mode requires 33% more comparisons than linear search to arrive at the same results.

Analysis

In the worst case, Timsort takes comparisons to sort an array of n elements. In the best case, which occurs when the input is already sorted, it runs in linear time, meaning that it is an adaptive sorting algorithm.

Formal Verification

In 2015, Dutch and German researchers in the EU FP7 ENVISAGE project found a bug in the standard implementation of Timsort.

Specifically, the invariants on stacked run sizes ensure a tight upper bound on the maximum size of the required stack. The implementation preallocated a stack sufficient to sort 2^{64} bytes of input, and avoided further overflow checks.

However, the guarantee requires the invariants to apply to *every* group of three consecutive runs, but the implementation only checked it for the top three. Using the KeY tool for formal verification of Java software, the researchers found that this check is not sufficient, and they were able to find run lengths (and inputs which generated those run lengths) which would result in the invariants being violated deeper in the stack after the top of the stack was merged.

As a consequence, for certain inputs the allocated size is not sufficient to hold all unmerged runs. In Java, this generates for those inputs an array-out-of-bound exception. The smallest input that triggers this exception in Java and Android v7 is of size 67108864. (Older Android versions already triggered this exception for certain inputs of size 65536)

The Java implementation was corrected by increasing the size of the preallocated stack based on an updated worst-case analysis. The study also showed by formal methods how to establish the intended invariant by checking that the *four* topmost runs in the stack satisfy the two rules above. This approach was adopted by Python and Android.

Introsort

Introsort being a hybrid sorting algorithm uses three sorting algorithm to minimise the running time, Quicksort, Heapsort and Insertion Sort

Working

Introsort begins with quicksort and if the recursion depth goes more than a particular limit it switches to Heapsort to avoid Quicksort's worse case $O(N^2)$ time complexity. It also uses insertion sort when the number of elements to sort is quite less.

So first it creates a partition. Three cases arise from here.

1. If the partition size is such that there is a possibility to exceed the maximum depth limit then the Introsort switches to Heapsort. We define the maximum depth limit as 2*log(N)

2. If the partition size is too small then Quicksort decays to Insertion Sort. We define this cut-off as 16 (due to research). So if the partition size is less than 16 then we will do insertion sort.

3. If the partition size is under the limit and not too small (i.e- between 16 and 2*log(N)), then it performs a simple quicksort.

Need of Introsort

Since Quicksort can have a worse case $O(N^2)$ time complexity and it also increases the recursion stack space (O(log N) if tail recursion applied), so to avoid all these, we need to switch the algorithm from Quicksort to another if there is a chance of worse case. So Introsort solves this problem by switching to Heapsort.

Also due to larger constant factor, quicksort can perform even worse than O(N2) sorting algorithm when N is small enough. So it switches to insertion sort to decrease the running time of sorting.

Also if a bad pivot-selection is done then the quicksort does no better than the bubble-sort.

Reasons for using Insertion Sort

Insertion sort offers following advantages.

1. It is a known and established fact that insertion sort is the most optimal comparison-based sorting algorithm for small arrays.

2. It has a good locality of reference

3. It is an adaptive sorting algorithm, i.e- it outperforms all the other algorithms if the array elements are partially sorted.

Reason for using Heapsort

This is solely because of memory requirements. Merge sort requires O(N) space whereas Heapsort is an in-place O(1) space algorithm.

Advantanges of using Quicksort over Heapsort

Although Heapsort also being O(N log N) in average as well as worse case and O(1) space also, we still don't use it when the partition size is under the limit because the extra hidden constant factor in Heapsort is quite larger than that of Quicksort.

Why is cut-off 16 for switching from quick sort to insertion sort, and 2*logN for switching from quick sort to heap sort

These values are chosen empirically as an approximate because of various tests and researches conducted.

```
/* A Program to sort the array using Introsort.

  The most popular C++ STL Algorithm- sort()

  uses Introsort. */


#include<bits/stdc++.h>

using namespace std;


// A utility function to swap the values pointed by

// the two pointers

void swapValue(int *a, int *b)
```

```
{
    int *temp = a;
    a = b;
    b = temp;
    return;
}


/* Function to sort an array using insertion sort*/
void InsertionSort(int arr[], int *begin, int *end)
{
    // Get the left and the right index of the subarray
    // to be sorted
    int left = begin - arr;
    int right = end - arr;

    for (int i = left+1; i <= right; i++)
    {
        int key = arr[i];
        int j = i-1;

        /* Move elements of arr[0..i-1], that are
           greater than key, to one position ahead
           of their current position */
        while (j >= left && arr[j] > key)
        {
            arr[j+1] = arr[j];
            j = j-1;
        }
        arr[j+1] = key;
    }
```

```
    return;

}


// A function to parition the array and return
// the partition point
int* Partition(int arr[], int low, int high)
{

    int pivot = arr[high];    // pivot
    int i = (low - 1);  // Index of smaller element


    for (int j = low; j <= high- 1; j++)
    {
        // If current element is smaller than or
        // equal to pivot
        if (arr[j] <= pivot)
        {

            // increment index of smaller element
            i++;


            swap(arr[i], arr[j]);
        }
    }
    swap(arr[i + 1], arr[high]);
    return (arr + i + 1);

}



// A function that find the middle of the
// values pointed by the pointers a, b, c
```

```
// and return that pointer
int *MedianOfThree(int * a, int * b, int * c)
{
    if (*a < *b && *b < *c)
        return (b);


    if (*a < *c && *c <= *b)
        return (c);


    if (*b <= *a && *a < *c)
        return (a);


    if (*b < *c && *c <= *a)
        return (c);


    if (*c <= *a && *a < *b)
        return (a);


    if (*c <= *b && *b <= *c)
        return (b);
}



// A Utility function to perform intro sort
void IntrosortUtil(int arr[], int * begin,
                int * end, int depthLimit)
{
    // Count the number of elements
    int size = end - begin;

        // If partition size is low then do insertion sort
```

```
    if (size < 16)
    {
        InsertionSort(arr, begin, end);
        return;
    }


    // If the depth is zero use heapsort
    if (depthLimit == 0)
    {
        make_heap(begin, end+1);
        sort_heap(begin, end+1);
        return;
    }


    // Else use a median-of-three concept to
    // find a good pivot
    int * pivot = MedianOfThree(begin, begin+size/2, end);


    // Swap the values pointed by the two pointers
    swapValue(pivot, end);

// Perform Quick Sort
    int * partitionPoint = Partition(arr, begin-arr, end-arr);
    IntrosortUtil(arr, begin, partitionPoint-1, depthLimit - 1);
    IntrosortUtil(arr, partitionPoint + 1, end, depthLimit - 1);


    return;
}


/* Implementation of introsort*/
```

```c
void Introsort(int arr[], int *begin, int *end)
{
    int depthLimit = 2 * log(end-begin);


    // Perform a recursive Introsort
    IntrosortUtil(arr, begin, end, depthLimit);


    return;
}



// A utility function ot print an array of size n
void printArray(int arr[], int n)
{
    for (int i=0; i < n; i++)
        printf("%d ", arr[i]);
    printf("\n");
}



// Driver program to test Introsort
int main()
{
    int arr[] = {3, 1, 23, -9, 233, 23, -313, 32, -9};
    int n = sizeof(arr) / sizeof(arr[0]);


    // Pass the array, the pointer to the first element and
    // the pointer to the last element
    Introsort(arr, arr, arr+n-1);
    printArray(arr, n);


    return(0);
```

}

Output:

5 6 **11 12 13**

Time Complexity

Best Case – O(N log N)

Average Case- O(N log N)

Worse Case- O(N log N)

where, N = number of elements to be sorted.

Block Sort

Block Merge Sort, also known as WikiSort, is a fast and stable O (n log n) shifting algorithm that uses O (1) memory designed by Mike McFadden.

The algorithm is even faster if the input is partially sorted or if a larger field can be used. It can also be modified to use additional extra memory to increase its speed.

Block Merge Sort as the name suggests consists of the distribution of a given list of elements into blocks, sorting them and then rewinding them. To achieve asymptotic complexity O (n log n), Block Merge Sort always combines at least two Merge sort and Insertion sort operations . So he got his name from comparing the two sorted A and B lists, which is in fact the equivalent distribution of the A list on a uniform section called block, inserting each block A into B by special rules and merging (Merge) pairs AB (Sort). One practical algorithm using the Block Merge Sort was published in 2008.

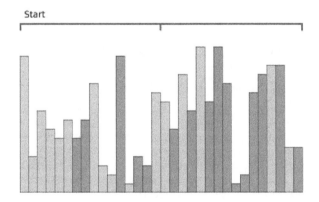

The Block Sort's outer loop is identical to the Merge Sortem and its bottom-up ranking, where each sorting level fills the pairs of auxiliary fields A and B, by size 1 then 2, then 4, 8, 16 and so on until both auxiliary fields are combined into separate field. However, instead of direct casting, A and B divide A into discrete blocks of size $\sqrt{A}$ (resulting in $\sqrt{A}$ blocks), insert each block A to B such that the first value of each block A is less than or equal to the B value located directly behind it. Then, each block A locally merges with each B value that is between it and the next block A. Since the casting still requires a buffer large enough to hold the cast block A, two array domains (known as an internal buffer) are reserved for this purpose.

The first two blocks are therefore modified to contain the first instance of each value inside A with the original content of those blocks that are dropped as needed. The remaining blocks A are then inserted into B and merged using one of the two buffers as a swap space. This procedure will reorganize the buffer values. Once the slots are all blocks A and B of each part of the field (auxiliary array) A and B for a given MargeSort level, the buffer values must be sorted to restore the original order, so they must come in the Insertion row. the values in the buffer are then rearranged to their first sorted positions in the array. This procedure is repeated for each level of top-down external sorting. At this point the field will be stably sorted.

Algorithm

The following operators are used in the code examples:

|	bitwise OR
>>	shift right
%	modulo
++ and +=	increment
$[x, y)$	range from $\geq x$ and $< y$
|range|	range.end - range.start
array[i]	i-th item of *array*

Additionally, block sort relies on the following operations as part of its overall algorithm:

- Swap: exchange the positions of two values in an array.

- Block swap: exchange a range of values within an array with values in a different range of the array.

- Binary search: assuming the array is sorted, check the middle value of the current search range, then if the value is lesser check the lower range, and if the value is greater check the upper range. Block sort uses two variants: one which finds the *first* position to insert a value in the sorted array, and one which finds the *last* position.

- Linear search: find a particular value in an array by checking every single element in order, until it is found.

- Insertion sort: for each item in the array, loop backward and find where it needs to be inserted, then insert it at that position.

- Array rotation: move the items in an array to the left or right by some number of spaces, with values on the edges wrapping around to the other side. Rotations can be implemented as three reversals.

Rotate(array, amount, range)

   Reverse(array, range)

   Reverse(array, [range.start, range.start + amount))

   Reverse(array, [range.start + amount, range.end))

- Floor power of two: floor a value to the next power of two. 63 becomes 32, 64 stays 64, and so forth.

FloorPowerOfTwo(x)

   x = x | (x >> 1)

   x = x | (x >> 2)

   x = x | (x >> 4)

   x = x | (x >> 8)

   x = x | (x >> 16)

   if (this is a 64-bit system)

      x = x | (x >> 32)

   return x - (x >> 1)

Outer Loop

As previously stated, the outer loop of a block sort is identical to a bottom-up merge sort. However, it benefits from the variant that ensures each A and B subarray are the same size to within one item:

BlockSort(array)

   power_of_two = **FloorPowerOfTwo**(array.size)

   scale = array.size/power_of_two // 1.0 ≤ scale < 2.0

   // insertion sort 16-31 items at a time

   for (merge = 0; merge < power_of_two; merge += 16)

      start = merge * scale

      end = start + 16 * scale

      InsertionSort(array, [start, end))

```
    for (length = 16; length < power_of_two; length += length)

        for (merge = 0; merge < power_of_two; merge += length * 2)

            start = merge * scale

            mid = (merge + length) * scale

            end = (merge + length * 2) * scale


            if (array[end - 1] < array[start])

                    // the two ranges are in reverse order, so a rotation is
enough to merge them

                    Rotate(array, mid - start, [start, end))

            else if (array[mid - 1] > array[mid])

                    Merge(array, A = [start, mid), B = [mid, end))

            // else the ranges are already correctly ordered
```

Fixed-point math may also be used, by representing the scale factor as a fraction integer_part + numerator/denominator:

```
power_of_two = FloorPowerOfTwo(array.size)

denominator = power_of_two/16

numerator_step = array.size % denominator

integer_step = floor(array.size/denominator)


// insertion sort 16-31 items at a time


while (integer_step < array.size)

    integer_part = numerator = 0

    while (integer_part < array.size)

        // get the ranges for A and B

        start = integer_part


        integer_part += integer_step

        numerator += numerator_step

        if (numerator ≥ denominator)
```

```
            numerator -= denominator
            integer_part++


      mid = integer_part


      integer_part += integer_step
      numerator += numerator_step
      if (numerator ≥ denominator)
            numerator -= denominator
            integer_part++


      end = integer_part


      if (array[end - 1] < array[start])
            Rotate(array, mid - start, [start, end))
      else if (array[mid - 1] > array[mid])
            Merge(array, A = [start, mid), B = [mid, end))


   integer_step += integer_step
   numerator_step += numerator_step
   if (numerator_step ≥ denominator)
      numerator_step -= denominator
      integer_step++
```

Extract Buffers

The two internal buffers needed for each level of the merge step are created by moving the first $2\sqrt{A}$ instances of each value within an A subarray to the start of A. First it iterates over the elements in A and counts off the unique values it needs, then it applies array rotations to move those unique values to the start. If A did not contain enough unique values to fill the two buffers (of size $\sqrt{A}$ each), B can be used just as well. In this case it moves the *last* instance of each value to the *end* of B, with that part of B not being included during the merges.

```
   while (integer_step < array.size)
      block_size = √integer_step
```

```
buffer_size = integer_step/block_size + 1

[extract two buffers of size 'buffer_size' each]
```

If B does not contain enough unique values either, it pulls out the largest number of unique values it *could* find, then adjusts the size of the A and B blocks such that the number of resulting A blocks is less than or equal to the number of unique items pulled out for the buffer. Only one buffer will be used in this case – the second buffer won't exist.

```
buffer_size = [number of unique values found]

block_size = integer_step/buffer_size + 1


integer_part = numerator = 0

while (integer_part < array.size)

    [get the ranges for A and B]

    [adjust A and B to not include the ranges used by the buffers]
```

Tag A Blocks

Once the one or two internal buffers have been created, it begins merging each A and B subarray for this level of the merge sort. To do so, it divides each A and B subarray into evenly sized blocks of the size calculated in the previous step, where the first A block and last B block are unevenly sized if needed. It then loops over each of the evenly sized A blocks and swaps the second value with a corresponding value from the first of the two internal buffers. This is known as *tagging* the blocks.

```
// blockA is the range of the remaining A blocks,

// and firstA is the unevenly sized first A block

blockA = [A.start, A.end)

firstA = [A.start, A.start + |blockA| % block_size)


// swap the second value of each A block with the value in buffer1

for (index = 0, indexA = firstA.end + 1; indexA < blockA.end; indexA += block_
size)

    Swap(array[buffer1.start + index], array[indexA])

    index++


lastA = firstA

blockB = [B.start, B.start + minimum(block_size, |B|))

blockA.start += |firstA|
```

Roll and Drop

Two A blocks rolling through the B blocks. Once the first A block is dropped behind, the unevenly sized A block is locally merged with the B values that follow it.

After defining and tagging the A blocks in this manner, the A blocks are *rolled* through the B blocks by block swapping the first evenly sized A block with the next B block. This process repeats until the first value of the A block with the smallest tag value is less than or equal to the last value of the B block that was just swapped with an A block.

At that point, the minimum A block (the A block with the smallest tag value) is swapped to the start of the rolling A blocks and the tagged value is restored with its original value from the first buffer. This is known as *dropping* a block behind, as it will no longer be rolled along with the remaining A blocks. That A block is then inserted into the previous B block, first by using a binary search on B to find the index where the first value of A is less than or equal to the value at that index of B, and then by rotating A into B at that index.

```
minA = blockA.start

indexA = 0


    while (true)
        // if there's a previous B block and the first value of the minimum A block
is ≤

        // the last value of the previous B block, then drop that minimum A block
behind.

        // or if there are no B blocks left then keep dropping the remaining A
blocks.
        if (((|lastB| > 0 and array[lastB.end - 1] ≥ array[minA]) or |blockB| = 0)
            // figure out where to split the previous B block, and rotate it at
the split
            B_split = BinaryFirst(array, array[minA], lastB)
            B_remaining = lastB.end - B_split


            // swap the minimum A block to the beginning of the rolling A blocks
            BlockSwap(array, blockA.start, minA, block_size)


            // restore the second value for the A block
            Swap(array[blockA.start + 1], array[buffer1.start + indexA])
            indexA++
```

```
        // rotate the A block into the previous B block
        Rotate(array, blockA.start - B_split, [B_split, blockA.start + block_
size))


        // locally merge the previous A block with the B values that follow it,
        // using the second internal buffer as swap space (if it exists)
        if (|buffer2| > 0)
            MergeInternal(array, lastA, [lastA.end, B_split), buffer2)
        else
            MergeInPlace(array, lastA, [lastA.end, B_split))


        // update the range for the remaining A blocks,
        // and the range remaining from the B block after it was split
        lastA = [blockA.start - B_remaining, blockA.start - B_remaining +
block_size)
        lastB = [lastA.end, lastA.end + B_remaining)


        // if there are no more A blocks remaining, this step is finished
        blockA.start = blockA.start + block_size
        if (|blockA| = 0)
            break


        minA = [new minimum A block]
    else if (|blockB| < block_size)
        // move the last B block, which is unevenly sized,
        // to before the remaining A blocks, by using a rotation
        Rotate(array, blockB.start - blockA.start, [blockA.start, blockB.end))


        lastB = [blockA.start, blockA.start + |blockB|)
        blockA.start += |blockB|
```

```
            blockA.end += |blockB|

            minA += |blockB|

            blockB.end = blockB.start

        else

            // roll the leftmost A block to the end by swapping it with the next
B block

            BlockSwap(array, blockA.start, blockB.start, block_size)

            lastB = [blockA.start, blockA.start + block_size)

            if (minA = blockA.start)

                minA = blockA.end


            blockA.start += block_size

            blockA.end += block_size

            blockB.start += block_size


            // this is equivalent to minimum(blockB.end + block_size, B.end),

            // but that has the potential to overflow

            if (blockB.end > B.end - block_size)

                blockB.end = B.end

            else

                blockB.end += block_size


    // merge the last A block with the remaining B values

    if (|buffer2| > 0)

        MergeInternal(array, lastA, [lastA.end, B.end), buffer2)

    else

        MergeInPlace(array, lastA, [lastA.end, B.end))
```

One optimization that can be applied during this step is the *floating-hole technique*. When the minimum A block is dropped behind and needs to be rotated into the previous B block, after which its contents are swapped into the second internal buffer for the local merges, it would be faster to swap the A block to the buffer beforehand, and to take advantage of the fact that the contents of that buffer do not need to retain any order. So rather than rotating the second buffer (which used to be the A block before the block swap) into the previous B block at position *index*, the values in the B block after *index* can simply be block swapped with the last items of the buffer.

The *floating hole* in this case refers to the contents of the second internal buffer *floating* around the array, and acting as a *hole* in the sense that the items do not need to retain their order.

Local Merges

Once the A block has been rotated into the B block, the previous A block is then merged with the B values that follow it, using the second buffer as swap space. When the first A block is dropped behind this refers to the unevenly sized A block at the start, when the second A block is dropped behind it means the first A block, and so forth.

```
MergeInternal(array, A, B, buffer)

    // block swap the values in A with those in 'buffer'

    BlockSwap(array, A.start, buffer.start, |A|)


    A_count = 0, B_count = 0, insert = 0

    while (A_count < |A| and B_count < |B|)

        if (array[buffer.start + A_count] ≤ array[B.start + B_count])

            Swap(array[A.start + insert], array[buffer.start + A_count])

            A_count++

        else

            Swap(array[A.start + insert], array[B.start + B_count])

            B_count++

        insert++


    // block swap the remaining part of the buffer with the remaining part
of the array

    BlockSwap(array, buffer.start + A_count, A.start + insert, |A| - A_count)
```

If the second buffer does not exist, a strictly in-place merge operation must be performed, such as a rotation-based version of the Hwang and Lin algorithm, the Dudzinski and Dydek algorithm, or a repeated binary search and rotate.

```
MergeInPlace(array, A, B)

    while (|A| > 0 and |B| > 0)

        // find the first place in B where the first item in A needs to be inserted
```

```
mid = BinaryFirst(array, array[A.start], B)


// rotate A into place
amount = mid - A.end
Rotate(array, amount, [A.start, mid))


// calculate the new A and B ranges
B = [mid, B.end)
A = [A.start + amount, mid)
A.start = BinaryLast(array, array[A.start], A)
```

After dropping the minimum A block and merging the previous A block with the B values that follow it, the new minimum A block must be found within the blocks that are still being rolled through the array. This is handled by running a linear search through those A blocks and comparing the tag values to find the smallest one.

```
minA = blockA.start
for (findA = minA + block_size; findA < blockA.end - 1; findA += block_size)
    if (array[findA + 1] < array[minA + 1])
        minA = findA
```

These remaining A blocks then continue rolling through the array and being dropped and inserted where they belong. This process repeats until all of the A blocks have been dropped and rotated into the previous B block.

Once the last remaining A block has been dropped behind and inserted into B where it belongs, it should be merged with the remaining B values that follow it. This completes the merge process for that particular pair of A and B subarrays. However, it must then repeat the process for the remaining A and B subarrays for the current level of the merge sort.

Note that the internal buffers can be reused for every set of A and B subarrays for this level of the merge sort, and do not need to be re-extracted or modified in any way.

Redistribute

After all of the A and B subarrays have been merged, the one or two internal buffers are still left over. The first internal buffer was used for tagging the A blocks, and its contents are still in the same order as before, but the second internal buffer may have had its contents rearranged when it was used as swap space for the merges. This means the contents of the second buffer will need to be sorted using a different algorithm, such as insertion sort. The two buffers must then be redistributed back into the array using the opposite process that was used to create them.

After repeating these steps for every level of the bottom-up merge sort, the block sort is completed.

Variants

Block sort works by extracting two internal buffers, breaking A and B subarrays into evenly sized blocks, rolling and dropping the A blocks into B (using the first buffer to track the order of the A blocks), locally merging using the second buffer as swap space, sorting the second buffer, and redistributing both buffers. While the steps do not change, these subsystems can vary in their actual implementation.

One variant of block sort allows it to use any amount of additional memory provided to it, by using this *external buffer* for merging an A subarray or A block with B whenever A fits into it. In this situation it would be identical to a merge sort.

Good choices for the buffer size include:

Size	Notes
(count + 1)/2	turns into a full-speed merge sort since all of the A subarrays will fit into it
$\sqrt{(count+1)/2}+1$	this will be the size of the A blocks at the largest level of merges, so block sort can skip using internal or in-place merges for anything
512	a fixed-size buffer large enough to handle the numerous merges at the smaller levels of the merge sort
0	if the system cannot allocate any extra memory, no memory works well

Rather than tagging the A blocks using the contents of one of the internal buffers, an indirect *movement-imitation buffer* can be used instead. This is an internal buffer defined as *s1 t s2*, where *s1* and *s2* are each as large as the number of A and B blocks, and *t* contains any values immediately following *s1* that are equal to the last value of *s1* (thus ensuring that no value in *s2* appears in *s1*). A second internal buffer containing √A unique values is still used. The first √A values of *s1* and *s2* are then swapped with each other to encode information into the buffer about which blocks are A blocks and which are B blocks. When an A block at index *i* is swapped with a B block at index *j* (where the first evenly sized A block is initially at index 0), s1[i] and s1[j] are swapped with s2[i] and s2[j], respectively. This *imitates the movements* of the A blocks through B. The unique values in the second buffer are used to determine the original order of the A blocks as they are rolled through the B blocks. Once all of the A blocks have been dropped, the movement-imitation buffer is used to decode whether a given block in the array is an A block or a B block, each A block is rotated into B, and the second internal buffer is used as swap space for the local merges.

The *second* value of each A block doesn't necessarily need to be tagged – the first, last, or any other element could be used instead. However, if the first value is tagged, the values will need to be read from the first internal buffer (where they were swapped) when deciding where to drop the minimum A block.

Many sorting algorithms can be used to sort the contents of the second internal buffer, including unstable sorts like quicksort, since the contents of the buffer are guaranteed to unique. Insertion sort is still recommended, though, for its situational performance and lack of recursion.

Analysis

Block sort is a well-defined and testable class of algorithms, with working implementations available as a merge and as a sort. This allows its characteristics to be measured and considered.

Complexity

Block sort begins by insertion sorting groups of 16–31 items in the array. Insertion sort is an $O(n^2)$ operation, so this leads to anywhere from $O(16^2 \times n/16)$ to $O(31^2 \times n/31)$, which is $O(n)$ once the constant factors are omitted. It must also apply an insertion sort on the second internal buffer after each level of merging is completed. However, as this buffer was limited to $\sqrt{A}$ in size, the $O(\sqrt{n}^2)$ operation also ends up being $O(n)$.

Next it must extract two internal buffers for each level of the merge sort. It does so by iterating over the items in the A and B subarrays and incrementing a counter whenever the value changes, and upon finding enough values it rotates them to the start of A or the end of B. In the worst case this will end up searching the entire array before finding $\sqrt{A}$ non-contiguous unique values, which requires $O(n)$ comparisons and $\sqrt{A}$ rotations for $\sqrt{A}$ values. This resolves to $O(n + \sqrt{n} \times \sqrt{})$, or $O(n)$.

When none of the A or B subarrays contained $\sqrt{A}$ unique values to create the internal buffers, a normally suboptimal in-place merge operation is performed where it repeatedly binary searches and rotates A into B. However, the known lack of unique values within any of the subarrays places a hard limit on the number of binary searches and rotations that will be performed during this step, which is again $\sqrt{A}$ items rotated up to $\sqrt{A}$ times, or $O(n)$. The size of each block is also adjusted to be smaller in the case where it found $\sqrt{A}$ unique values but not $2\sqrt{A}$, which further limits the number of unique values contained within any A or B block.

Tagging the A blocks is performed $\sqrt{A}$ times for each A subarray, then the A blocks are rolled through and inserted into the B blocks up to $\sqrt{A}$ times. The local merges retain the same $O(n)$ complexity of a standard merge, albeit with more assignments since the values must be swapped rather than copied. The linear search for finding the new minimum A block iterates over $\sqrt{A}$ blocks $\sqrt{A}$ times. And the buffer redistribution process is identical to the buffer extraction but in reverse, and therefore has the same $O(n)$ complexity.

After omitting all but the highest complexity and considering that there are $log\ n$ levels in the outer merge loop, this leads to a final asymptotic complexity of $O(n \log n)$ for the worst and average cases. For the best case, where the data is already in order, the merge step performs $n/16$ comparisons for the first level, then $n/32$, $n/64$, $n/128$, etc. This is a well-known mathematical series which resolves to $O(n)$.

Memory

As block sort is non-recursive and does not require the use of dynamic allocations, this leads to constant stack and heap space. It uses $O(1)$ auxiliary memory in a transdichotomous model, which accepts that the O(log n) bits needed to keep track of the ranges for A and B cannot be any greater than 32 or 64 on 32-bit or 64-bit computing systems, respectively, and therefore simplifies to O(1) space for any array that can feasibly be allocated.

Stability

Although items in the array are moved out of order during a block sort, each operation is fully reversible and will have restored the original order of equivalent items by its completion.

Stability requires the first instance of each value in an array before sorting to still be the first instance of that value after sorting. Block sort moves these first instances to the start of the array to create the two internal buffers, but when all of the merges are completed for the current level of the block sort, those values are distributed back to the first sorted position within the array. This maintains stability.

Before rolling the A blocks through the B blocks, each A block has its second value swapped with a value from the first buffer. At that point the A blocks are moved out of order to roll through the B blocks. However, once it finds where it should insert the smallest A block into the previous B block, that smallest A block is moved back to the start of the A blocks and its second value is restored. By the time all of the A blocks have been inserted, the A blocks will be in order again and the first buffer will contain its original values in the original order.

Using the second buffer as swap space when merging an A block with some B values causes the contents of that buffer to be rearranged. However, as the algorithm already ensured the buffer only contains unique values, sorting the contents of the buffer is sufficient to restore their original stable order.

Adaptivity

Block sort is an adaptive sort on two levels: first, it skips merging A and B subarrays that are already in order. Next, when A and B need to be merged and are broken into evenly sized blocks, the A blocks are only rolled through B as far as is necessary, and each block is only merged with the B values immediately following it. The more ordered the data originally was, the fewer B values there will be that need to be merged into A.

Advantages

BlockSort is a stable sorting algorithm that does not require additional computer memory, which is especially useful if we do not have enough memory to allocate buffer O (n). If we use BlockSort with an external buffer, we can reduce the memory from the default O (n) to smaller and smaller buffers, and the algorithm will continue to function efficiently.

Disadvantages

BlockSort does not use ranges as efficiently as other algorithms, such as Timsort. BlockSort checks these graded ranges only in two levels: as auxiliary fields A and B and as blocks A and B. It is also worse to implement in comparison to the Merge Sort algorithm and can not be easily parallelized.

Code In C++

```
0002./***********************************************************
0003.WikiSort (public domain license)
0004.
0005.
0006.to run:
0007.clang -o WikiSort.x WikiSort.c -O3
0008.(or replace 'clang' with 'gcc')
0009../WikiSort.x
0010.***********************************************************/
0011.
0012.#include <stdio.h>
0013.#include <stdlib.h>
0014.#include <stdint.h>
0015.#include <stdarg.h>
0016.#include <string.h>
0017.#include <math.h>
0018.#include <assert.h>
0019.#include <time.h>
0020.#include <limits.h>
0021.
0022./* record the number of comparisons */
0023./* note that this reduces WikiSort's performance when enabled */
0024.#define PROFILE false
0025.
0026./* verify that WikiSort is actually correct */
0027./* (this also reduces performance slightly) */
0028.#define VERIFY false
0029.
```

```
0030./* simulate comparisons that have a bit more overhead than just an inlined
(int < int) */

0031./* (so we can tell whether reducing the number of comparisons was worth the
added complexity) */

0032.#define SLOW_COMPARISONS false

0033.

0034./* whether to give WikiSort a full-size cache, to see how it performs when
given more memory */

0035.#define DYNAMIC_CACHE false

0036.

0037.

0038.double Seconds() { return clock() * 1.0/CLOCKS_PER_SEC; }

0039.

0040./* various #defines for the C code */

0041.#ifndef true

0042.#define true 1

0043.#define false 0

0044.typedef uint8_t bool;

0045.#endif

0046.

0047.#define Var(name, value)                    __typeof__(value) name = value

0048.#define Allocate(type, count)                (type *)malloc((count) * sizeof(type))

0049.

0050.size_t Min(const size_t a, const size_t b) {

0051.if (a < b) return a;

0052.return b;

0053.}

0054.

0055.size_t Max(const size_t a, const size_t b) {

0056.if (a > b) return a;

0057.return b;
```

```
0058.}

0059.

0060.

0061./* structure to test stable sorting (index will contain its original index
in the array, to make sure it doesn't switch places with other items) */

0062.typedef struct {

0063.size_t value;

0064.#if VERIFY

0065.size_t index;

0066.#endif

0067.} Test;

0068.

0069.#if PROFILE

0070./* global for testing how many comparisons are performed for each sorting
algorithm */

0071.size_t comparisons;

0072.#endif

0073.

0074.#if SLOW_COMPARISONS

0075.#define NOOP_SIZE 50

0076.size_t noop1[NOOP_SIZE], noop2[NOOP_SIZE];

0077.#endif

0078.

0079.bool TestCompare(Test item1, Test item2) {

0080.#if SLOW_COMPARISONS

0081./* test slow comparisons by adding some fake overhead */

0082./* (in real-world use this might be string comparisons, etc.) */

0083.size_t index;

0084.for (index = 0; index < NOOP_SIZE; index++)

0085.noop1[index] = noop2[index];

0086.#endif
```

```
0087.

0088.#if PROFILE

0089.comparisons++;

0090.#endif

0091.

0092.return (item1.value < item2.value);

0093.}

0094.

0095.typedef bool (*Comparison)(Test, Test);

0096.

0097.

0098.

0099./* structure to represent ranges within the array */

0100.typedef struct {

0101.size_t start;

0102.size_t end;

0103.} Range;

0104.

0105.size_t Range_length(Range range) { return range.end - range.start; }

0106.

0107.Range Range_new(const size_t start, const size_t end) {

0108.Range range;

0109.range.start = start;

0110.range.end = end;

0111.return range;

0112.}

0113.

0114.

0115./* toolbox functions used by the sorter */

0116.
```

```
0117./* swap value1 and value2 */
0118.#define Swap(value1, value2) { \
0119.Var(a, &(value1)); \
0120.Var(b, &(value2)); \
0121.\
0122.Var(c, *a); \
0123.*a = *b; \
0124.*b = c; \
0125.}
0126.
0127./* 63 -> 32, 64 -> 64, etc. */
0128./* this comes from Hacker's Delight */
0129.size_t FloorPowerOfTwo (const size_t value) {
0130.size_t x = value;
0131.x = x | (x >> 1);
0132.x = x | (x >> 2);
0133.x = x | (x >> 4);
0134.x = x | (x >> 8);
0135.x = x | (x >> 16);
0136.#if __LP64__
0137.x = x | (x >> 32);
0138.#endif
0139.return x - (x >> 1);
0140.}
0141.
0142./* find the index of the first value within the range that is equal to ar-
ray[index] */
0143.size_t BinaryFirst(const Test array[], const Test value, const Range range,
constComparison compare) {
0144.size_t start = range.start, end = range.end - 1;
0145.if (range.start >= range.end) return range.start;
```

```
0146.while (start < end) {

0147.size_t mid = start + (end - start)/2;

0148.if (compare(array[mid], value))

0149.start = mid + 1;

0150.else

0151.end = mid;

0152.}

0153.if (start == range.end - 1 && compare(array[start], value)) start++;

0154.return start;

0155.}

0156.

0157./* find the index of the last value within the range that is equal to ar-
ray[index], plus 1 */

0158.size_t BinaryLast(const Test array[], const Test value, const Range range,
constComparison compare) {

0159.size_t start = range.start, end = range.end - 1;

0160.if (range.start >= range.end) return range.end;

0161.while (start < end) {

0162.size_t mid = start + (end - start)/2;

0163.if (.compare(value, array[mid]))

0164.start = mid + 1;

0165.else

0166.end = mid;

0167.}

0168.if (start == range.end - 1 && .compare(value, array[start])) start++;

0169.return start;

0170.}

0171.

0172./* combine a linear search with a binary search to reduce the number of
comparisons in situations */

0173./* where have some idea as to how many unique values there are and where
the next value might be */
```

```
0174.size_t FindFirstForward(const Test array[], const Test value, const Range
range, constComparison compare, const size_t unique) {

0175.size_t skip, index;

0176.if (Range_length(range) == 0) return range.start;

0177.skip = Max(Range_length(range)/unique, 1);

0178.

0179.for (index = range.start + skip; compare(array[index - 1], value); index
+= skip)

0180.if (index >= range.end - skip)

0181.return BinaryFirst(array, value, Range_new(index, range.end), compare);

0182.

0183.return BinaryFirst(array, value, Range_new(index - skip, index), compare);

0184.}

0185.

0186.size_t FindLastForward(const Test array[], const Test value, const Range
range, constComparison compare, const size_t unique) {

0187.size_t skip, index;

0188.if (Range_length(range) == 0) return range.start;

0189.skip = Max(Range_length(range)/unique, 1);

0190.

0191.for (index = range.start + skip; .compare(value, array[index - 1]); index
+= skip)

0192.if (index >= range.end - skip)

0193.return BinaryLast(array, value, Range_new(index, range.end), compare);

0194.

0195.return BinaryLast(array, value, Range_new(index - skip, index), compare);

0196.}

0197.

0198.size_t FindFirstBackward(const Test array[], const Test value, const Range
range, constComparison compare, const size_t unique) {

0199.size_t skip, index;

0200.if (Range_length(range) == 0) return range.start;

0201.skip = Max(Range_length(range)/unique, 1);
```

```
0202.

0203.for (index = range.end - skip; index > range.start && .compare(array[index
- 1], value); index -= skip)

0204.if (index < range.start + skip)

0205.return BinaryFirst(array, value, Range_new(range.start, index), compare);

0206.

0207.return BinaryFirst(array, value, Range_new(index, index + skip), compare);

0208.}

0209.

0210.size_t FindLastBackward(const Test array[], const Test value, const Range
range, constComparison compare, const size_t unique) {

0211.size_t skip, index;

0212.if (Range_length(range) == 0) return range.start;

0213.skip = Max(Range_length(range)/unique, 1);

0214.

0215.for (index = range.end - skip; index > range.start && compare(value, ar-
ray[index - 1]); index -= skip)

0216.if (index < range.start + skip)

0217.return BinaryLast(array, value, Range_new(range.start, index), compare);

0218.

0219.return BinaryLast(array, value, Range_new(index, index + skip), compare);

0220.}

0221.

0222./* n^2 sorting algorithm used to sort tiny chunks of the full array */

0223.void InsertionSort(Test array[], const Range range, const Comparison com-
pare) {

0224.size_t i, j;

0225.for (i = range.start + 1; i < range.end; i++) {

0226.const Test temp = array[i];

0227.for (j = i; j > range.start && compare(temp, array[j - 1]); j--)

0228.array[j] = array[j - 1];

0229.array[j] = temp;
```

```
0230.}

0231.}

0232.

0233./* reverse a range of values within the array */

0234.void Reverse(Test array[], const Range range) {

0235.size_t index;

0236.for (index = Range_length(range)/2; index > 0; index--)

0237.Swap(array[range.start + index - 1], array[range.end - index]);

0238.}

0239.

0240./* swap a series of values in the array */

0241.void BlockSwap(Test array[], const size_t start1, const size_t start2,
const size_t block_size) {

0242.size_t index;

0243.for (index = 0; index < block_size; index++)

0244.Swap(array[start1 + index], array[start2 + index]);

0245.}

0246.

0247./* rotate the values in an array ([0 1 2 3] becomes [1 2 3 0] if we rotate
by 1) */

0248./* this assumes that 0 <= amount <= range.length() */

0249.void Rotate(Test array[], const size_t amount, const Range range, Test
cache[], constsize_t cache_size) {

0250.size_t split; Range range1, range2;

0251.if (Range_length(range) == 0) return;

0252.

0253.split = range.start + amount;

0254.range1 = Range_new(range.start, split);

0255.range2 = Range_new(split, range.end);

0256.

0257./* if the smaller of the two ranges fits into the cache, it's *slightly*
faster copying it there and shifting the elements over */
```

```
0258.if (Range_length(range1) <= Range_length(range2)) {

0259.if (Range_length(range1) <= cache_size) {

0260.memcpy(&cache[0], &array[range1.start], Range_length(range1) * sizeof(ar-
ray[0]));

0261.memmove(&array[range1.start], &array[range2.start], Range_length(range2) *
sizeof(array[0]));

0262.memcpy(&array[range1.start + Range_length(range2)], &cache[0], Range_
length(range1) * sizeof(array[0]));

0263.return;

0264.}

0265.} else {

0266.if (Range_length(range2) <= cache_size) {

0267.memcpy(&cache[0], &array[range2.start], Range_length(range2) * sizeof(ar-
ray[0]));

0268.memmove(&array[range2.end - Range_length(range1)], &array[range1.start],
Range_length(range1) * sizeof(array[0]));

0269.memcpy(&array[range1.start], &cache[0], Range_length(range2) * sizeof(ar-
ray[0]));

0270.return;

0271.}

0272.}

0273.

0274.Reverse(array, range1);

0275.Reverse(array, range2);

0276.Reverse(array, range);

0277.}

0278.

0279./* calculate how to scale the index value to the range within the array */

0280./* the bottom-up merge sort only operates on values that are powers of two,
*/

0281./* so scale down to that power of two, then use a fraction to scale back
again */

0282.typedef struct {

0283.size_t size, power_of_two;
```

```
0284.size_t numerator, decimal;

0285.size_t denominator, decimal_step, numerator_step;

0286.} WikiIterator;

0287.

0288.void WikiIterator_begin(WikiIterator *me) {

0289.me->numerator = me->decimal = 0;

0290.}

0291.

0292.Range WikiIterator_nextRange(WikiIterator *me) {

0293.size_t start = me->decimal;

0294.

0295.me->decimal += me->decimal_step;

0296.me->numerator += me->numerator_step;

0297.if (me->numerator >= me->denominator) {

0298.me->numerator -= me->denominator;

0299.me->decimal++;

0300.}

0301.

0302.return Range_new(start, me->decimal);

0303.}

0304.

0305.bool WikiIterator_finished(WikiIterator *me) {

0306.return (me->decimal >= me->size);

0307.}

0308.

0309.bool WikiIterator_nextLevel(WikiIterator *me) {

0310.me->decimal_step += me->decimal_step;

0311.me->numerator_step += me->numerator_step;

0312.if (me->numerator_step >= me->denominator) {

0313.me->numerator_step -= me->denominator;
```

```
0314.me->decimal_step++;

0315.}

0316.

0317.return (me->decimal_step < me->size);

0318.}

0319.

0320.size_t WikiIterator_length(WikiIterator *me) {

0321.return me->decimal_step;

0322.}

0323.

0324.WikiIterator WikiIterator_new(size_t size2, size_t min_level) {

0325.WikiIterator me;

0326.me.size = size2;

0327.me.power_of_two = FloorPowerOfTwo(me.size);

0328.me.denominator = me.power_of_two/min_level;

0329.me.numerator_step = me.size % me.denominator;

0330.me.decimal_step = me.size/me.denominator;

0331.WikiIterator_begin(&me);

0332.return me;

0333.}

0334.

0335./* merge two ranges from one array and save the results into a different array */

0336.void MergeInto(Test from[], const Range A, const Range B, const Comparison compare, Test into[]) {

0337.Test *A_index = &from[A.start], *B_index = &from[B.start];

0338.Test *A_last = &from[A.end], *B_last = &from[B.end];

0339.Test *insert_index = &into[0];

0340.

0341.while (true) {

0342.if (.compare(*B_index, *A_index)) {
```

```
0343. *insert_index = *A_index;

0344. A_index++;

0345. insert_index++;

0346. if (A_index == A_last) {

0347. /* copy the remainder of B into the final array */

0348. memcpy(insert_index, B_index, (B_last - B_index) * sizeof(from[0]));

0349. break;

0350. }

0351. } else {

0352. *insert_index = *B_index;

0353. B_index++;

0354. insert_index++;

0355. if (B_index == B_last) {

0356. /* copy the remainder of A into the final array */

0357. memcpy(insert_index, A_index, (A_last - A_index) * sizeof(from[0]));

0358. break;

0359. }

0360. }

0361. }

0362. }

0363.

0364. /* merge operation using an external buffer, */

0365. void MergeExternal(Test array[], const Range A, const Range B, const Comparison compare, Test cache[]) {

0366. /* A fits into the cache, so use that instead of the internal buffer */

0367. Test *A_index = &cache[0];

0368. Test *B_index = &array[B.start];

0369. Test *insert_index = &array[A.start];

0370. Test *A_last = &cache[Range_length(A)];

0371. Test *B_last = &array[B.end];

0372.
```

```
0373.if (Range_length(B) > 0 && Range_length(A) > 0) {

0374.while (true) {

0375.if (.compare(*B_index, *A_index)) {

0376.*insert_index = *A_index;

0377.A_index++;

0378.insert_index++;

0379.if (A_index == A_last) break;

0380.} else {

0381.*insert_index = *B_index;

0382.B_index++;

0383.insert_index++;

0384.if (B_index == B_last) break;

0385.}

0386.}

0387.}

0388.

0389./* copy the remainder of A into the final array */

0390.memcpy(insert_index, A_index, (A_last - A_index) * sizeof(array[0]));

0391.}

0392.

0393./* merge operation using an internal buffer */

0394.void MergeInternal(Test array[], const Range A, const Range B, const Comparison compare, const Range buffer) {

0395./* whenever we find a value to add to the final array, swap it with the value that's already in that spot */

0396./* when this algorithm is finished, 'buffer' will contain its original contents, but in a different order */

0397.size_t A_count = 0, B_count = 0, insert = 0;

0398.

0399.if (Range_length(B) > 0 && Range_length(A) > 0) {

0400.while (true) {

0401.if (.compare(array[B.start + B_count], array[buffer.start + A_count])) {
```

```
0402.Swap(array[A.start + insert], array[buffer.start + A_count]);

0403.A_count++;

0404.insert++;

0405.if (A_count >= Range_length(A)) break;

0406.} else {

0407.Swap(array[A.start + insert], array[B.start + B_count]);

0408.B_count++;

0409.insert++;

0410.if (B_count >= Range_length(B)) break;

0411.}

0412.}

0413.}

0414.

0415./* swap the remainder of A into the final array */

0416.BlockSwap(array, buffer.start + A_count, A.start + insert, Range_length(A)
- A_count);

0417.}

0418.

0419./* merge operation without a buffer */

0420.void MergeInPlace(Test array[], Range A, Range B, const Comparison compare,
Test cache[], const size_t cache_size) {

0421.if (Range_length(A) == 0 || Range_length(B) == 0) return;

0422.

0423./*

0424.this just repeatedly binary searches into B and rotates A into position.

0425.the paper suggests using the 'rotation-based Hwang and Lin algorithm' here,

0426.but I decided to stick with this because it had better situational perfor-
mance

0427.

0428.(Hwang and Lin is designed for merging subarrays of very different sizes,

0429.but WikiSort almost always uses subarrays that are roughly the same size)

0430.
```

0431.normally this is incredibly suboptimal, but this function is only called

0432.when none of the A or B blocks in any subarray contained 2√A unique values,

0433.which places a hard limit on the number of times this will ACTUALLY need

0434.to binary search and rotate.

0435.

0436.according to my analysis the worst case is √A rotations performed on √A items

0437.once the constant factors are removed, which ends up being O(n)

0438.

0439.again, this is NOT a general-purpose solution - it only works well in this case.

0440.kind of like how the O(n^2) insertion sort is used in some places

0441.*/

0442.

0443.while (true) {

0444./* find the first place in B where the first item in A needs to be inserted */

0445.size_t mid = BinaryFirst(array, array[A.start], B, compare);

0446.

0447./* rotate A into place */

0448.size_t amount = mid - A.end;

0449.Rotate(array, Range_length(A), Range_new(A.start, mid), cache, cache_size);

0450.if (B.end == mid) break;

0451.

0452./* calculate the new A and B ranges */

0453.B.start = mid;

0454.A = Range_new(A.start + amount, B.start);

0455.A.start = BinaryLast(array, array[A.start], A, compare);

0456.if (Range_length(A) == 0) break;

0457.}

0458.}

0459.

```
0460./* bottom-up merge sort combined with an in-place merge algorithm for O(1)
memory use */

0461.void WikiSort(Test array[], const size_t size, const Comparison compare) {

0462./* use a small cache to speed up some of the operations */

0463.#if DYNAMIC_CACHE

0464.size_t cache_size;

0465.Test *cache = NULL;

0466.#else

0467./* since the cache size is fixed, it's still O(1) memory. */

0468./* just keep in mind that making it too small ruins the point (nothing will
fit into it), */

0469./* and making it too large also ruins the point (so much for "low memory".)
*/

0470./* removing the cache entirely still gives 70% of the performance of a
standard merge */

0471.#define CACHE_SIZE 512

0472.const size_t cache_size = CACHE_SIZE;

0473.Test cache[CACHE_SIZE];

0474.#endif

0475.

0476.WikiIterator iterator;

0477.

0478./* if the array is of size 0, 1, 2, or 3, just sort them like so: */

0479.if (size < 4) {

0480.if (size == 3) {

0481./* hard-coded insertion sort */

0482.if (compare(array[1], array[0])) Swap(array[0], array[1]);

0483.if (compare(array[2], array[1])) {

0484.Swap(array[1], array[2]);

0485.if (compare(array[1], array[0])) Swap(array[0], array[1]);

0486.}

0487.} else if (size == 2) {
```

```
0488./* swap the items if they're out of order */

0489.if (compare(array[1], array[0])) Swap(array[0], array[1]);

0490.}

0491.

0492.return;

0493.}

0494.

0495./* sort groups of 4-8 items at a time using an unstable sorting network, */

0496./* but keep track of the original item orders to force it to be stable */

0497.

0498.iterator = WikiIterator_new(size, 4);

0499.WikiIterator_begin(&iterator);

0500.while (.WikiIterator_finished(&iterator)) {

0501.uint8_t order[] = { 0, 1, 2, 3, 4, 5, 6, 7 };

0502.Range range = WikiIterator_nextRange(&iterator);

0503.

0504.#define SWAP(x, y) if (compare(array[range.start + y], array[range.start + x]) || \

0505.(order[x] > order[y] && .compare(array[range.start + x], array[range.start + y]))) { \

0506.Swap(array[range.start + x], array[range.start + y]); Swap(order[x], order[y]); }

0507.

0508.if (Range_length(range) == 8) {

0509.SWAP(0, 1); SWAP(2, 3); SWAP(4, 5); SWAP(6, 7);

0510.SWAP(0, 2); SWAP(1, 3); SWAP(4, 6); SWAP(5, 7);

0511.SWAP(1, 2); SWAP(5, 6); SWAP(0, 4); SWAP(3, 7);

0512.SWAP(1, 5); SWAP(2, 6);

0513.SWAP(1, 4); SWAP(3, 6);

0514.SWAP(2, 4); SWAP(3, 5);

0515.SWAP(3, 4);

0516.
```

```
0517.} else if (Range_length(range) == 7) {
0518.SWAP(1, 2); SWAP(3, 4); SWAP(5, 6);
0519.SWAP(0, 2); SWAP(3, 5); SWAP(4, 6);
0520.SWAP(0, 1); SWAP(4, 5); SWAP(2, 6);
0521.SWAP(0, 4); SWAP(1, 5);
0522.SWAP(0, 3); SWAP(2, 5);
0523.SWAP(1, 3); SWAP(2, 4);
0524.SWAP(2, 3);
0525.
0526.} else if (Range_length(range) == 6) {
0527.SWAP(1, 2); SWAP(4, 5);
0528.SWAP(0, 2); SWAP(3, 5);
0529.SWAP(0, 1); SWAP(3, 4); SWAP(2, 5);
0530.SWAP(0, 3); SWAP(1, 4);
0531.SWAP(2, 4); SWAP(1, 3);
0532.SWAP(2, 3);
0533.
0534.} else if (Range_length(range) == 5) {
0535.SWAP(0, 1); SWAP(3, 4);
0536.SWAP(2, 4);
0537.SWAP(2, 3); SWAP(1, 4);
0538.SWAP(0, 3);
0539.SWAP(0, 2); SWAP(1, 3);
0540.SWAP(1, 2);
0541.
0542.} else if (Range_length(range) == 4) {
0543.SWAP(0, 1); SWAP(2, 3);
0544.SWAP(0, 2); SWAP(1, 3);
0545.SWAP(1, 2);
0546.}
```

```
0547.}

0548.if (size < 8) return;

0549.

0550.#if DYNAMIC_CACHE

0551./* good choices for the cache size are: */

0552./* (size + 1)/2 - turns into a full-speed standard merge sort since every-
thing fits into the cache */

0553.cache_size = (size + 1)/2;

0554.cache = (Test *)malloc(cache_size * sizeof(array[0]));

0555.

0556.if (.cache) {

0557./* sqrt((size + 1)/2) + 1 - this will be the size of the A blocks at the
largest level of merges, */

0558./* so a buffer of this size would allow it to skip using internal or in-
place merges for anything */

0559.cache_size = sqrt(cache_size) + 1;

0560.cache = (Test *)malloc(cache_size * sizeof(array[0]));

0561.

0562.if (.cache) {

0563./* 512 - chosen from careful testing as a good balance between fixed-size
memory use and run time */

0564.if (cache_size > 512) {

0565.cache_size = 512;

0566.cache = (Test *)malloc(cache_size * sizeof(array[0]));

0567.}

0568.

0569./* 0 - if the system simply cannot allocate any extra memory whatsoever, no
memory works just fine */

0570.if (.cache) cache_size = 0;

0571.}

0572.}

0573.#endif

0574.
```

```
0575./* then merge sort the higher levels, which can be 8-15, 16-31, 32-63, 64-
127, etc. */

0576.while (true) {

0577.

0578./* if every A and B block will fit into the cache, use a special branch spe-
cifically for merging with the cache */

0579./* (we use < rather than <= since the block size might be one more than
iterator.length()) */

0580.if (WikiIterator_length(&iterator) < cache_size) {

0581.

0582./* if four subarrays fit into the cache, it's faster to merge both pairs of
subarrays into the cache, */

0583./* then merge the two merged subarrays from the cache back into the orig-
inal array */

0584.if ((WikiIterator_length(&iterator) + 1) * 4 <= cache_size && WikiItera-
tor_length(&iterator) * 4 <= size) {

0585.WikiIterator_begin(&iterator);

0586.while (.WikiIterator_finished(&iterator)) {

0587./* merge A1 and B1 into the cache */

0588.Range A1, B1, A2, B2, A3, B3;

0589.A1 = WikiIterator_nextRange(&iterator);

0590.B1 = WikiIterator_nextRange(&iterator);

0591.A2 = WikiIterator_nextRange(&iterator);

0592.B2 = WikiIterator_nextRange(&iterator);

0593.

0594.if (compare(array[B1.end - 1], array[A1.start])) {

0595./* the two ranges are in reverse order, so copy them in reverse order into
the cache */

0596.memcpy(&cache[Range_length(B1)],   &array[A1.start],   Range_length(A1)   *
sizeof(array[0]));

0597.memcpy(&cache[0], &array[B1.start], Range_length(B1) * sizeof(array[0]));

0598.} else if (compare(array[B1.start], array[A1.end - 1])) {

0599./* these two ranges weren't already in order, so merge them into the cache
*/
```

```
0600.MergeInto(array, A1, B1, compare, &cache[0]);

0601.} else {

0602./* if A1, B1, A2, and B2 are all in order, skip doing anything else */

0603.if (.compare(array[B2.start], array[A2.end - 1]) && .compare(array[A2.
start], array[B1.end - 1])) continue;

0604.

0605./* copy A1 and B1 into the cache in the same order */

0606.memcpy(&cache[0], &array[A1.start], Range_length(A1) * sizeof(array[0]));

0607.memcpy(&cache[Range_length(A1)], &array[B1.start], Range_length(B1) *
sizeof(array[0]));

0608.}

0609.A1 = Range_new(A1.start, B1.end);

0610.

0611./* merge A2 and B2 into the cache */

0612.if (compare(array[B2.end - 1], array[A2.start])) {

0613./* the two ranges are in reverse order, so copy them in reverse order into
the cache */

0614.memcpy(&cache[Range_length(A1) + Range_length(B2)], &array[A2.start],
Range_length(A2) * sizeof(array[0]));

0615.memcpy(&cache[Range_length(A1)], &array[B2.start], Range_length(B2) *
sizeof(array[0]));

0616.} else if (compare(array[B2.start], array[A2.end - 1])) {

0617./* these two ranges weren't already in order, so merge them into the cache
*/

0618.MergeInto(array, A2, B2, compare, &cache[Range_length(A1)]);

0619.} else {

0620./* copy A2 and B2 into the cache in the same order */

0621.memcpy(&cache[Range_length(A1)], &array[A2.start], Range_length(A2) *
sizeof(array[0]));

0622.memcpy(&cache[Range_length(A1) + Range_length(A2)], &array[B2.start],
Range_length(B2) * sizeof(array[0]));

0623.}

0624.A2 = Range_new(A2.start, B2.end);

0625.
```

```
0626./* merge A1 and A2 from the cache into the array */

0627.A3 = Range_new(0, Range_length(A1));

0628.B3 = Range_new(Range_length(A1), Range_length(A1) + Range_length(A2));

0629.

0630.if (compare(cache[B3.end - 1], cache[A3.start])) {

0631./* the two ranges are in reverse order, so copy them in reverse order into
the array */

0632.memcpy(&array[A1.start + Range_length(A2)], &cache[A3.start], Range_
length(A3) * sizeof(array[0]));

0633.memcpy(&array[A1.start], &cache[B3.start], Range_length(B3) * sizeof(ar-
ray[0]));

0634.} else if (compare(cache[B3.start], cache[A3.end - 1])) {

0635./* these two ranges weren't already in order, so merge them back into the
array */

0636.MergeInto(cache, A3, B3, compare, &array[A1.start]);

0637.} else {

0638./* copy A3 and B3 into the array in the same order */

0639.memcpy(&array[A1.start], &cache[A3.start], Range_length(A3) * sizeof(ar-
ray[0]));

0640.memcpy(&array[A1.start + Range_length(A1)], &cache[B3.start], Range_
length(B3) * sizeof(array[0]));

0641.}

0642.}

0643.

0644./* we merged two levels at the same time, so we're done with this level
already */

0645./* (iterator.nextLevel() is called again at the bottom of this outer merge
loop) */

0646.WikiIterator_nextLevel(&iterator);

0647.

0648.} else {

0649.WikiIterator_begin(&iterator);

0650.while (.WikiIterator_finished(&iterator)) {

0651.Range A = WikiIterator_nextRange(&iterator);
```

```
0652.Range B = WikiIterator_nextRange(&iterator);

0653.

0654.if (compare(array[B.end - 1], array[A.start])) {

0655./* the two ranges are in reverse order, so a simple rotation should fix it */

0656.Rotate(array, Range_length(A), Range_new(A.start, B.end), cache, cache_
size);

0657.} else if (compare(array[B.start], array[A.end - 1])) {

0658./* these two ranges weren't already in order, so we'll need to merge them.
*/

0659.memcpy(&cache[0], &array[A.start], Range_length(A) * sizeof(array[0]));

0660.MergeExternal(array, A, B, compare, cache);

0661.}

0662.}

0663.}

0664.} else {

0665./* this is where the in-place merge logic starts.

0666.1. pull out two internal buffers each containing √A unique values

0667.1a. adjust block_size and buffer_size if we couldn't find enough unique val-
ues

0668.2. loop over the A and B subarrays within this level of the merge sort

0669.3. break A and B into blocks of size 'block_size'

0670.4. "tag" each of the A blocks with values from the first internal buffer

0671.5. roll the A blocks through the B blocks and drop/rotate them where they
belong

0672.6. merge each A block with any B values that follow, using the cache or the
second internal buffer

0673.7. sort the second internal buffer if it exists

0674.8. redistribute the two internal buffers back into the array */

0675.

0676.size_t block_size = sqrt(WikiIterator_length(&iterator));

0677.size_t buffer_size = WikiIterator_length(&iterator)/block_size + 1;

0678.

0679./* as an optimization, we really only need to pull out the internal buffers
```

once for each level of merges */

0680./* after that we can reuse the same buffers over and over, then redistribute it when we're finished with this level */

0681.Range buffer1, buffer2, A, B; bool find_separately;

0682.size_t index, last, count, find, start, pull_index = 0;

0683.struct { size_t from, to, count; Range range; } pull[2];

0684.pull[0].from = pull[0].to = pull[0].count = 0; pull[0].range = Range_new(0, 0);

0685.pull[1].from = pull[1].to = pull[1].count = 0; pull[1].range = Range_new(0, 0);

0686.

0687.buffer1 = Range_new(0, 0);

0688.buffer2 = Range_new(0, 0);

0689.

0690./* find two internal buffers of size 'buffer_size' each */

0691.find = buffer_size + buffer_size;

0692.find_separately = false;

0693.

0694.if (block_size <= cache_size) {

0695./* if every A block fits into the cache then we won't need the second internal buffer, */

0696./* so we really only need to find 'buffer_size' unique values */

0697.find = buffer_size;

0698.} else if (find > WikiIterator_length(&iterator)) {

0699./* we can't fit both buffers into the same A or B subarray, so find two buffers separately */

0700.find = buffer_size;

0701.find_separately = true;

0702.}

0703.

0704./* we need to find either a single contiguous space containing $2\sqrt{A}$ unique values (which will be split up into two buffers of size $\sqrt{A}$ each), */

0705./* or we need to find one buffer of $< 2\sqrt{A}$ unique values, and a second buffer of √A unique values, */

0706./* OR if we couldn't find that many unique values, we need the largest possible buffer we can get */

0707.

0708./* in the case where it couldn't find a single buffer of at least √A unique values, */

0709./* all of the Merge steps must be replaced by a different merge algorithm (MergeInPlace) */

0710.WikiIterator_begin(&iterator);

0711.while (.WikiIterator_finished(&iterator)) {

0712.A = WikiIterator_nextRange(&iterator);

0713.B = WikiIterator_nextRange(&iterator);

0714.

0715./* just store information about where the values will be pulled from and to, */

0716./* as well as how many values there are, to create the two internal buffers */

0717.#define PULL(_to) \

0718.pull[pull_index].range = Range_new(A.start, B.end); \

0719.pull[pull_index].count = count; \

0720.pull[pull_index].from = index; \

0721.pull[pull_index].to = _to

0722.

0723./* check A for the number of unique values we need to fill an internal buffer */

0724./* these values will be pulled out to the start of A */

0725.for (last = A.start, count = 1; count < find; last = index, count++) {

0726.index = FindLastForward(array, array[last], Range_new(last + 1, A.end), compare, find - count);

0727.if (index == A.end) break;

0728.}

0729.index = last;

0730.

0731.if (count >= buffer_size) {

0732./* keep track of the range within the array where we'll need to "pull out" these values to create the internal buffer */

0733.PULL(A.start);

0734.pull_index = 1;

0735.

0736.if (count == buffer_size + buffer_size) {

0737./* we were able to find a single contiguous section containing 2√A unique values, */

0738./* so this section can be used to contain both of the internal buffers we'll need */

0739.buffer1 = Range_new(A.start, A.start + buffer_size);

0740.buffer2 = Range_new(A.start + buffer_size, A.start + count);

0741.break;

0742.} else if (find == buffer_size + buffer_size) {

0743./* we found a buffer that contains at least √A unique values, but did not contain the full 2√A unique values, */

0744./* so we still need to find a second separate buffer of at least √A unique values */

0745.buffer1 = Range_new(A.start, A.start + count);

0746.find = buffer_size;

0747.} else if (block_size <= cache_size) {

0748./* we found the first and only internal buffer that we need, so we're done. */

0749.buffer1 = Range_new(A.start, A.start + count);

0750.break;

0751.} else if (find_separately) {

0752./* found one buffer, but now find the other one */

0753.buffer1 = Range_new(A.start, A.start + count);

0754.find_separately = false;

0755.} else {

0756./* we found a second buffer in an 'A' subarray containing √A unique values, so we're done. */

```
0757.buffer2 = Range_new(A.start, A.start + count);

0758.break;

0759.}

0760.} else if (pull_index == 0 && count > Range_length(buffer1)) {

0761./* keep track of the largest buffer we were able to find */

0762.buffer1 = Range_new(A.start, A.start + count);

0763.PULL(A.start);

0764.}

0765.

0766./* check B for the number of unique values we need to fill an internal buf-
fer */

0767./* these values will be pulled out to the end of B */

0768.for (last = B.end - 1, count = 1; count < find; last = index - 1, count++) {

0769.index = FindFirstBackward(array, array[last], Range_new(B.start, last),
compare, find - count);

0770.if (index == B.start) break;

0771.}

0772.index = last;

0773.

0774.if (count >= buffer_size) {

0775./* keep track of the range within the array where we'll need to "pull out"
these values to create the internal buffer */

0776.PULL(B.end);

0777.pull_index = 1;

0778.

0779.if (count == buffer_size + buffer_size) {

0780./* we were able to find a single contiguous section containing 2√A unique
values, */

0781./* so this section can be used to contain both of the internal buffers we'll
need */

0782.buffer1 = Range_new(B.end - count, B.end - buffer_size);

0783.buffer2 = Range_new(B.end - buffer_size, B.end);

0784.break;
```

```
0785.} else if (find == buffer_size + buffer_size) {

0786./* we found a buffer that contains at least √A unique values, but did not
contain the full 2√A unique values, */

0787./* so we still need to find a second separate buffer of at least √A unique
values */

0788.buffer1 = Range_new(B.end - count, B.end);

0789.find = buffer_size;

0790.} else if (block_size <= cache_size) {

0791./* we found the first and only internal buffer that we need, so we're done.
*/

0792.buffer1 = Range_new(B.end - count, B.end);

0793.break;

0794.} else if (find_separately) {

0795./* found one buffer, but now find the other one */

0796.buffer1 = Range_new(B.end - count, B.end);

0797.find_separately = false;

0798.} else {

0799./* buffer2 will be pulled out from a 'B' subarray, so if the first buffer
was pulled out from the corresponding 'A' subarray, */

0800./* we need to adjust the end point for that A subarray so it knows to stop
redistributing its values before reaching buffer2 */

0801.if (pull[0].range.start == A.start) pull[0].range.end -= pull[1].count;

0802.

0803./* we found a second buffer in an 'B' subarray containing √A unique values,
so we're done. */

0804.buffer2 = Range_new(B.end - count, B.end);

0805.break;

0806.}

0807.} else if (pull_index == 0 && count > Range_length(buffer1)) {

0808./* keep track of the largest buffer we were able to find */

0809.buffer1 = Range_new(B.end - count, B.end);

0810.PULL(B.end);

0811.}
```

```
0812.}

0813.

0814./* pull out the two ranges so we can use them as internal buffers */

0815.for (pull_index = 0; pull_index < 2; pull_index++) {

0816.Range range;

0817.size_t length = pull[pull_index].count;

0818.

0819.if (pull[pull_index].to < pull[pull_index].from) {

0820./* we're pulling the values out to the left, which means the start of an A
subarray */

0821.index = pull[pull_index].from;

0822.for (count = 1; count < length; count++) {

0823.index = FindFirstBackward(array, array[index - 1], Range_new(pull[pull_in-
dex].to, pull[pull_index].from - (count - 1)), compare, length - count);

0824.range = Range_new(index + 1, pull[pull_index].from + 1);

0825.Rotate(array, Range_length(range) - count, range, cache, cache_size);

0826.pull[pull_index].from = index + count;

0827.}

0828.} else if (pull[pull_index].to > pull[pull_index].from) {

0829./* we're pulling values out to the right, which means the end of a B sub-
array */

0830.index = pull[pull_index].from + 1;

0831.for (count = 1; count < length; count++) {

0832.index = FindLastForward(array, array[index], Range_new(index, pull[pull_
index].to), compare, length - count);

0833.range = Range_new(pull[pull_index].from, index - 1);

0834.Rotate(array, count, range, cache, cache_size);

0835.pull[pull_index].from = index - 1 - count;

0836.}

0837.}

0838.}

0839.
```

```
0840./* adjust block_size and buffer_size based on the values we were able to
pull out */

0841.buffer_size = Range_length(buffer1);

0842.block_size = WikiIterator_length(&iterator)/buffer_size + 1;

0843.

0844./* the first buffer NEEDS to be large enough to tag each of the evenly sized
A blocks, */

0845./* so this was originally here to test the math for adjusting block_size
above */

0846./* assert((WikiIterator_length(&iterator) + 1)/block_size <= buffer_size);
*/

0847.

0848./* now that the two internal buffers have been created, it's time to merge
each A+B combination at this level of the merge sort. */

0849.WikiIterator_begin(&iterator);

0850.while (.WikiIterator_finished(&iterator)) {

0851.A = WikiIterator_nextRange(&iterator);

0852.B = WikiIterator_nextRange(&iterator);

0853.

0854./* remove any parts of A or B that are being used by the internal buffers */

0855.start = A.start;

0856.if (start == pull[0].range.start) {

0857.if (pull[0].from > pull[0].to) {

0858.A.start += pull[0].count;

0859.

0860./* if the internal buffer takes up the entire A or B subarray, then there's
nothing to merge */

0861./* this only happens for very small subarrays, like √4 = 2, 2 * (2 internal
buffers) = 4, */

0862./* which also only happens when cache_size is small or 0 since it'd other-
wise use MergeExternal */

0863.if (Range_length(A) == 0) continue;

0864.} else if (pull[0].from < pull[0].to) {

0865.B.end -= pull[0].count;
```

```
0866.if (Range_length(B) == 0) continue;

0867.}

0868.}

0869.if (start == pull[1].range.start) {

0870.if (pull[1].from > pull[1].to) {

0871.A.start += pull[1].count;

0872.if (Range_length(A) == 0) continue;

0873.} else if (pull[1].from < pull[1].to) {

0874.B.end -= pull[1].count;

0875.if (Range_length(B) == 0) continue;

0876.}

0877.}

0878.

0879.if (compare(array[B.end - 1], array[A.start])) {

0880./* the two ranges are in reverse order, so a simple rotation should fix it */

0881.Rotate(array, Range_length(A), Range_new(A.start, B.end), cache, cache_
size);

0882.} else if (compare(array[A.end], array[A.end - 1])) {

0883./* these two ranges weren't already in order, so we'll need to merge them.
*/

0884.Range blockA, firstA, lastA, lastB, blockB;

0885.size_t indexA, findA;

0886.

0887./* break the remainder of A into blocks. firstA is the uneven-sized first A
block */

0888.blockA = Range_new(A.start, A.end);

0889.firstA = Range_new(A.start, A.start + Range_length(blockA) % block_size);

0890.

0891./* swap the first value of each A block with the value in buffer1 */

0892.for (indexA = buffer1.start, index = firstA.end; index < blockA.end; in-
dexA++, index += block_size)

0893.Swap(array[indexA], array[index]);
```

```
0894.

0895./* start rolling the A blocks through the B blocks. */

0896./* whenever we leave an A block behind, we'll need to merge the previous
A block with any B blocks that follow it, so track that information as well */

0897.lastA = firstA;

0898.lastB = Range_new(0, 0);

0899.blockB = Range_new(B.start, B.start + Min(block_size, Range_length(B)));

0900.blockA.start += Range_length(firstA);

0901.indexA = buffer1.start;

0902.

0903./* if the first unevenly sized A block fits into the cache, copy it there for
when we go to Merge it */

0904./* otherwise, if the second buffer is available, block swap the contents
into that */

0905.if (Range_length(lastA) <= cache_size)

0906.memcpy(&cache[0], &array[lastA.start], Range_length(lastA) * sizeof(ar-
ray[0]));

0907.else if (Range_length(buffer2) > 0)

0908.BlockSwap(array, lastA.start, buffer2.start, Range_length(lastA));

0909.

0910.if (Range_length(blockA) > 0) {

0911.while (true) {

0912./* if there's a previous B block and the first value of the minimum A block
is <= the last value of the previous B block, */

0913./* then drop that minimum A block behind. or if there are no B blocks left
then keep dropping the remaining A blocks. */

0914.if ((Range_length(lastB) > 0 && .compare(array[lastB.end - 1], array[in-
dexA])) || Range_length(blockB) == 0) {

0915./* figure out where to split the previous B block, and rotate it at the
split */

0916.size_t B_split = BinaryFirst(array, array[indexA], lastB, compare);

0917.size_t B_remaining = lastB.end - B_split;

0918.

0919./* swap the minimum A block to the beginning of the rolling A blocks */
```

```
0920.size_t minA = blockA.start;

0921.for (findA = minA + block_size; findA < blockA.end; findA += block_size)

0922.if (compare(array[findA], array[minA]))

0923.minA = findA;

0924.BlockSwap(array, blockA.start, minA, block_size);

0925.

0926./* swap the first item of the previous A block back with its original value,
which is stored in buffer1 */

0927.Swap(array[blockA.start], array[indexA]);

0928.indexA++;

0929.

0930./*

0931.locally merge the previous A block with the B values that follow it

0932.if lastA fits into the external cache we'll use that (with MergeExternal),

0933.or if the second internal buffer exists we'll use that (with MergeInter-
nal),

0934.or failing that we'll use a strictly in-place merge algorithm (MergeIn-
Place)

0935.*/

0936.if (Range_length(lastA) <= cache_size)

0937.MergeExternal(array, lastA, Range_new(lastA.end, B_split), compare, cache);

0938.else if (Range_length(buffer2) > 0)

0939.MergeInternal(array, lastA, Range_new(lastA.end, B_split), compare, buf-
fer2);

0940.else

0941.MergeInPlace(array, lastA, Range_new(lastA.end, B_split), compare, cache,
cache_size);

0942.

0943.if (Range_length(buffer2) > 0 || block_size <= cache_size) {

0944./* copy the previous A block into the cache or buffer2, since that's where
we need it to be when we go to merge it anyway */

0945.if (block_size <= cache_size)

0946.memcpy(&cache[0], &array[blockA.start], block_size * sizeof(array[0]));
```

```
0947.else

0948.BlockSwap(array, blockA.start, buffer2.start, block_size);

0949.

0950./* this is equivalent to rotating, but faster */

0951./* the area normally taken up by the A block is either the contents of buf-
fer2, or data we don't need anymore since we memcopied it */

0952./* either way, we don't need to retain the order of those items, so instead
of rotating we can just block swap B to where it belongs */

0953.BlockSwap(array, B_split, blockA.start + block_size - B_remaining, B_re-
maining);

0954.} else {

0955./* we are unable to use the 'buffer2' trick to speed up the rotation oper-
ation since buffer2 doesn't exist, so perform a normal rotation */

0956.Rotate(array, blockA.start - B_split, Range_new(B_split, blockA.start +
block_size), cache, cache_size);

0957.}

0958.

0959./* update the range for the remaining A blocks, and the range remaining from
the B block after it was split */

0960.lastA = Range_new(blockA.start - B_remaining, blockA.start - B_remaining +
block_size);

0961.lastB = Range_new(lastA.end, lastA.end + B_remaining);

0962.

0963./* if there are no more A blocks remaining, this step is finished. */

0964.blockA.start += block_size;

0965.if (Range_length(blockA) == 0)

0966.break;

0967.

0968.} else if (Range_length(blockB) < block_size) {

0969./* move the last B block, which is unevenly sized, to before the remaining
A blocks, by using a rotation */

0970./* the cache is disabled here since it might contain the contents of the
previous A block */

0971.Rotate(array, blockB.start - blockA.start, Range_new(blockA.start, blockB.
end), cache, 0);
```

```
0972.
0973.lastB = Range_new(blockA.start, blockA.start + Range_length(blockB));
0974.blockA.start += Range_length(blockB);
0975.blockA.end += Range_length(blockB);
0976.blockB.end = blockB.start;
0977.} else {
0978./* roll the leftmost A block to the end by swapping it with the next B
block */
0979.BlockSwap(array, blockA.start, blockB.start, block_size);
0980.lastB = Range_new(blockA.start, blockA.start + block_size);
0981.
0982.blockA.start += block_size;
0983.blockA.end += block_size;
0984.blockB.start += block_size;
0985.
0986.if (blockB.end > B.end - block_size) blockB.end = B.end;
0987.else blockB.end += block_size;
0988.}
0989.}
0990.}
0991.
0992./* merge the last A block with the remaining B values */
0993.if (Range_length(lastA) <= cache_size)
0994.MergeExternal(array, lastA, Range_new(lastA.end, B.end), compare, cache);
0995.else if (Range_length(buffer2) > 0)
0996.MergeInternal(array, lastA, Range_new(lastA.end, B.end), compare, buffer2);
0997.else
0998.MergeInPlace(array, lastA, Range_new(lastA.end, B.end), compare, cache,
cache_size);
0999.}
1000.}
```

```
1001.

1002./* when we're finished with this merge step we should have the one or two
internal buffers left over, where the second buffer is all jumbled up */

1003./* insertion sort the second buffer, then redistribute the buffers back
into the array using the opposite process used for creating the buffer */

1004.

1005./* while an unstable sort like quicksort could be applied here, in bench-
marks it was consistently slightly slower than a simple insertion sort, */

1006./* even for tens of millions of items. this may be because insertion sort
is quite fast when the data is already somewhat sorted, like it is here */

1007.InsertionSort(array, buffer2, compare);

1008.

1009.for (pull_index = 0; pull_index < 2; pull_index++) {

1010.size_t amount, unique = pull[pull_index].count * 2;

1011.if (pull[pull_index].from > pull[pull_index].to) {

1012./* the values were pulled out to the left, so redistribute them back to the
right */

1013.Range buffer = Range_new(pull[pull_index].range.start, pull[pull_index].
range.start + pull[pull_index].count);

1014.while (Range_length(buffer) > 0) {

1015.index = FindFirstForward(array, array[buffer.start], Range_new(buffer.end,
pull[pull_index].range.end), compare, unique);

1016.amount = index - buffer.end;

1017.Rotate(array, Range_length(buffer), Range_new(buffer.start, index), cache,
cache_size);

1018.buffer.start += (amount + 1);

1019.buffer.end += amount;

1020.unique -= 2;

1021.}

1022.} else if (pull[pull_index].from < pull[pull_index].to) {

1023./* the values were pulled out to the right, so redistribute them back to
the left */

1024.Range buffer = Range_new(pull[pull_index].range.end - pull[pull_index].
count, pull[pull_index].range.end);

1025.while (Range_length(buffer) > 0) {
```

```
1026.index = FindLastBackward(array, array[buffer.end - 1], Range_new(pull[pull_
index].range.start, buffer.start), compare, unique);

1027.amount = buffer.start - index;

1028.Rotate(array, amount, Range_new(index, buffer.end), cache, cache_size);

1029.buffer.start -= amount;

1030.buffer.end -= (amount + 1);

1031.unique -= 2;

1032.}

1033.}

1034.}

1035.}

1036.

1037./* double the size of each A and B subarray that will be merged in the next
level */

1038.if (.WikiIterator_nextLevel(&iterator)) break;

1039.}

1040.

1041.#if DYNAMIC_CACHE

1042.if (cache) free(cache);

1043.#endif

1044.

1045.#undef CACHE_SIZE

1046.}

1047.

1048.

1049.

1050.

1051./* standard merge sort, so we have a baseline for how well WikiSort works */

1052.void MergeSortR(Test array[], const Range range, const Comparison compare,
Test buffer[]) {

1053.size_t mid, A_count = 0, B_count = 0, insert = 0;

1054.Range A, B;
```

```
1055.
1056.if (Range_length(range) < 32) {
1057.InsertionSort(array, range, compare);
1058.return;
1059.}
1060.
1061.mid = range.start + (range.end - range.start)/2;
1062.A = Range_new(range.start, mid);
1063.B = Range_new(mid, range.end);
1064.
1065.MergeSortR(array, A, compare, buffer);
1066.MergeSortR(array, B, compare, buffer);
1067.
1068./* standard merge operation here (only A is copied to the buffer, and only
the parts that weren't already where they should be) */
1069.A = Range_new(BinaryLast(array, array[B.start], A, compare), A.end);
1070.memcpy(&buffer[0], &array[A.start], Range_length(A) * sizeof(array[0]));
1071.while (A_count < Range_length(A) && B_count < Range_length(B)) {
1072.if (.compare(array[A.end + B_count], buffer[A_count])) {
1073.array[A.start + insert] = buffer[A_count];
1074.A_count++;
1075.} else {
1076.array[A.start + insert] = array[A.end + B_count];
1077.B_count++;
1078.}
1079.insert++;
1080.}
1081.
1082.memcpy(&array[A.start + insert], &buffer[A_count], (Range_length(A) - A_
count) * sizeof(array[0]));
1083.}
```

```
1084.
1085.void MergeSort(Test array[], const size_t array_count, const Comparison
compare) {
1086.Var(buffer, Allocate(Test, (array_count + 1)/2));
1087.MergeSortR(array, Range_new(0, array_count), compare, buffer);
1088.free(buffer);
1089.}
1090.
1091.
1092.
1093.
1094.size_t TestingRandom(size_t index, size_t total) {
1095.return rand();
1096.}
1097.
1098.size_t TestingRandomFew(size_t index, size_t total) {
1099.return rand() * (100.0/RAND_MAX);
1100.}
1101.
1102.size_t TestingMostlyDescending(size_t index, size_t total) {
1103.return total - index + rand() * 1.0/RAND_MAX * 5 - 2.5;
1104.}
1105.
1106.size_t TestingMostlyAscending(size_t index, size_t total) {
1107.return index + rand() * 1.0/RAND_MAX * 5 - 2.5;
1108.}
1109.
1110.size_t TestingAscending(size_t index, size_t total) {
1111.return index;
1112.}
1113.
```

```
1114.size_t TestingDescending(size_t index, size_t total) {
1115.return total - index;
1116.}
1117.
1118.size_t TestingEqual(size_t index, size_t total) {
1119.return 1000;
1120.}
1121.
1122.size_t TestingJittered(size_t index, size_t total) {
1123.return (rand() * 1.0/RAND_MAX <= 0.9) ? index : (index - 2);
1124.}
1125.
1126.size_t TestingMostlyEqual(size_t index, size_t total) {
1127.return 1000 + rand() * 1.0/RAND_MAX * 4;
1128.}
1129.
1130./* the last 1/5 of the data is random */
1131.size_t TestingAppend(size_t index, size_t total) {
1132.if (index > total - total/5) return rand() * 1.0/RAND_MAX * total;
1133.return index;
1134.}
1135.
1136./* make sure the items within the given range are in a stable order */
1137./* if you want to test the correctness of any changes you make to the main WikiSort function,
1138.move this function to the top of the file and call it from within WikiSort after each step */
1139.#if VERIFY
1140.void WikiVerify(const Test array[], const Range range, const Comparison compare, constchar *msg) {
1141.size_t index;
1142.for (index = range.start + 1; index < range.end; index++) {
```

```
1143./* if it's in ascending order then we're good */

1144./* if both values are equal, we need to make sure the index values are as-
cending */

1145.if (.(compare(array[index - 1], array[index]) ||

1146.(.compare(array[index], array[index - 1]) && array[index].index > array[in-
dex - 1].index))) {

1147.

1148./*for (index2 = range.start; index2 < range.end; index2++) */

1149./*  printf("%lu (%lu) ", array[index2].value, array[index2].index); */

1150.

1151.printf("failed with message: %s\n", msg);

1152.assert(false);

1153.}

1154.}

1155.}

1156.#endif

1157.

1158.int main() {

1159.size_t total, index;

1160.double total_time, total_time1, total_time2;

1161.const size_t max_size = 1500000;

1162.Var(array1, Allocate(Test, max_size));

1163.Var(array2, Allocate(Test, max_size));

1164.Comparison compare = TestCompare;

1165.

1166.#if PROFILE

1167.size_t compares1, compares2, total_compares1 = 0, total_compares2 = 0;

1168.#endif

1169.#if .SLOW_COMPARISONS && VERIFY

1170.size_t test_case;

1171.__typeof__(&TestingRandom) test_cases[] = {
```

```
1172.TestingRandom,

1173.TestingRandomFew,

1174.TestingMostlyDescending,

1175.TestingMostlyAscending,

1176.TestingAscending,

1177.TestingDescending,

1178.TestingEqual,

1179.TestingJittered,

1180.TestingMostlyEqual,

1181.TestingAppend

1182.};

1183.#endif

1184.

1185./* initialize the random-number generator */

1186.srand(time(NULL));

1187./*srand(10141985);*/ /* in case you want the same random numbers */

1188.

1189.total = max_size;

1190.

1191.#if .SLOW_COMPARISONS && VERIFY

1192.printf("running test cases... ");

1193.fflush(stdout);

1194.

1195.for (test_case = 0; test_case < sizeof(test_cases)/sizeof(test_cases[0]);
test_case++) {

1196.

1197.for (index = 0; index < total; index++) {

1198.Test item;

1199.

1200.item.value = test_cases[test_case](index, total);

1201.item.index = index;
```

```
1202.
1203.array1[index] = array2[index] = item;
1204.}
1205.
1206.WikiSort(array1, total, compare);
1207.
1208.MergeSort(array2, total, compare);
1209.
1210.WikiVerify(array1, Range_new(0, total), compare, "test case failed");
1211.for (index = 0; index < total; index++)
1212.assert(.compare(array1[index], array2[index]) && .compare(array2[index],
array1[index]));
1213.}
1214.printf("passed.\n");
1215.#endif
1216.
1217.total_time = Seconds();
1218.total_time1 = total_time2 = 0;
1219.
1220.for (total = 0; total < max_size; total += 2048 * 16) {
1221.double time1, time2;
1222.
1223.for (index = 0; index < total; index++) {
1224.Test item;
1225.
1226./* TestingRandom, TestingRandomFew, TestingMostlyDescending, TestingMost-
lyAscending, */
1227./* TestingAscending, TestingDescending, TestingEqual, TestingJittered,
TestingMostlyEqual, TestingAppend */
1228.item.value = TestingRandom(index, total);
1229.#if VERIFY
1230.item.index = index;
```

```
1231.#endif

1232.

1233.array1[index] = array2[index] = item;

1234.}

1235.

1236.time1 = Seconds();

1237.#if PROFILE

1238.comparisons = 0;

1239.#endif

1240.WikiSort(array1, total, compare);

1241.time1 = Seconds() - time1;

1242.total_time1 += time1;

1243.#if PROFILE

1244.compares1 = comparisons;

1245.total_compares1 += compares1;

1246.#endif

1247.

1248.time2 = Seconds();

1249.#if PROFILE

1250.comparisons = 0;

1251.#endif

1252.MergeSort(array2, total, compare);

1253.time2 = Seconds() - time2;

1254.total_time2 += time2;

1255.#if PROFILE

1256.compares2 = comparisons;

1257.total_compares2 += compares2;

1258.#endif

1259.

1260.printf("[%zu]\n", total);
```

```
1261.

1262.if (time1 >= time2)

1263.printf("WikiSort: %f seconds, MergeSort: %f seconds (%f%% as fast)\n",
time1, time2, time2/time1 * 100.0);

1264.else

1265.printf("WikiSort: %f seconds, MergeSort: %f seconds (%f%% faster)\n",
time1, time2, time2/time1 * 100.0 - 100.0);

1266.

1267.#if PROFILE

1268.if (compares1 <= compares2)

1269.printf("WikiSort: %zu compares, MergeSort: %zu compares (%f%% as many)\n",
compares1, compares2, compares1 * 100.0/compares2);

1270.else

1271.printf("WikiSort: %zu compares, MergeSort: %zu compares (%f%% more)\n",
compares1, compares2, compares1 * 100.0/compares2 - 100.0);

1272.#endif

1273.

1274.#if VERIFY

1275./* make sure the arrays are sorted correctly, and that the results were
stable */

1276.printf("verifying... ");

1277.fflush(stdout);

1278.

1279.WikiVerify(array1, Range_new(0, total), compare, "testing the final array");

1280.for (index = 0; index < total; index++)

1281.assert(.compare(array1[index], array2[index]) && .compare(array2[index],
array1[index]));

1282.

1283.printf("correct.\n");

1284.#endif

1285.}

1286.

1287.total_time = Seconds() - total_time;
```

```
1288.printf("tests completed in %f seconds\n", total_time);

1289.if (total_time1 >= total_time2)

1290.printf("WikiSort: %f seconds, MergeSort: %f seconds (%f%% as fast)\n", to-
tal_time1, total_time2, total_time2/total_time1 * 100.0);

1291.else

1292.printf("WikiSort: %f seconds, MergeSort: %f seconds (%f%% faster)\n", to-
tal_time1, total_time2, total_time2/total_time1 * 100.0 - 100.0);

1293.

1294.#if PROFILE

1295.if (total_compares1 <= total_compares2)

1296.printf("WikiSort: %zu compares, MergeSort: %zu compares (%f%% as many)\n",
total_compares1, total_compares2, total_compares1 * 100.0/total_compares2);

1297.else

1298.printf("WikiSort: %zu compares, MergeSort: %zu compares (%f%% more)\n",
total_compares1, total_compares2, total_compares1 * 100.0/total_compares2 -
100.0);

1299.#endif

1300.

1301.free(array1); free(array2);

1302.return 0;

1303.}

1304.

1305.</limits.h></time.h></assert.h></math.h></string.h></stdarg.h></stdint.
h></stdlib.h></stdio.h>
```

References

- Edmonds, Jeff (2008), "5.2 Counting Sort (a Stable Sort)", How to Think about Algorithms, Cambridge University Press, pp. 72–75, ISBN 978-0-521-84931-9

- Sorting-algorithm: whatis.techtarget.com, Retrieved 27 May 2018

- Burris, David S.; Schember, Kurt (1980), "Sorting sequential files with limited auxiliary storage", Proceedings of the 18th annual Southeast Regional Conference, New York, NY, USA: ACM, pp. 23–31, doi:10.1145/503838.503855, ISBN 0897910141

- Bubble-sort-algorithm, data-structures-algorithms: tutorialspoint.com, Retrieved 13 July 2018

- MacIver, David R. (11 January 2010). "Understanding timsort, Part 1: Adaptive Mergesort". Retrieved 2015-12-05

- Selection-sorting, data-structures: studytonight.com, Retrieved 26 June 2018

- Pardo, Luis Trabb (1977). Stable Sorting and Merging with Optimal Space and Time Bounds. SIAM Journal on Computing. 6. pp. 351–372

- Know-your-sorting-algorithm-set-2-introsort-cs-sorting-weapon: geeksforgeeks.org, Retrieved 24 June 2018

- Knuth, D. E. (1998), The Art of Computer Programming, Volume 3: Sorting and Searching (2nd ed.), Addison-Wesley, ISBN 0-201-89685-0. Section 5.2, Sorting by counting, pp. 75–80, and historical notes, p. 170

- Block-Merge-Sort-51222: algoritmy.net, Retrieved 09 March 2018

- Mannila, Heikki; Ukkonen, Esko (1984). A Simple Linear Time Algorithm for In-Situ Merging. Information Processing Letters. 18. Elsevier B.V. pp. 203–208. doi:10.1016/0020-0190(84)90112-1

Graph Algorithms

An understanding of graph algorithms is vital for a holistic understanding of computer algorithms. This chapter discusses in extensive detail the varied graph algorithms, such as Hopcroft–Karp algorithm, Edmonds' algorithm, Boruvka's algorithm, Bellman–Ford algorithm, etc.

A graph is an abstract notation used to represent the connection between pairs of objects. A graph consists of –

- Vertices: Interconnected objects in a graph are called vertices. Vertices are also known as nodes.

- Edges: Edges are the links that connect the vertices.

There are two types of graphs –

- Directed graph: In a directed graph, edges have direction, i.e., edges go from one vertex to another.

- Undirected graph: In an undirected graph, edges have no direction.

Graph Coloring

Graph coloring is a method to assign colors to the vertices of a graph so that no two adjacent vertices have the same color. Some graph coloring problems are –

- Vertex coloring – A way of coloring the vertices of a graph so that no two adjacent vertices share the same color.

- Edge Coloring – It is the method of assigning a color to each edge so that no two adjacent edges have the same color.

- Face coloring – It assigns a color to each face or region of a planar graph so that no two faces that share a common boundary have the same color.

Chromatic Number

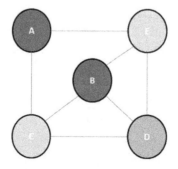

Chromatic number is the minimum number of colors required to color a graph. For example, the chromatic number of the following graph is 3.

The concept of graph coloring is applied in preparing timetables, mobile radio frequency assignment, Suduku, register allocation, and coloring of maps.

Steps for Graph Coloring

- Set the initial value of each processor in the n-dimensional array to 1.

- Now to assign a particular color to a vertex, determine whether that color is already assigned to the adjacent vertices or not.

- If a processor detects same color in the adjacent vertices, it sets its value in the array to 0.

- After making n^2 comparisons, if any element of the array is 1, then it is a valid coloring.

Pseudocode for graph coloring

```
begin

    create the processors P(i₀,i₁,...iₙ₋₁) where 0_iᵥ < m, 0 _ v < n
    status[i0,..iₙ₋₁] = 1

    for j varies from 0 to n-1 do
       begin

           for k varies from 0 to n-1 do
           begin
               if a_{j,k}=1 and i_j=i_k then
                  status[i₀,..iₙ₋₁] =0
           end

       end
       ok = ΣStatus

    if ok > 0, then display valid coloring exists
    else
```

```
    display invalid coloring
```

end

Minimal Spanning Tree

A spanning tree whose sum of weight (or length) of all its edges is less than all other possible spanning tree of graph G is known as a minimal spanning tree or minimum cost spanning tree. The following figure shows a weighted connected graph.

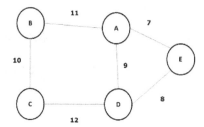

Some possible spanning trees of the above graph are shown below –

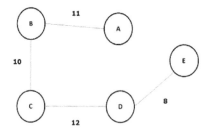

Total weight =11+10+12+8=41

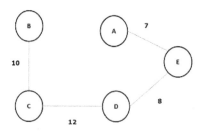

Total weight =10+12+8+7=37

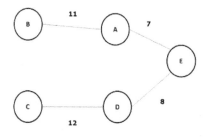

Total weight =12+8+7+11=38

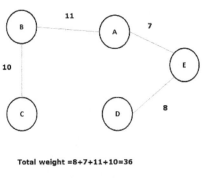

Total weight =8+7+11+10=36

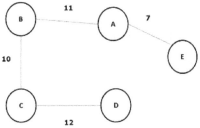

Total weight =7+11+10+12=40

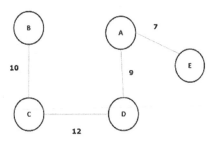

Total weight =10+12+9+7=38

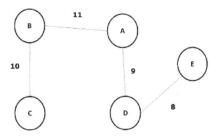

Total weight =10+11+9+8=38

Among all the above spanning trees, figure (d) is the minimum spanning tree. The concept of minimum cost spanning tree is applied in travelling salesman problem, designing electronic circuits, Designing efficient networks, and designing efficient routing algorithms.

To implement the minimum cost-spanning tree, the following two methods are used –

- Prim's Algorithm
- Kruskal's Algorithm

Prim's Algorithm

Prim's algorithm is a greedy algorithm, which helps us find the minimum spanning tree for a weighted undirected graph. It selects a vertex first and finds an edge with the lowest weight incident on that vertex.

Steps of Prim's Algorithm

- Select any vertex, say v_1 of Graph G.

- Select an edge, say e_1 of G such that $e_1 = v_1 v_2$ and $v_1 \neq v_2$ and e_1 has minimum weight among the edges incident on v_1 in graph G.

- Now, following step 2, select the minimum weighted edge incident on v_2.

- Continue this till n–1 edges have been chosen. Here n is the number of vertices.

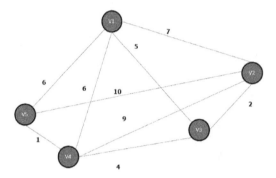

The minimum spanning tree is –

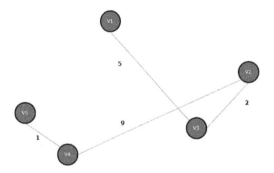

Kruskal's Algorithm

Kruskal's algorithm is a greedy algorithm, which helps us find the minimum spanning tree for a connected weighted graph, adding increasing cost arcs at each step. It is a minimum-spanning-tree algorithm that finds an edge of the least possible weight that connects any two trees in the forest.

Steps of Kruskal's Algorithm

- Select an edge of minimum weight; say e_1 of Graph G and e_1 is not a loop.

- Select the next minimum weighted edge connected to e_1.

- Continue this till n−1 edges have been chosen. Here n is the number of vertices.

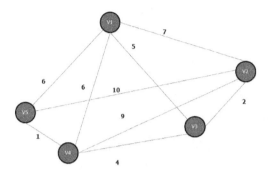

The minimum spanning tree of the above graph is −

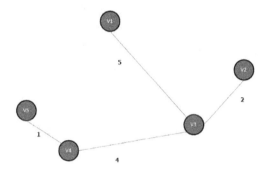

Shortest Path Algorithm

Shortest Path algorithm is a method of finding the least cost path from the source node(S) to the destination node (D). Here, we will discuss Moore's algorithm, also known as Breadth First Search Algorithm.

Moore's algorithm

- Label the source vertex, S and label it i and set i=0.

- Find all unlabeled vertices adjacent to the vertex labeled i. If no vertices are connected to the vertex, S, then vertex, D, is not connected to S. If there are vertices connected to S, label them i+1.

- If D is labeled, then go to step 4, else go to step 2 to increase i=i+1.

- Stop after the length of the shortest path is found.

Hopcroft–Karp Algorithm

A matching in a Bipartite Graph is a set of the edges chosen in such a way that no two edges share an endpoint. A maximum matching is a matching of maximum size (maximum number of edges).

In a maximum matching, if any edge is added to it, it is no longer a matching. There can be more than one maximum matching for a given Bipartite Graph.

Free Node or Vertex: Given a matching M, a node that is not part of matching is called free node. Initially all vertices as free. In second graph, u2 and v2 are free. In third graph, no vertex is free.

Matching and Not-Matching edges: Given a matching M, edges that are part of matching are called Matching edges and edges that are not part of M (or connect free nodes) are called Not-Matching edges. In first graph, all edges are non-matching. In second graph, (u0, v1), (u1, v0) and (u3, v3) are matching and others not-matching.

Alternating Paths: Given a matching M, an alternating path is a path in which the edges belong alternatively to the matching and not matching. All single edges paths are alternating paths. Examples of alternating paths in middle graph are u0-v1-u2 and u2-v1-u0-v2.

Augmenting path: Given a matching M, an augmenting path is an alternating path that starts from and ends on free vertices. All single edge paths that start and end with free vertices are augmenting paths. In below diagram, augmenting paths are highlighted with blue color. Note that the augmenting path always has one extra matching edge.

The Hopcroft Karp algorithm is based on below concept.

A matching M is not maximum if there exists an augmenting path. It is also true other way, i.e, a matching is maximum if no augmenting path exists

So the idea is to one by one look for augmenting paths. And add the found paths to current matching.

The algorithm

```
1) Initialize Maximal Matching M as empty.

2) While there exists an Augmenting Path p

     Remove matching edges of p from M and add not-matching edges of p to M

     (This increases size of M by 1 as p starts and ends with a free vertex)

3) Return M.
```

Below diagram shows working of the algorithm.

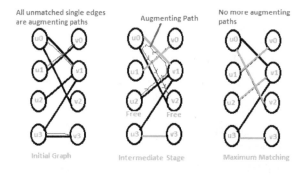

In the initial graph all single edges are augmenting paths and we can pick in any order. In the middle stage, there is only one augmenting path. We remove matching edges of this path from M and add not-matching edges. In final matching, there are no augmenting paths so the matching is maximum.

There are few important things to note before we start implementation.

1. We need to find an augmenting path (A path that alternates between matching and not matching edges, and has free vertices as starting and ending points).

2. Once we find alternating path, we need to add the found path to existing Matching. Here adding path means, making previous matching edges on this path as not-matching and previous not-matching edges as matching.

The idea is to use BFS (Breadth First Search) to find augmenting paths. Since BFS traverses level by level, it is used to divide the graph in layers of matching and not matching edges. A dummy vertex NIL is added that is connected to all vertices on left side and all vertices on right side. Following arrays are used to find augmenting path. Distance to NIL is initialized as INF (infinite). If we start from dummy vertex and come back to it using alternating path of distinct vertices, then there is an augmenting path.

1. pairU[]: An array of size m+1 where m is number of vertices on left side of Bipartite Graph. pairU[u] stores pair of u on right side if u is matched and NIL otherwise.

2. pairV[]: An array of size n+1 where n is number of vertices on right side of Bipartite Graph. pairV[v] stores pair of v on left side if v is matched and NIL otherwise.

3. dist[]: An array of size m+1 where m is number of vertices on left side of Bipartite Graph. dist[u] is initialized as 0 if u is not matching and INF (infinite) otherwise. dist[] of NIL is also initialized as INF

Once an augmenting path is found, DFS (Depth First Search) is used to add augmenting paths to current matching. DFS simply follows the distance array setup by BFS. It fills values in pairU[u] and pairV[v] if v is next to u in BFS.

Below is C++ implementation of above Hopkroft Karp algorithm.

```
// C++ implementation of Hopcroft Karp algorithm for

// maximum matching

#include<bits/stdc++.h>

using namespace std;

#define NIL 0

#define INF INT_MAX


// A class to represent Bipartite graph for Hopcroft
```

```cpp
// Karp implementation
class BipGraph
{
    // m and n are number of vertices on left
    // and right sides of Bipartite Graph
    int m, n;

    // adj[u] stores adjacents of left side
    // vertex <u'. The value of u ranges from 1 to m.
    // 0 is used for dummy vertex
    list<int> *adj;

    // These are basically pointers to arrays needed
    // for hopcroftKarp()
    int *pairU, *pairV, *dist;

public:
    BipGraph(int m, int n); // Constructor
    void addEdge(int u, int v); // To add edge

    // Returns true if there is an augmenting path
    bool bfs();

    // Adds augmenting path if there is one beginning
    // with u
    bool dfs(int u);

    // Returns size of maximum matcing
    int hopcroftKarp();
};
```

```cpp
// Returns size of maximum matching
int BipGraph::hopcroftKarp()
{

    // pairU[u] stores pair of u in matching where u
    // is a vertex on left side of Bipartite Graph.
    // If u doesn't have any pair, then pairU[u] is NIL
    pairU = new int[m+1];


    // pairV[v] stores pair of v in matching. If v
    // doesn't have any pair, then pairU[v] is NIL
    pairV = new int[n+1];


    // dist[u] stores distance of left side vertices
    // dist[u] is one more than dist[u'] if u is next
    // to u'in augmenting path
    dist = new int[m+1];


    // Initialize NIL as pair of all vertices
    for (int u=0; u<m; u++)
        pairU[u] = NIL;
    for (int v=0; v<n; v++)
        pairV[v] = NIL;


    // Initialize result
    int result = 0;


    // Keep updating the result while there is an
    // augmenting path.
    while (bfs())
```

```
    {
        // Find a free vertex

        for (int u=1; u<=m; u++)


            // If current vertex is free and there is
            // an augmenting path from current vertex
            if (pairU[u]==NIL && dfs(u))
                result++;
    }
    return result;
}


// Returns true if there is an augmenting path, else returns
// false
bool BipGraph::bfs()
{
    queue<int> Q; //an integer queue


    // First layer of vertices (set distance as 0)
    for (int u=1; u<=m; u++)
    {
        // If this is a free vertex, add it to queue
        if (pairU[u]==NIL)
        {
            // u is not matched
            dist[u] = 0;
            Q.push(u);
        }


        // Else set distance as infinite so that this vertex
```

```
        // is considered next time
        else dist[u] = INF;
}


// Initialize distance to NIL as infinite
dist[NIL] = INF;


// Q is going to contain vertices of left side only.
while (.Q.empty())
{
    // Dequeue a vertex
    int u = Q.front();
    Q.pop();


    // If this node is not NIL and can provide a shorter path to NIL
    if (dist[u] < dist[NIL])
    {
        // Get all adjacent vertices of the dequeued vertex u
        list<int>::iterator i;
        for (i=adj[u].begin(); i.=adj[u].end(); ++i)
        {
            int v = *i;


            // If pair of v is not considered so far
            // (v, pairV[V]) is not yet explored edge.
            if (dist[pairV[v]] == INF)
            {
                // Consider the pair and add it to queue
                dist[pairV[v]] = dist[u] + 1;
                Q.push(pairV[v]);
```

```
            }

        }

    }

}


    // If we could come back to NIL using alternating path of distinct
    // vertices then there is an augmenting path
    return (dist[NIL] .= INF);
}


// Returns true if there is an augmenting path beginning with free vertex u
bool BipGraph::dfs(int u)
{
    if (u .= NIL)
    {
        list<int>::iterator i;
        for (i=adj[u].begin(); i.=adj[u].end(); ++i)
        {
            // Adjacent to u
            int v = *i;

            // Follow the distances set by BFS
            if (dist[pairV[v]] == dist[u]+1)
            {
                // If dfs for pair of v also returns
                // true
                if (dfs(pairV[v]) == true)
                {
                    pairV[v] = u;
                    pairU[u] = v;
```

```
                        return true;
                }
            }
        }


        // If there is no augmenting path beginning with u.
        dist[u] = INF;
        return false;
    }
    return true;
}


// Constructor
BipGraph::BipGraph(int m, int n)
{
    this->m = m;
    this->n = n;
    adj = new list<int>[m+1];
}


// To add edge from u to v and v to u
void BipGraph::addEdge(int u, int v)
{
    adj[u].push_back(v); // Add u to v's list.
    adj[v].push_back(u); // Add u to v's list.
}


// Driver Program
int main()
{
```

```
BipGraph g(4, 4);

g.addEdge(1, 2);

g.addEdge(1, 3);

g.addEdge(2, 1);

g.addEdge(3, 2);

g.addEdge(4, 2);

g.addEdge(4, 4);


cout << "Size of maximum matching is " << g.hopcroftKarp();


return 0;
}
```

Edmonds' Algorithm

Edmonds's Blossom Algorithm is an algorithm that computes a maximum matching in an undirected graph. In contrast to some other matching algorithms, the graph need not be bipartite. The algorithm was introduced by Jack Edmonds in 1965 and has been further improved since then. Many exact modern algorithms for the maximum matching problem on general graphs are still based on the ideas of the Blossom Algorithm.

Edmonds's Blossom Algorithm uses and extends the essential ideas of the Hopcroft-Karp algorithm, which computes a maximum matching for bipartite graphs.

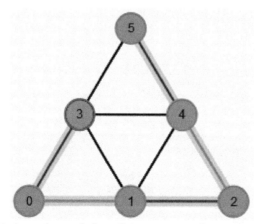

Augmenting path from free vertex 3 to free vertex 5.

We consider an undirected graph $G = (V, E)$ with a set of vertices V and a set of edges E. A matching $M \subseteq E$ is a subset of edges such that every vertex is covered by at most one edge of M. In the figure above, we illustrate a valid matching in a graph. Its edges are colored blue. Each node is incident to at most one edge. If we added e.g. the edge between 0 and 3 to the current matching, the result would not be a matching anymore because 0 would then be contained twice in the matching.

We call a vertex that is not covered by the matching a free vertex. Given an edge $e = \{v, m\} \in M$, v is the mate of w and vice versa. In our example, 3 and 5 are free vertices because they are not incident to any of the blue edges, 0 and 1 are mates of each other and 2 and 4 as well.

A matching M is called a maximum matching if its number of edges is maximum, i.e. if there does not exist any other matching M' in G with $|M'| > |M|$. The matching in figure below is not maximum. We could evidently add the edge between the free vertices 3 and 5 to our matching and, by doing so, increase its number of edges to 3.

A graph is called bipartite if its vertices can be partitioned into two sets V1 and V2 such that every edge has one endpoint in V1 and the other one in V2. We know that a graph is bipartite if and only if it does not contain any odd cycles. Obviously, the graph in our example is not bipartite because it contains triangles.

Edmonds's Blossom Algorithm computes a maximum matching in a general graph. In contrast to many other algorithms, the graph is not required to be bipartite. It extends the idea of the Hopcroft-Karp Algorithm, which computes a maximum matching for a bipartite graph, by treating odd cycles appropriately

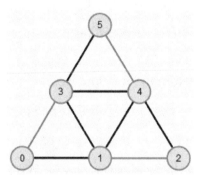

Matching after inverting the augmenting path. Since there are no free vertices anymore, the matching must be maximum.

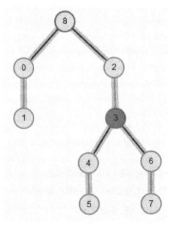

Layered BFS tree (in grey) with root 8 and currently active node 3.
Layer 0: 8, Layer 1: 0 and 2, Layer 2: 1 and 3, ...

Algorithm for Bipartite Graphs

We shortly recapitulate the basic concepts of the Hopcroft-Karp Algorithm that are also relevant for Edmonds's Blossom Algorithm. In order to improve a given matching, we try to find an augmenting path. An augmenting path is a path starting with a free node, ending with a free node and alternating between unmatched and matched edges.

The following theorem by C. Berge is essential for the algorithm: A matching M is not maximum if there exists an augmenting path in G. Thus, if we cannot find an augmenting path in G anymore, the resulting matching must be maximum.

But how can we find augmenting paths in a graph? We first pick an arbitrary free node r and start a modified Breadth-First Search (BFS) from there. While traversing the graph we construct a layered tree with root r. Edges from even to odd layers are unmatched edges, edges from odd to even layers are matched ones. Such a layered BFS tree is shown in figure above.

If we check a new node v during the execution of the BFS, one of the following cases may occur:

- Case 1: v is a free node

  Then we have found an augmenting path from r to v. We invert the path and are done with the BFS.

- Case 2: v is already matched and not contained in the tree so far

  Then we add v and its mate to the tree and push the mate of v to the BFS queue to continue the search from there later.

- Case 3: v is already contained in the tree and we have detected a cycle of even length

  There is nothing to do in this case, we ignore v and continue the BFS.

- Case 4: v is already contained in the tree and we have detected a cycle of odd length

  Since our graph is bipartite, this case cannot occur. When developing an algorithm for general graphs, however, we have to deal with this case as well.

General Graphs: Ways to Deal with Odd-length Cycles

In general graphs, we also use the procedure explained above to find augmenting paths. However, we might detect odd-length cycles now (case 4) and have to treat this case appropriately. The idea is the following: We ignore the entire cycle by contracting it to a single supernode and continue the BFS in the new graph. When we have found an augmenting path at some point we have to expand all supernodes again (in reversed order) before inverting the matching. We call such odd-length cycles blossoms and this is why the algorithm is often referred to as the Blossom Algorithm.

We illustrate the procedure of contracting an odd-length cycle to a supernode and expanding it again with the following small example. In the picture to the left, we see a layered BFS tree with root 4. At the moment, the active node is 1 and we check the edge between 1 and 3. Since 3 is already contained in the tree, we know that there must be a cycle. The cycle has odd length, so we end up in case 4 and have to contract the whole blossom (1, 0, 4, 2, 3) to a new supernode 7 (on the right).

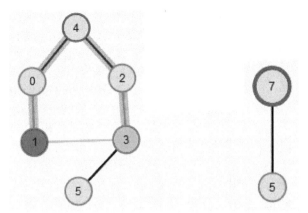

From 7 we continue the Breadth-First Search and find an augmenting path between 7 and 5. When we have found an augmenting path, we have to check if there are any contracted nodes that must be expanded again. Thus, we expand the supernode 7 to the original blossom (1, 0, 4, 2, 3) again (picture to the right). In addition, we have to reconstruct the augmenting path through the blossom correctly. Now that there are not any contracted nodes left we can invert the augmenting path.

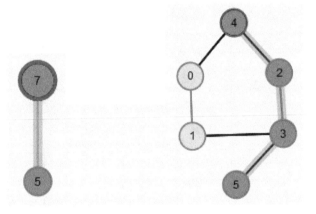

Working of Shrinking Method

We illustrate the idea behind the contraction of blossoms by having a look at the following example graph. The picture shows a snapshot of the algorithm: We have already constructed a layered tree with root 8 and now we are detecting the blossom (3,4,5,6,7) when exploring the edge between 5 and 6. We call the path from the root to the blossom (in this case 8 to 3) the stem and the intersecting node 3 the tip of the stem.

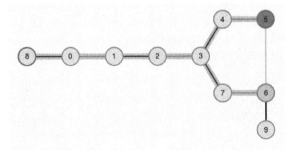

First note that the last edge of the stem must always be a matched edge (edge from 2 to 3 in the example). Then, for each node v contained in the blossom (except for the tip itself), there are two distinct paths from the tip to v. To reach node 6 from the tip, for instance, we could either traverse the blossom clockwise and choose the path (3,4,5,6) or we traverse it counter-clockwise and choose the path (3,7,6). One of the paths always ends with a matched edge, the other one with an unmatched edge. Thus, one of the two paths will make it possible to complete an augmenting path correctly later. At this point of the algorithm, however, we cannot make this decision because we do not know yet where the augmenting path (if there is any) will lead to. Thus, we postpone the decision of correctly traversing the blossom by shrinking the entire blossom to a supernode. When we find a free node, we expand the supernodes again and can reconstruct the augmenting path correctly. Have a look at the two examples above. In both graphs, we find the free node 9 and have to reconstruct the path through the blossom. The edge from 9 to the blossom is unmatched in both cases so we have to start the traversal of the blossom with a matched edge (between 6 and 7). Thus, in the first graph, we go clockwise until we reach the tip 3 and in the second graph we go counter-clockwise.

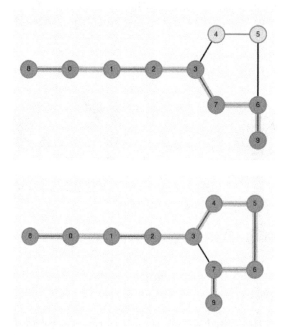

Boruvka's Algorithm

Boruvka's Algorithm is a way to find a minimum spanning tree — a spanning tree where the sum of edge weights is minimized. It was the first algorithm developed (in 1926) to find MSTs; Otakar Boruvka used it to find the most efficient routing for an electrical grid.

There are many ways to find minimum spanning trees. Boruvka's Algorithm is a greedy algorithm and is similar to Kruskal's algorithm and Prim's algorithm. It is basically a cross between the two algorithms. It is also known as Sollin's algorithm, especially in computing.

Boruvka's Algorithm Example

Find the minimum spanning tree for the following graph using Buruvka's Algorithm.

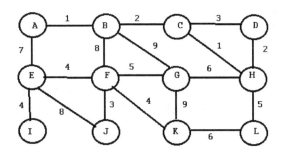

Step 1: Write out a list of components. For this graph, we have: A,B,C,D,E,F,G,H,I,J,K,L. This step is optional but helps you to keep track.

Step 2: Highlight the cheapest outgoing edge for each node in your list. For example, node A has outgoing edges with weights 1 and 7, so we'll highlight 1. Continue sequentially (for this list, go to B, then C...). Guidelines:

1. At this stage, only highlight one cheapest edge for each node.

2. For a tie (node E has two edges with a weight of 4), assign a lower weight to one of the edges. This is arbitrary, but must stay consistent throughout the process. For this example, we'll make the edge to the left the lowest weight.

3. Always highlight the cheapest edge, *even if it has been highlighted before*. Do not choose the edge with the next lowest weight. For practical purposes, this means you might not have to highlight anything for some nodes, if the cheapest weight has already been highlighted.

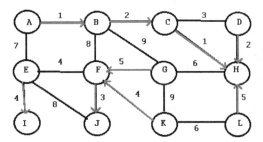

Step 3: Highlight the separate tree clusters. These are the sets of connected nodes, which we'll call *components*.

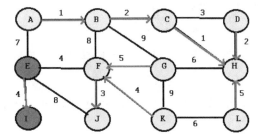

Step 4: Repeat the algorithm for each component (each differently colored set). This time, for each node, choose the cheapest edge outside of the component. For example, ABCDHL is one component (blue nodes). For node A, the cheapest edge outside the component is node 7 (because node 1 is connected inside the component). We're highlighting in blue for clarity: you can use whatever color you like.

Guidelines:

1. Make sure you are choosing the cheapest edge *outside* of the component. For this graph and this iteration, those edges are colored black.

2. As in the first iteration, skip highlighting an edge if it's already been highlighted this time around.

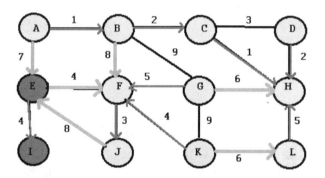

Step 5: If your nodes are all connected in a single component, you're done. If not, repeat step 4.

The following graph shows the final MST. We've remove any unused (black) edges.

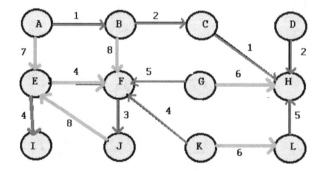

Bellman–Ford Algorithm

Bellman Ford algorithm helps us find the shortest path from a vertex to all other vertices of a weighted graph.

It is similar to Dijkstra's algorithm but it can work with graphs in which edges can have negative weights.

Reasons for having Edges with Negative Weights in Real Life

Negative weight edges might seem useless at first but they can explain a lot of phenomena like cashflow, heat released/absorbed in a chemical reaction etc.

For instance, if there are different ways to reach from one chemical A to another chemical B, each method will have sub-reactions involving both heat dissipation and absorption.

If we want to find the set of reactions where minimum energy is required, then we will need to be able to factor in the heat absorption as negative weights and heat dissipation as positive weights.

Reason for being Careful with Negative Weights

Negative weight edges can create negative weight cycles i.e. a cycle which will reduce the total path distance by coming back to the same point.

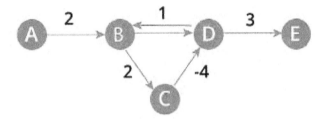

Shortest path algorithms like Dijkstra's Algorithm that aren't able to detect such a cycle can give an incorrect result because they can go through a negative weight cycle and reduce the path length.

Working of Bellman Ford's Algorithm

Bellman Ford algorithm works by overestimating the length of the path from the starting vertex to all other vertices. Then it iteratively relaxes those estimates by finding new paths that are shorter than the previously overestimated paths.

By doing this repeatedly for all vertices, we are able to guarantee that the end result is optimized.

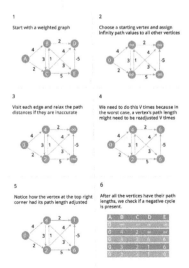

Bellman Ford Pseudocode

We need to maintain the path distance of every vertex. We can store that in an array of size v, where v is the number of vertices.

We also want to able to get the shortest path, not only know the length of the shortest path. For this, we map each vertex to the vertex that last updated its path length.

Once the algorithm is over, we can backtrack from the destination vertex to the source vertex to find the path.

```
function bellmanFord(G, S)

        for each vertex V in G

                        distance[V] <- infinite

                        previous[V] <- NULL

        distance[S] <- 0

        for each vertex V in G

                for each edge (U,V) in G

                        tempDistance <- distance[U] + edge_weight(U, V)

                        if tempDistance < distance[V]

                            distance[V] <- tempDistance

                            previous[V] <- U


        for each edge (U,V) in G

                If distance[U] + edge_weight(U, V) < distance[V}

                        Error: Negative Cycle Exists



        return distance[], previous[]
```

Bellman Ford vs Dijkstra

```
function bellmanFord(G, S)                          function dijkstra(G, S)
    for each vertex V in G                              for each vertex V in G
        distance[V] <- infinite                            distance[V] <- infinite
        previous[V] <- NULL                                previous[V] <- NULL
                                                           If V != S, add V to Priority Queue Q

    distance[S] <- 0                                    distance[S] <- 0

    for each vertex V in G                              while Q IS NOT EMPTY
                                                           U <- Extract MIN from Q
        for each edge (U,V) in G                           for each unvisited neighbour V of U
            tempDistance <- distance[U] + edge_weight(U, V)    tempDistance <- distance[U] + edge_weight(U, V)
            if tempDistance < distance[V]                      if tempDistance < distance[V]
                distance[V] <- tempDistance                        distance[V] <- tempDistance
                previous[V] <- U                                   previous[V] <- U

    for each edge (U,V) in G
        If distance[U] + edge_weight(U, V) < distance[V}
            Error: Negative Cycle Exists

    return distance[], previous[]                       return distance[], previous[]
```

Bellman Ford's algorithm and Dijkstra's algorithm are very similar in structure. While Dijkstra looks only to the immediate neighbours of a vertex, Bellman goes through each edge in every iteration.

Bellman Ford's Algorithm Code

The code for Bellman Ford's Algorithm in C is given below.

```c
#include <stdio.h>

#include <stdlib.h>


#define INFINITY 99999


//struct for the edges of the graph
struct Edge {
        int u;   //start vertex of the edge
        int v;   //end vertex of the edge
        int w;   //weight of the edge (u,v)
};


//Graph - it consists of edges
struct Graph {
        int V;   //total number of vertices in the graph
        int E;   //total number of edges in the graph
        struct Edge *edge;       //array of edges
};


void bellmanford(struct Graph *g, int source);
void display(int arr[], int size);


int main(void) {
        //create graph
        struct Graph *g = (struct Graph*)malloc(sizeof(struct Graph));
        g->V = 4;        //total vertices
```

```
        g->E = 5;          //total edges


        //array of edges for graph
        g->edge = (struct Edge*)malloc(g->E * sizeof(struct Edge));


        //------- adding the edges of the graph
        /*
                edge(u, v)

                where    u = start vertex of the edge (u,v)

                                v = end vertex of the edge (u,v)


                w is the weight of the edge (u,v)
        */


        //edge 0 --> 1
        g->edge[0].u = 0;

        g->edge[0].v = 1;

        g->edge[0].w = 5;


        //edge 0 --> 2
        g->edge[1].u = 0;

        g->edge[1].v = 2;

        g->edge[1].w = 4;


        //edge 1 --> 3
        g->edge[2].u = 1;

        g->edge[2].v = 3;

        g->edge[2].w = 3;


        //edge 2 --> 1
        g->edge[3].u = 2;
```

```
        g->edge[3].v = 1;

        g->edge[3].w = -6;


        //edge 3 --> 2

        g->edge[4].u = 3;

        g->edge[4].v = 2;

        g->edge[4].w = 2;


        bellmanford(g, 0);                        //0 is the source vertex


        return 0;

}


void bellmanford(struct Graph *g, int source) {

        //variables

        int i, j, u, v, w;


        //total vertex in the graph g

        int tV = g->V;


        //total edge in the graph g

        int tE = g->E;


        //distance array

        //size equal to the number of vertices of the graph g

        int d[tV];


        //predecessor array

        //size equal to the number of vertices of the graph g

        int p[tV];
```

```
//step 1: fill the distance array and predecessor array
for (i = 0; i < tV; i++) {
        d[i] = INFINITY;
        p[i] = 0;
}


//mark the source vertex
d[source] = 0;


//step 2: relax edges |V| - 1 times
for(i = 1; i <= tV-1; i++) {
        for(j = 0; j < tE; j++) {
                //get the edge data
                u = g->edge[j].u;
                v = g->edge[j].v;
                w = g->edge[j].w;

                if(d[u] .= INFINITY && d[v] > d[u] + w) {
                        d[v] = d[u] + w;
                        p[v] = u;
                }
        }
}


//step 3: detect negative cycle
//if value changes then we have a negative cycle in the graph
//and we cannot find the shortest distances
for(i = 0; i < tE; i++) {
        u = g->edge[i].u;
        v = g->edge[i].v;
        w = g->edge[i].w;
```

```
            if(d[u] .= INFINITY && d[v] > d[u] + w) {

                    printf("Negative weight cycle detected.\n");

                    return;

            }

    }


    //No negative weight cycle found.

    //print the distance and predecessor array

    printf("Distance array: ");

    display(d, tV);

    printf("Predecessor array: ");

    display(p, tV);

}


void display(int arr[], int size) {

    int i;

    for(i = 0; i < size; i ++) {

            printf("%d ", arr[i]);

    }

    printf("\n");

}
```

Dijkstra's Algorithm

Dijkstra's algorithm generates a SPT with given source as root.

We maintain two sets, one set contains vertices included in shortest path tree, other set includes vertices not yet included in shortest path tree. At every step of the algorithm, we find a vertex which is in the other set (set of not yet included) and has a minimum distance from the source.

Below are the detailed steps used in Dijkstra's algorithm to find the shortest path from a single source vertex to all other vertices in the given graph.

Algorithm

1) Create a set sptSet (shortest path tree set) that keeps track of vertices included in shortest path tree, i.e., whose minimum distance from source is calculated and finalized. Initially, this set is empty.

2) Assign a distance value to all vertices in the input graph. Initialize all distance values as IN-FINITE. Assign distance value as 0 for the source vertex so that it is picked first.

3) While sptSet doesn't include all vertices

a) Pick a vertex u which is not there in sptSet and has minimum distance value.

b) Include u to sptSet.

c) Update distance value of all adjacent vertices of u. To update the distance values, iterate through all adjacent vertices. For every adjacent vertex v, if sum of distance value of u (from source) and weight of edge u-v, is less than the distance value of v, then update the distance value of v.

Let us understand with the following example:

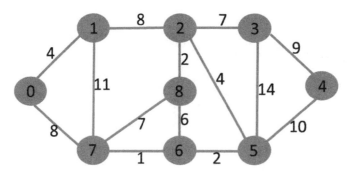

The set *sptSet* is initially empty and distances assigned to vertices are {0, INF, INF, INF, INF, INF, INF, INF} where INF indicates infinite. Now pick the vertex with minimum distance value. The vertex 0 is picked, include it in *sptSet*. So *sptSet* becomes {0}. After including 0 to *sptSet*, update distance values of its adjacent vertices. Adjacent vertices of 0 are 1 and 7. The distance values of 1 and 7 are updated as 4 and 8. Following sub graph shows vertices and their distance values, only the vertices with finite distance values are shown. The vertices included in SPT are shown in green color.

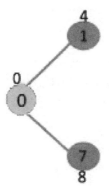

Pick the vertex with minimum distance value and not already included in SPT (not in sptSET). The vertex 1 is picked and added to sptSet. So sptSet now becomes {0, 1}. Update the distance values of adjacent vertices of 1. The distance value of vertex 2 becomes 12.

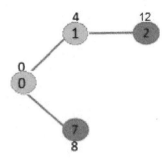

Pick the vertex with minimum distance value and not already included in SPT (not in sptSET). Vertex 7 is picked. So sptSet now becomes {0, 1, 7}. Update the distance values of adjacent vertices of 7. The distance value of vertex 6 and 8 becomes finite (15 and 9 respectively).

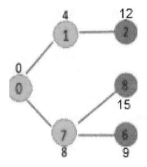

Pick the vertex with minimum distance value and not already included in SPT (not in sptSET). Vertex 6 is picked. So sptSet now becomes {0, 1, 7, 6}. Update the distance values of adjacent vertices of 6. The distance value of vertex 5 and 8 are updated.

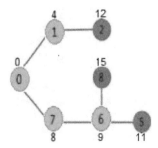

We repeat the above steps until *sptSet* doesn't include all vertices of given graph. Finally, we get the following Shortest Path Tree (SPT).

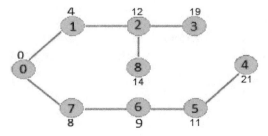

Implementation of the above algorithm

We use a boolean array sptSet[] to represent the set of vertices included in SPT. If a value sptSet[v] is true, then vertex v is included in SPT, otherwise not. Array dist[] is used to store shortest distance values of all vertices.

Johnson's Algorithm

Using Johnson's algorithm, we can find all pair shortest paths in $O(V^2\log V + VE)$ time. Johnson's algorithm uses both Dijkstra and Bellman-Ford as subroutines.

If we apply Dijkstra's Single Source shortest path algorithm for every vertex, considering every vertex as source, we can find all pair shortest paths in O(V*VLogV) time. So using Dijkstra's single source shortest path seems to be a better option than Floyd Warshell, but the problem with Dijkstra's algorithm is, it doesn't work for negative weight edge. The idea of Johnson's algorithm is to re-weight all edges and make them all positive, then apply Dijkstra's algorithm for every vertex.

Transforming a given Graph to a Graph with all Non-negative Weight Edges

One may think of a simple approach of finding the minimum weight edge and adding this weight to all edges. Unfortunately, this doesn't work as there may be different number of edges in different paths. If there are multiple paths from a vertex u to v, then all paths must be increased by same amount, so that the shortest path remains the shortest in the transformed graph. The idea of Johnson's algorithm is to assign a weight to every vertex. Let the weight assigned to vertex u be h[u]. We reweight edges using vertex weights. For example, for an edge (u, v) of weight w(u, v), the new weight becomes w(u, v) + h[u] – h[v]. The great thing about this reweighting is, all set of paths between any two vertices are increased by same amount and all negative weights become non-negative. Consider any path between two vertices s and t, weight of every path is increased by h[s] – h[t], all h[] values of vertices on path from s to t cancel each other.

How do we calculate h[] values? Bellman-Ford algorithm is used for this purpose. Following is the complete algorithm. A new vertex is added to the graph and connected to all existing vertices. The shortest distance values from new vertex to all existing vertices are h[] values.

Algorithm

1) Let the given graph be G. Add a new vertex s to the graph, add edges from new vertex to all vertices of G. Let the modified graph be G'.

2) Run Bellman-Ford algorithm on G' with s as source. Let the distances calculated by Bellman-Ford be h[0], h[1], .. h[V-1]. If we find a negative weight cycle, then return. Note that the negative weight cycle cannot be created by new vertex s as there is no edge to s. All edges are from s.

3) Reweight the edges of original graph. For each edge (u, v), assign the new weight as "original weight + h[u] – h[v]".

4) Remove the added vertex s and run Dijkstra's algorithm for every vertex.

How does the transformation ensure nonnegative weight edges

The following property is always true about h[] values as they are shortest distances.

```
h[v] <= h[u] + w(u, v)
```

The property simply means, shortest distance from s to v must be smaller than or equal to shortest distance from s to u plus weight of edge (u, v). The new weights are w(u, v) + h[u] - h[v]. The value of the new weights must be greater than or equal to zero because of the inequality "h[v] <= h[u] + w(u, v)". Example:

Let us consider the following graph.

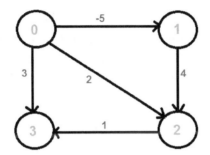

We add a source s and add edges from s to all vertices of the original graph. In the following figure s is 4.

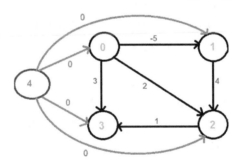

We calculate the shortest distances from 4 to all other vertices using Bellman-Ford algorithm. The shortest distances from 4 to 0, 1, 2 and 3 are 0, -5, -1 and 0 respectively, i.e., h[] = {0, -5, -1, 0}. Once we get these distances, we remove the source vertex 4 and reweight the edges using following formula. w(u, v) = w(u, v) + h[u] - h[v].

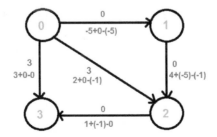

Distances from 4 to 0, 1, 2 and 3 are 0, -5, -1 and 0 respectievely.

Since all weights are positive now, we can run Dijkstra's shortest path algorithm for every vertex as source.

Time Complexity: The main steps in algorithm are Bellman Ford Algorithm called once and Dijkstra called V times. Time complexity of Bellman Ford is O(VE) and time complexity of Dijkstra is O(VLogV). So overall time complexity is O(V²log V + VE).

The time complexity of Johnson's algorithm becomes same as Floyd Warshell when the graphs is complete (For a complete graph E = O(V²). But for sparse graphs, the algorithm performs much better than Floyd Warshell.

Floyd–Warshall Algorithm

Floyd-Warshall algorithm is a procedure, which is used to find the shortest (longest) paths among all pairs of nodes in a graph, which does not contain any cycles of negative length. The main advantage of Floyd-Warshall algorithm is its simplicity.

Description

Floyd-Warshall algorithm uses a matrix of lengths D_0 as its input. If there is an edge between nodes i and j, than the matrix D_0 contains its length at the corresponding coordinates. The diagonal of the matrix contains only zeros. If there is no edge between edges i and j, than the position (i, j) contains positive infinity. In other words, the matrix represents lengths of all paths between nodes that does not contain any intermediate node.

In each iteration of Floyd-Warshall algorithm is this matrix recalculated, so it contains lengths of paths among all pairs of nodes using gradually enlarging set of intermediate nodes. The matrix D_1, which is created by the first iteration of the procedure, contains paths among all nodes using exactly one (predefined) intermediate node. D_2 contains lengths using two predefined intermediate nodes. Finally the matrix D_n uses n intermediate nodes.

This transformation can be described using the following recurrent formula:

$$D_{ij}^n = \min\left(D_{ij}^{n-1}, D_{ik}^{n-1} + D_{kj}^{n-1}\right)$$

Because this transformation never rewrites elements, which are to be used to calculate the new matrix, we can use the same matrix for both D^i and D^{i+1}.

Code

- Pseudocode

- Java

```
1.procedure [array] FloydWarshall(D, P)
```

```
2.for k in 1 to n do

3.for i in 1 to n do

4.for j in 1 to n do

5.if D[i][j] > D[i][k] + D[k][j] then

6.D[i][j] = D[i][k] + D[k][j]

7.P[i][j] = P[k][j]

8.return P

01./**

02.* Floyd-Warshall algorithm. Finds all shortest paths among all pairs of nodes

03.* @param d matrix of distances (Integer.MAX_VALUE represents positive infin-
ity)

04.* @return matrix of predecessors

05.*/

06.public static int[][] floydWarshall(int[][] d) {

07.int[][] p = constructInitialMatixOfPredecessors(d);

08.for (int k = 0; k < d.length; k++) {

09.for (int i = 0; i < d.length; i++) {

10.for (int j = 0; j < d.length; j++) {

11.if (d[i][k] == Integer.MAX_VALUE || d[k][j] == Integer.MAX_VALUE) {

12.continue;

13.}

14.

15.if (d[i][j] > d[i][k] + d[k][j]) {

16.d[i][j] = d[i][k] + d[k][j];

17.p[i][j] = p[k][j];

18.}

19.

20.}

21.}

22.}

23.return p;
```

```
24.}
25.
26./**
27.* Constructs matrix P0
28.* @param d matrix of lengths
29.* @return P0
30.*/
31.private static int[][] constructInitialMatixOfPredecessors(int[][] d) {
32.int[][] p = new int[d.length][d.length];
33.for (int i = 0; i < d.length; i++) {
34.for (int j = 0; j < d.length; j++) {
35.if (d[i][j] .= 0 && d[i][j] .= Integer.MAX_VALUE) {
36.p[i][j] = i;
37.} else {
38.p[i][j] = -1;
39.}
40.}
41.}
42.return p;
43.}
```

Asymptotic Complexity

The algorithm consists of three loops over all nodes, and the most inner loop contains only operations of a constant complexity. Hence the asymptotic complexity of the whole Floyd-Warshall algorithm is $O(|N|^3)$, where $|N|$ is number of nodes of the graph.

Example

$$D_0 = \begin{pmatrix} 0 & 5 & \infty & 2 & \infty \\ \infty & 0 & 2 & \infty & \infty \\ 3 & \infty & 0 & \infty & 7 \\ \infty & \infty & 4 & 0 & 1 \\ 1 & 3 & \infty & \infty & 0 \end{pmatrix} \quad D_1 = \begin{pmatrix} 0 & 5 & \infty & 2 & \infty \\ \infty & 0 & 2 & \infty & \infty \\ 3 & 8 & 0 & 5 & 7 \\ \infty & \infty & 4 & 0 & 1 \\ 1 & 3 & \infty & 3 & 0 \end{pmatrix} \quad \begin{pmatrix} 0 & 5 & 7 & 2 & \infty \\ \infty & 0 & 2 & \infty & \infty \\ 3 & 8 & 0 & 5 & 7 \\ \infty & \infty & 4 & 0 & 1 \\ 1 & 3 & 5 & 3 & 0 \end{pmatrix}$$

$$D_3 = \begin{pmatrix} 0 & 5 & 7 & 2 & 14 \\ 5 & 0 & 2 & 7 & 9 \\ 3 & 8 & 0 & 5 & 7 \\ 7 & 12 & 4 & 0 & 1 \\ 1 & 3 & 5 & 3 & 0 \end{pmatrix} \quad D_4 = \begin{pmatrix} 0 & 5 & 6 & 2 & 3 \\ 5 & 0 & 2 & 7 & 8 \\ 3 & 8 & 0 & 5 & 6 \\ 7 & 12 & 4 & 0 & 1 \\ 1 & 3 & 5 & 3 & 0 \end{pmatrix} \quad D_5 = \begin{pmatrix} 0 & 5 & 6 & 2 & 3 \\ 5 & 0 & 2 & 7 & 8 \\ 3 & 8 & 0 & 5 & 6 \\ 2 & 4 & 4 & 0 & 1 \\ 1 & 3 & 5 & 3 & 0 \end{pmatrix}$$

Matrix of Predecessors

In order to return shortest (longest) paths among all pairs of nodes, we construct during transformations of matrix D_k also output matrix P (matrix of predecessors). The matrix can be read as follows: if we want to reconstruct the (shortest) path between nodes i and i, than we look at the element at corresponding coordinates. If its value is 0, than there is no path between these nodes, otherwise the value of the element denotes predecessor of j on the path from i to i. So we repeat this procedure, while the preceding node is not equal to i.

$$P_{ij}^{(0)} = \begin{cases} 0 & \text{if } i = j \text{ or } D_{ij} = \infty \\ i & \text{in all other cases} \end{cases}$$

$$P_{ij}^{(n)} = \begin{cases} P_{ij}^{(n-1)} & \text{if } D_{ij}^{(n-1)} \leq D_{ik}^{(n-1)} + D_{kj}^{(n-1)} \\ P_{kj}^{(n-1)} & \text{if } D_{ij}^{(n-1)} \leq D_{ik}^{(n-1)} + D_{kj}^{(n-1)} \end{cases}$$

Code

Pseudocode

```
1.function getPath(P, i, j)

2.if i == j then

3.write(i)

4.else if P[i][j] = 0 then

5.write("Path does not exist")

6.else

7.getPath(P, i, P[i][j])

8.write(j)
```

Example

$$P_0 = \begin{pmatrix} 0 & 1 & 0 & 1 & 0 \\ 0 & 0 & 2 & 0 & 0 \\ 3 & 0 & 0 & 0 & 3 \\ 0 & 0 & 4 & 0 & 4 \\ 5 & 5 & 0 & 0 & 0 \end{pmatrix} \quad P_1 = \begin{pmatrix} 0 & 1 & 0 & 1 & 0 \\ 0 & 0 & 2 & 0 & 0 \\ 3 & 1 & 0 & 1 & 3 \\ 0 & 0 & 4 & 0 & 4 \\ 5 & 5 & 0 & 1 & 0 \end{pmatrix} \quad P_2 = \begin{pmatrix} 0 & 1 & 2 & 1 & 0 \\ 0 & 0 & 2 & 0 & 0 \\ 3 & 1 & 0 & 1 & 3 \\ 0 & 0 & 4 & 0 & 4 \\ 5 & 5 & 2 & 1 & 0 \end{pmatrix}$$

$$P_3 = \begin{pmatrix} 0 & 1 & 2 & 1 & 3 \\ 3 & 0 & 2 & 1 & 3 \\ 3 & 1 & 0 & 1 & 3 \\ 3 & 1 & 4 & 0 & 4 \\ 5 & 5 & 2 & 1 & 0 \end{pmatrix} \quad P_4 = \begin{pmatrix} 0 & 1 & 4 & 1 & 4 \\ 3 & 0 & 2 & 1 & 4 \\ 3 & 1 & 0 & 1 & 4 \\ 3 & 1 & 4 & 0 & 4 \\ 5 & 5 & 2 & 1 & 0 \end{pmatrix} \quad P_5 = \begin{pmatrix} 0 & 1 & 4 & 1 & 4 \\ 3 & 0 & 2 & 1 & 4 \\ 3 & 1 & 0 & 1 & 4 \\ 5 & 5 & 4 & 0 & 4 \\ 5 & 5 & 2 & 1 & 0 \end{pmatrix}$$

Detection of Cycles of Non-negative Length

Floyd-Warshall algorithm can be easily modified to detect cycles. If we fill negative infinity value at the diagonal of the matrix and run the algorithm, than the matrix of predecessors will contain also all cycles in the graph (the diagonal will not contain only zeros, if there is a cycle in the graph).

References

- Graph-algorithm, parallel-algorithm: tutorialspoint.com, Retrieved 11 May 2018

- Boruvkas-algorithm: statisticshowto.com, Retrieved 18 July 2018

- Bellman-ford-algorithm: programiz.com, Retrieved 30 June 2018

- Dijkstras-shortest-path-algorithm-greedy-algo-7: geeksforgeeks.org, Retrieved 17 May 2018

- Floyd-Warshall-algorithm-45708: programming-algorithms.net, Retrieved 27 March 2018

Parallel and Distributed Algorithms

Parallel algorithm is an algorithm that can be executed one piece at a time on different processing devices and thereafter combined to produce the desired result. A distributed algorithm is a type of parallel algorithm that is designed to operate on hardware that is constructed from interconnected processors. All the diverse aspects of parallel and distributed algorithms, such as algorithm structures, algorithm models, matrix-matrix multiplication, etc. have been carefully analyzed in this chapter.

Parallel Algorithm

Algorithms in which several operations may be executed simultaneously are referred to as parallel algorithms. A parallel algorithm for a parallel computer can be defined as set of processes that may be executed simultaneously and may communicate with each other in order to solve a given problem. The term process may be defined as a part of a program that can be run on a processor.

In designing a parallel algorithm, it is important to determine the efficiency of its use of available resources. Once a parallel algorithm has been developed, a measurement should be used for evaluating its performance (or efficiency) on a parallel machine. A common measurement often used is run time. Run time (also referred to as elapsed time or completion time) refers to the time the algorithm takes on a parallel machine in order to solve a problem. More specifically, it is the elapsed time between the start of the first processor (or the first set of processors) and the termination of the last processor (or the last set of processors).

Various approaches may be used to design a parallel algorithm for a given problem. One approach is to attempt to convert a sequential algorithm to a parallel algorithm. If a sequential algorithm already exists for the problem, then inherent parallelism in that algorithm may be recognized and implemented in parallel. Inherent parallelism is parallelism that occurs naturally within an algorithm, not as a result of any special effort on the part of the algorithm or machine designer. It should be noted that exploiting inherent parallelism in a sequential algorithm might not always lead to an efficient parallel algorithm. It turns out that for certain types of problems a better approach is to adopt a parallel algorithm that solves a problem similar to, but different from, the given problem. Another approach is to design a totally new parallel algorithm that is more efficient than the existing one.

In either case, in the development of a parallel algorithm, a few important considerations cannot be ignored. The cost of communication between processes has to be considered, for instance. Communication aspects are important since, for a given algorithm, communication time may be greater than the actual computation time. Another consideration is that the algorithm should take into account the architecture of the computer on which it is to be executed. This is particularly important, since the same algorithm may be very efficient on one architecture and very inefficient on another architecture.

Parallel Models of Computation

Developing a standard parallel model of computation for analyzing algorithms has proven diffi-cult because different parallel computers tend to vary significantly in their organizations. In spite of this difficulty, useful parallel models have emerged, along with a deeper understanding of the modeling process. Here we describe three important principles that have emerged.

1. Work-efficiency. In designing a parallel algorithm, it is more important to make it efficient than to make it asymptotically fast. The efficiency of an algorithm is determined by the total number of operations, or *work* that it performs. On a sequential machine, an algorithm's work is the same as its time. On a parallel machine, the work is simply the processor-time product. Hence, an algorithm that takes time t on a P-processor machine performs work $W = Pt$. In either case, the work roughly captures the actual cost to perform the computation, assuming that the cost of a parallel machine is proportional to the number of processors in the machine. We call an algorithm *work-efficient* (or just efficient) if it performs the same amount of work, to within a constant factor, as the fastest known sequential algorithm. For example, a parallel algorithm that sorts n keys in $O(\sqrt{n} \log n)$ time using $\sqrt{n}$ processors is efficient since the work, $O(n \log n)$, is as good as any (comparison-based) sequential algorithm. However, a sorting algorithm that runs in $O(\log n)$ time using n^2 processors is not efficient. The first algorithm is better than the second - even though it is slower - because it's work, or cost, is smaller. Of course, given two parallel algorithms that perform the same amount of work, the faster one is generally better.

2. Emulation. The notion of work-efficiency leads to another important observation: a model can be useful without mimicking any real or even realizable machine. Instead, it suffices that any algorithm that runs efficiently in the model can be translated into an algorithm that runs efficiently on real machines. As an example, consider the widely-used parallel random-access machine (PRAM) model. In the PRAM model, a set of processors share a single memory system. In a single unit of time, each processor can perform an arithmetic, logical, or memory access operation. This model has often been criticized as unrealistically powerful, primarily because no shared memory system can perform memory accesses as fast as processors can execute local arithmetic and logical operations. The important observation, however, is that for a model to be useful we only require that algorithms that are efficient in the model can be mapped to algorithms that are efficient on realistic machines, not that the model is realistic. In particular, any algorithm that runs efficiently in a P-processor PRAM model can be translated into an algorithm that runs efficiently on a P/L -processor machine with a latency L memory system, a much more realistic machine. In the translated algorithm, each of the P/L processors emulates L PRAM processors. The latency is "hidden" because a processor has useful work to perform while waiting for a memory access to complete. Although the translated algorithm is a factor of L slower than the PRAM algorithm, it uses a factor of L fewer processors, and hence is equally efficient.

3. Modeling Communication. To get the best performance out of a parallel machine, it is often helpful to model the communication capabilities of the machine, such as its latency, explic-itly. The most important measure is the communication bandwidth. The bandwidth avail-able to a processor is the maximum rate at which it can communicate with other processors

or the memory system. Because it is more difficult to hide insufficient bandwidth than large latency, some measure of bandwidth is often included in parallel models. Sometimes the specific topology of the communication network is modeled as well. Although including this level of detail in the model often complicates the design of parallel algorithms, it's essential for designing the low-level communication primitives for the machine. In addition to modeling basic communication primitives, other operations supported by hardware, including synchronization and concurrent memory accesses, are often modeled, as well as operations that mix computation and communication, such as fetch-and-add and scans. A final consideration is whether the machine supports shared memory, or whether all communication relies on passing messages between the processors.

Algorithmic Techniques

A major advance in parallel algorithms has been the identification of fundamental algorithmic techniques. Some of these techniques are also used by sequential algorithms, but play a more prominent role in parallel algorithms, while others are unique to parallelism. Here we list some of these techniques with a brief description of each.

1. Divide-and-Conquer: Divide-and-conquer is a natural paradigm for parallel algorithms. After dividing a problem into two or more subproblems, the subproblems can be solved in parallel. Typically the subproblems are solved recursively and thus the next divide step yields even more subproblems to be solved in parallel. For example, suppose we want to compute the convex-hull of a set of n points in the plane (i.e., compute the smallest convex polygon that encloses all of the points). This can be implemented by splitting the points into the leftmost $n/2$ and right most $n/2$, recursively finding the convex hull of each set in parallel, and then merging the two resulting hulls. Divide-and-conquer has proven to be one of the most powerful techniques for solving problems in parallel with applications ranging from linear systems to computer graphics and from factoring large numbers to n-body simulations.

2. Randomization: The use of random numbers is ubiquitous in parallel algorithms. Intuitively, randomness is helpful because it allows processors to make local decisions which, with high probability, add up to good global decisions. For example, suppose we want to sort a collection of integer keys. This can be accomplished by partitioning the keys into buckets then sorting within each bucket. For this to work well, the buckets must represent non-overlapping intervals of integer values, and contain approximately the same number of keys. Randomization is used to determine the boundaries of the intervals. First each processor selects a random sample of its keys. Next all of the selected keys are sorted together. Finally these keys are used as the boundaries. Such random sampling is also used in many parallel computational geometry, graph, and string matching algorithms. Other uses of randomization include symmetry breaking, load balancing, and routing algorithms.

3. Parallel Pointer Manipulations: Many of the traditional sequential techniques for manipulating lists, trees, and graphs do not translate easily into parallel techniques. For example techniques such as traversing the elements of a linked list, visiting the nodes of a tree in post order, or performing a depth-first traversal of a graph appear to be inherently

sequential. Fortunately, each of these techniques can be replaced by efficient parallel techniques. These parallel techniques include pointer jumping, the Euler-tour technique, ear decomposition, and graph contraction. For example, one way to label each node of an n-node list (or tree) with the label of the last node (or root) is to use pointer jumping. In each pointer-jumping step each node in parallel replaces its pointer with that of its successor (or parent). After at most $\log n$ steps, every node points to the same node, the end of the list (or root of the tree).

4. Others: Other useful techniques include finding small graph separators for partitioning data among processors to reduce communication, hashing for balancing load across processors and mapping addresses to memory, and iterative techniques as a replacement for direct methods for solving linear systems.

These techniques have led to efficient parallel algorithms in most problem areas for which efficient sequential algorithms are known. In fact, some of the techniques originally developed for parallel algorithms have led to improvements in sequential algorithms.

Analysis of Parallel Algorithms

Analysis of an algorithm helps us determine whether the algorithm is useful or not. Generally, an algorithm is analyzed based on its execution time (Time Complexity) and the amount of space (Space Complexity) it requires.

Since we have sophisticated memory devices available at reasonable cost, storage space is no longer an issue. Hence, space complexity is not given so much of importance.

Parallel algorithms are designed to improve the computation speed of a computer. For analyzing a Parallel Algorithm, we normally consider the following parameters –

- Time complexity (Execution Time),
- Total number of processors used, and
- Total cost.

Time Complexity

The main reason behind developing parallel algorithms was to reduce the computation time of an algorithm. Thus, evaluating the execution time of an algorithm is extremely important in analyzing its efficiency.

Execution time is measured on the basis of the time taken by the algorithm to solve a problem. The total execution time is calculated from the moment when the algorithm starts executing to the moment it stops. If all the processors do not start or end execution at the same time, then the total execution time of the algorithm is the moment when the first processor started its execution to the moment when the last processor stops its execution.

Time complexity of an algorithm can be classified into three categories–

- Worst-case complexity: When the amount of time required by an algorithm for a given input is maximum.

- Average-case complexity: When the amount of time required by an algorithm for a given input is average.

- Best-case complexity: When the amount of time required by an algorithm for a given input is minimum.

Asymptotic Analysis

The complexity or efficiency of an algorithm is the number of steps executed by the algorithm to get the desired output. Asymptotic analysis is done to calculate the complexity of an algorithm in its theoretical analysis. In asymptotic analysis, a large length of input is used to calculate the complexity function of the algorithm.

Asymptotic is a condition where a line tends to meet a curve, but they do not intersect. Here the line and the curve is asymptotic to each other.

Asymptotic notation is the easiest way to describe the fastest and slowest possible execution time for an algorithm using high bounds and low bounds on speed. For this, we use the following notations –

- Big O notation

- Omega notation

- Theta notation

Big O Notation

In mathematics, Big O notation is used to represent the asymptotic characteristics of functions. It represents the behavior of a function for large inputs in a simple and accurate method. It is a method of representing the upper bound of an algorithm's execution time. It represents the longest amount of time that the algorithm could take to complete its execution. The function –

$f(n) = O(g(n))$

if there exists positive constants c and n_0 such that $f(n) \leq c * g(n)$ for all n where $n \geq n_0$.

Omega Notation

Omega notation is a method of representing the lower bound of an algorithm's execution time. The function –

$f(n) = \Omega(g(n))$

if there exists positive constants c and n_0 such that $f(n) \geq c * g(n)$ for all n where $n \geq n_0$.

Theta Notation

Theta notation is a method of representing both the lower bound and the upper bound of an algorithm's execution time. The function –

$$f(n) = \theta(g(n))$$

if there exists positive constants c_1, c_2, and n_0 such that $c1 * g(n) \leq f(n) \leq c2 * g(n)$ for all n where $n \geq n_0$.

Speedup of an Algorithm

The performance of a parallel algorithm is determined by calculating its speedup. Speedup is defined as the ratio of the worst-case execution time of the fastest known sequential algorithm for a particular problem to the worst-case execution time of the parallel algorithm.

$$speedup = \frac{\text{Worst case execution time of the fastest known sequential for a particular problem}}{\text{Worst case execution time of the parallel algorithm}}$$

Number of Processors Used

The number of processors used is an important factor in analyzing the efficiency of a parallel algorithm. The cost to buy, maintain, and run the computers are calculated. Larger the number of processors used by an algorithm to solve a problem, more costly becomes the obtained result.

Total Cost

Total cost of a parallel algorithm is the product of time complexity and the number of processors used in that particular algorithm.

Total Cost = Time complexity × Number of processors used

Therefore, the efficiency of a parallel algorithm is –

$$Efficiency = \frac{\text{Worst case execution time of sequential algorithm}}{\text{Worst case execution time of the parallel algorithm}}$$

Algorithm Structures

A parallel algorithm for parallel computers can be defined as a collection of concurrent processes operating simultaneously to solve a given problem. These algorithms can be divided into three categories: synchronous, asynchronous, and pipeline structures.

Synchronous Structure

In this category of algorithms, two or more processes are linked by a common execution point used for synchronization purposes. A process will come to a point in its execution where it must wait for other (one or more) processes to reach a certain point. After processes have reached the synchronization point, they can continue their execution. This leads to the fact that all processes that have to synchronize at a given point in their execution must wait for the slowest one. This waiting period is the main drawback for this type of algorithm. Synchronous algorithms are also referred to as *partitioning algorithms.*

Large-scale numerical problems (such as those solving large systems of equations) expose an opportunity for developing synchronous algorithms. Often, techniques used for these problems involve a series of iterations on large arrays. Each iteration uses the partial result produced from the previous iteration and makes a step of progress toward the final solution. The computation of each iteration can be parallelized by letting many processes work on different parts of the data array. However, after each iteration, processes should be synchronized because the partial result produced by one process is to be used by other processes on the next iteration.

Synchronous parallel algorithms can be implemented on both shared-memory models and message-passing models. When synchronous algorithms are implemented on a message-passing model, communication between processes is achieved *explicitly* using some kind of message-passing mechanism. When implemented on a shared-memory model, depending on the type of problem to be solved, two kinds of communication strategies may be used. Processes may communicate *explicitly* using message passing or *implicitly* by referring to certain parts of memory.

Consider the following computation on four vectors A, B, C, and D using two processors.

```
for (i=1; i<=10; i++){

    Z[i] = (A[i]*B[i]) + (C[i]/D[i]);

}
```

The parallel algorithm used for this computation is straightforward and consists of two processes, process $P1$ and $P2$. For each index i (for i=1 to 10), $P1$ evaluates $x = A[i] * B[i]$ and process $P2$ evaluates two statements, $y = C[i] / D[i]$ and $Z[i] = x + y$.

When the processes communicate explicitly, then, for each index i, process $P1$ evaluates x and sends a message packet consisting of the value of x to process $P2$. Process $P2$ in turn evaluates y and, after it receives the message, evaluates $Z[i]$.

When the processes communicate implicitly, no message-passing is required. Instead, process $P2$ evaluates y and checks if process $P1$ has evaluated x. If yes, it picks the value of x from memory and proceeds to evaluate $Z[i]$. Otherwise, it waits until $P1$ evaluates x. When $P2$ finishes computation of $Z[i]$, it will start the computation of y for the next index, i+1. At the same time, $P1$ starts the computation of x for the next index. This process continues until all the indexes are processed.

The following code gives the main steps of the preceding algorithm when the processes communicate implicitly. In the code, the process $P1$ is denoted as the slave process and the process $P2$ is denoted as master process.

```
struct global_memory
```

```
        {                               -- creates the following variables as shared variables  shared
        int next_index; .

        shared int A[10],B[10],C[10],D[10],Z[10]; .

        shared int x;

        shared char turn [6];

        }

        main()

        {
int y; next_

index = 1;

turn = 'slave';

CREATE(slave)          -- create a process, called slave.

                       -- This process starts execution at the slave routine

while ( next_index <= 10 ) {

        y = C[next_index] / D[next_index];

        while (turn = = 'slave') NOP; Z[next_index] = x + y;

        next_index = next_index + 1;

        turn = 'slave';

        }

        PRINT_RESULT


        }

        slave()

        {
while (next_index <= 10) {

        while (turn = = 'master') NOP;

        x = A[next_index] * B[next_index]; turn = 'master';

                }

        }
```

The vectors A, B, C, D, and Z are in global shared-memory and are accessible to both processes. Once the main process, called the master process, has allocated shared memory, it executes the CREATE macro.

Execution of CREATE causes a new process to be created. The created process, called the slave process, starts execution at the slave routine, which is specified as an argument in the CREATE statement.

Asynchronous Structure

Asynchronous parallel algorithms are characterized by letting the processes work with the most recently available data. These kinds of algorithms can be implemented on both shared-memory models and message-passing models. In the shared-memory model, there is a set of global variables accessible to all processes. Whenever a process completes a stage of its program, it reads some global variables. Based on the values of these variables and the results obtained from the last stage, the process activates its next stage and updates some of the global variables.

When asynchronous algorithms are implemented on a message-passing model, a process reads some input messages after completing a stage of its program. Based on these messages and the results obtained from the last stage, the process starts its next stage and sends messages to other processes.

Thus an asynchronous algorithm continues or terminates its process according to values in some global variables (or some messages) and does not wait for an input set as a synchronous algorithm does. That is, in an asynchronous algorithm, synchronizations are not needed for ensuring that certain input is available for processes at various times. Asynchronous algorithms are also referred to as *relaxed algorithms* due to their less restrictive synchronization constraints.

As an example, consider the computation of the four vectors that have been described previously. Using two processes to evaluate, we have:

$$Z[i]=(A[i]*B[i])+(C[i]/D[i]) \text{ for } i=1 \text{ to } 10$$

An asynchronous algorithm can be created by letting each process compute above expression for a specific i. At any time, each process requests an index. Once it obtains a valid subscript, say i, it evaluates: $Z[i]=(A[i]*B[i])+(C[i]/D[i])$ and then claims another subscript. That is, process P_1 may evaluate $Z[1]$ while process P_2 evaluates $Z[2]$. This action continues until the processes exhaust all the subscripts in the range 1 to 10.

The following code gives the main steps of a parallel program for the preceding algorithm.

```
struct global_memory

    {

    shared int next_index;

    shared int A[10],B[10],C[10],D[10],Z[10];
```

```
        }
        main()
        {
                CREATE(slave)              -- create a process, called slave.

                                           -- This process starts execution at the slave routine
task();
WAIT_FOR_END            -- wait for slave to be terminated PRINT_RESULT
        }
        slave()
        {


task();

        }
        task()
  {
                int i; GET_NEXT_INDEX(i);
                while (i>0) {
                     Z[i] = (A[i] * B[i]) + (C[i] / D[i]); GET_NEXT_INDEX(i);
                }
        }
```

The vectors A, B, C, D, and Z are in global shared-memory and are accessible to both processes. Once the master process has allocated shared memory, it creates a slave process. In the slave routine, the slave process simply calls *task*. The master process also calls task immediately after creating the slave. In the task routine, each process executes the macro GET_NEXT_INDEX(i). The macro GET_NEXT_INDEX is a monitor operation, that is, at any time only one process is allowed to execute and modify some statements and the variables of this macro.

Execution of GET_NEXT_INDEX returns in i the next available subscript (in the range 1 to 10) while valid subscripts exist; otherwise, it returns -1 in i. The macro GET_NEXT_INDEX uses the shared variable next_index to keep the next available subscript. When a process obtains a valid subscript, it evaluates $Z[i]$ and again calls GET_NEXT_INDEX to claim another subscript. This process continues until all the subscripts in the range 1 to 10 are claimed. If the slave process receives -1 in i, it dies by returning from *task* to *slave* and then exiting from *slave*. If the master process receives -1 in i, it returns back to the main routine and executes the macro WAIT_FOR_END. This macro causes the master process to wait until the slave process has terminated. This ensures that all the subscripts have been processed.

In comparison to synchronous algorithms, asynchronous algorithms require less access to shared variables and as a result tend to reduce memory contention problems. Memory contention occurs when different processes access the same memory module within a short time interval. When a large number of processes accesses a set of shared variables for the purpose of synchronization or communication, a severe memory contention may occur. These shared variables, sometimes called memory *hot spots*, may cause a large number of memory accesses to occur. The memory accesses may then create congestion on the interconnection network between processors and memory modules. The congestion will increase the access time to memory modules and, as a result, cause performance degradation. Therefore, it is important to reduce memory hot spots. This can be achieved in asynchronous algorithms by distributing data in a proper way among the memory modules.

In general, asynchronous algorithms are more efficient than synchronous for the following four reasons.

1. Processes never wait on other processes for input. This often results in decreasing run time.

2. The result of the processes that are run faster may be used to abort the slower processes, which are doing useless computations.

3. More reliable.

4. Less memory contention problems, in particular when the algorithm is based on the data partitioning approach.

However, asynchronous algorithms have the drawback that their analysis is more difficult than synchronous algorithms. At times, due to the dynamic way in which asynchronous processes execute and communicate, analysis can even be impossible.

Pipeline Structure

In algorithms using a pipeline structure, processes are ordered and data are moved from one process to the next as though through a pipeline. Computation proceeds in steps as on an assembly line. At each step, each process receives its input from some other process, computes a result based on the input, and then passes the result to some neighboring processes.

This type of processing is also referred to as *macro pipelining* and is useful when the algorithm can be decomposed into a finite set of processes with relationships as defined in the previous paragraph.

In a pipeline structure, the communication of data between processes can be synchronous or asynchronous. In a synchronous design, a global synchronizing mechanism, such as a clock, is used. When the clock pulses, each process starts the computation of its next step.

In an asynchronized design, the processes synchronize only with some of their neighbors using some local mechanism, such as message passing. Thus, in this type of design, the total computation requires less synchronization overhead than a synchronized design.

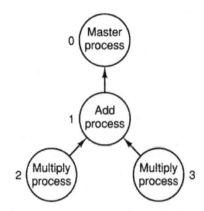

Communication of data between processes in a pipeline algorithm.

As an example, consider the computation of $Z[i] = (A[i]*B[i])+(C[i]*D[i])$ for i = 1 to 10, with four processes, including one master and three slaves. The basic communication structure for the processes that cooperate to do this computation is shown in the figure above. The master process simply creates the other three processes, sends off an initial message to each of them, and waits for them to complete their task and send back the result. The processes at the bottom of the figure are multiply processes. For each index i, one multiply process computes $A[i]*B[i]$ and the other process computes $C[i]*D[i]$, and they send their computed values up to an add process. The add process takes two input values and adds them and then sends the result to the master process. The following is an outline of code for each of these types of processes.

Pseudo Code for the Master Process

Master: process {

        Initialize the environment and read in data create the multiply and add processes

        for each of the multiply processes {

                send the multiply process a pair of vectors to be multiplied along with the process id of the add

                process that receives the output of this multiply process

        }

        send to the add process a message that gives it the process ids of the multiply processes and the process id of the master process.

        while (all of the computed Zs have not been received yet) { receive a message from add process and move the Z's value into the Z vector

        }

        print the Z vector.

        wait for all of the multiply and add processes to die

}

Pseudo Code for the Multiply Process

Multiply: process {

receive the vectors to be multiplied, along with the process id of the add process.

Move the received vector into vectors x and y

for (i=1; i<=10; i++) {

RESULT = $x[i]*y[i]$;

Send the RESULT to add process

}

send an END_MESSAGE to add process

}

Pseudo Code for the Add Process

Add: process {

Receive the message giving the process ids of the two producers (multiply process-es) and the single consumer (master process)

Receive the first message from the left child, and move its value to LEFT_RESULT Receive the first message from the right child, and move its value to RIGHT_RESULT

While (an END_MESSAGE has not yet received) { RESULT = LEFT_RE-SULT + RIGHT_RESULT

Send the RESULT to master process Receive the next message from the left child, and move its value to LEFT_RESULT

Receive the next message from the right child, and move its value to RIGHT_RESULT

}

Send an END_MESSAGE to master process

}

Parallel Algorithm Models

An algorithm model is the representation of a parallel algorithm by selecting a strategy for dividing the data and processing technique and applying the appropriate method to reduce interactions. The various models available are:

1. The data parallel model

2. The task graph model

3. The work pool model

4. The master slave model

5. The pipeline or producer consumer model

6. Hybrid models

Data-Parallel Model

In this model, the tasks are statically or semi-statically attached onto processes and each task performs identical operations on a variety of data. This type of parallelism that is a result of single operations being applied on multiple data items is called data parallelism. The task may be executed in phases and the data operated upon in different phases may be different. Typically, data-parallel computation phases are interspersed with interactions to synchronize the tasks or to get fresh data to the tasks. Since all tasks perform same computations, the decomposition of the problem into tasks is usually based on data partitioning because a uniform partitioning of data followed by a static mapping is sufficient to guarantee load balance. Data-parallel algorithms can be implemented in both shared-address-space and message-passing paradigms. However, the partitioned address- space in a message-passing paradigm may allow better control of placement, and thus may offer a better handle on locality. On the other hand, shared-address space can ease the programming effort, especially if the distribution of data is different in different phases of the algorithm. Interaction overheads in the data-parallel model can be minimized by choosing a locality preserving decomposition and, if applicable, by overlapping computation and interaction and by using optimized collective interaction routines. A key characteristic of data-parallel problems is that for most problems, the degree of data parallelism increases with the size of the problem, making it possible to use more processes to effectively solve larger problems. An example of a data-parallel algorithm is dense matrix multiplication problem.

Task Graph Model

The computations in any parallel algorithm can be viewed as a task graph. The task graph may be either trivial or nontrivial. The type of parallelism that is expressed by the task graph is called task parallelism. In certain parallel algorithms, the taskgraph is explicitly used in establishing relationship between various tasks. In the task graph model, the interrelationships among the tasks are utilized to promote locality or to reduce interaction costs. This model is applied to solve problems in which the amount of data associated with the tasks is huge relative to the amount of computation associated with them. The tasks are mapped statically to help optimize the cost of data movement among tasks. Sometimes a decentralized dynamic mapping may be used. This mapping uses the information concerning the task-dependency graph structure and the interaction pattern of tasks to minimize interaction overhead. Work is more easily shared in paradigms with globally addressable space, but mechanisms are available to share work in disjoint address space. Typical interaction-reducing techniques applicable to this model include reducing the volume and frequency of interaction by promoting locality while mapping the tasks based on the interaction pattern of tasks, and using asynchronous interaction methods to overlap the interaction with computation. Examples of algorithms based on the task graph model include parallel quicksort, sparse matrix factorization, and many parallel algorithms derived via divide-and-conquer approach.

Work Pool Model

The work pool or the task pool model is characterized by a dynamic mapping of tasks onto processes for load balancing in which any task may potentially be executed by any process. There is no desired pre-mapping of tasks onto processes. The mapping may be centralized or decentralized. Pointers to the tasks may be stored in a physically shared list, priority queue, hash table, or tree, or they could be stored in a physically distributed data structure. The work may be statically available in the beginning, or could be dynamically generated; i.e., the processes may generate work and add it to the global (possibly distributed) work pool. If the work is generated dynamically and a decentralized mapping is used, then a termination detection algorithm would be required so that all processes can actually detect the completion of the entire program (i.e., exhaustion of all potential tasks) and stop looking for more work. In the message-passing paradigm, the work pool model is typically used when the amount of data associated with tasks is relatively small compared to the computation associated with the tasks. As a result, tasks can be readily moved around without causing too much data interaction overhead. The granularity of the tasks can be adjusted to attain the desired level of tradeoff between load-imbalance and the overhead of accessing the work pool for adding and extracting tasks .Parallelization of loops by chunk scheduling or related methods is an example of the use of the work pool model with centralized mapping when the tasks are statically available. Parallel tree search where the work is represented by a centralized or distributed data structure is an example of the use of the work pool model where the tasks are generated dynamically.

Master-Slave Model

In the master-slave or the manager-worker model, one or more master processes generate work and allocate it to slave processes. The tasks may be allocated a priori if the manager can estimate the size of the tasks or if a random mapping can do an adequate job of load balancing. In another scenario, workers are assigned smaller pieces of work at different times. The latter scheme is preferred if it is time consuming for the master to generate work and hence it is not desirable to make all workers wait until the master has generated all work pieces. In some cases, work may need to be performed in phases, and work in each phase must finish before work in the next phases can be generated. In this case, the manager may cause all workers to synchronize after each phase. Usually, there is no desired pre-mapping of work to processes, and any worker can do any job assigned to it. The manager-worker model can be generalized to the hierarchical or multi-level manager-worker model in which the top level manager feeds large chunks of tasks to second-level managers, who further subdivide the tasks among their own workers and may perform part of the work themselves. This model is generally equally suitable to shared-address-space or message-passing paradigms since the interaction is naturally two- way; i.e., the manager knows that it needs to give out work and workers know that they need to get work from the manager. While using the master-slave model, care should be taken to ensure that the master does not become a bottleneck, which may happen if the tasks are too small (or the workers are relatively fast). The granularity of tasks should be chosen such that the cost of doing work dominates the cost of communication and the cost of synchronization. Asynchronous interaction may help overlap interaction and the computation associated with work generation by the master. It may also reduce waiting times if the nature of requests from workers is nondeterministic.

Pipeline or Producer-Consumer Model

In the pipeline model, a stream of data is passed on through a succession of processes, each of which performs some task on it. This simultaneous execution of different programs on a data stream is called stream parallelism. With the exception of the process initiating the pipeline, the arrival of new data triggers the execution of a new task by a process in the pipeline. The process-es could form such pipelines in the shape of linear or multidimensional arrays, trees, or general graphs with or without cycles. A pipeline is a chain of producers and consumers. Each process in the pipeline can be viewed as a consumer of a sequence of data items for the process preceding it in the pipeline and as a producer of data for the process following it in the pipeline. The pipeline does not need to be a linear chain; it can be a directed graph. The pipeline model usually involves a static mapping of tasks onto processes. Load balancing is a function of task granularity. The larger the granularity, the longer it takes to fill up the pipeline, i.e. for the trigger produced by the first process in the chain to propagate to the last process, thereby keeping some of the processes waiting. However, too fine a granularity may increase interaction overheads because processes will need to interact to receive fresh data after smaller pieces of computation. The most common inter-action reduction technique applicable to this model is overlapping interaction with computation. An example of a two-dimensional pipeline is the parallel LU factorization algorithm.

Hybrid Models

In some cases, more than one model may be applicable to the problem at hand, resulting in a hybrid algorithm model. A hybrid model may be composed either of multiple models applied hierarchically or multiple models applied sequentially to different phases of a parallel algorithm. In some cases, an algorithm formulation may have characteristics of more than one algorithm model. For instance, data may flow in a pipelined manner in a pattern guided by a task graph. In another scenario, the major computation may be described by a task graph, but each node of the graph may represent a su-per task comprising multiple subtasks that may be suitable for data-parallel or pipelined parallelism. Parallel quicksort is one of the applications for which a hybrid model is ideally suited.

Matrix-Matrix Multiplication

Here we discuss parallel algorithms for multiplying two n x n dense, square matrices A and B to yield the product matrix $C = A$ x B. All parallel matrix multiplication algorithms here are based on the conventional serial algorithm shown in Algorithm below. If we assume that an addition and multiplication pair (line 8) takes unit time, then the sequential run time of this algorithm is n^3. Matrix multiplication algorithms with better asymptotic sequential complexities are available, for example Strassen's algorithm. However, for the sake of simplicity, in this book we assume that the conventional algorithm is the best available serial algorithm.

Algorithm: The conventional serial algorithm for multiplication of two n x n matrices.

```
1.    procedure MAT_MULT (A, B, C)

2.    begin

3.        for i := 0 to n - 1 do

4.            for j := 0 to n - 1 do

5.                begin

6.                    C[i, j] := 0;

7.                    for k := 0 to n - 1 do

8.                        C[i, j] := C[i, j] + A[i, k] x B[k, j];

9.                endfor;

10.   end MAT_MULT
```

Algorithm: The block matrix multiplication algorithm for n x n matrices with a block size of (n/q) x (n/q).

```
1.    procedure BLOCK_MAT_MULT (A, B, C)

2.    begin

3.        for i := 0 to q - 1 do

4.            for j := 0 to q - 1 do

5.                begin

6.                    Initialize all elements of C_{i,j} to zero;

7.                    for k := 0 to q - 1 do

8.                        C_{i,j} := C_{i,j} + A_{i,k} x B_{k,j};

9.                endfor;

10.   end BLOCK_MAT_MULT
```

A concept that is useful in matrix multiplication as well as in a variety of other matrix algorithms is that of block matrix operations. We can often express a matrix computation involving scalar algebraic operations on all its elements in terms of identical matrix algebraic operations on blocks or sub matrices of the original matrix. Such algebraic operations on the sub matrices are called *block matrix operations*. For example, an n x n matrix A can be regarded as a q x q array of blocks $A_{i,j}$

$(0 \leq i, j < q)$ such that each block is an (n/q) x (n/q) sub matrix. The matrix multiplication algorithm in Conventional serial algorithm can then be rewritten as Block matrix multiplication algorithm, in which the multiplication and addition operations on line 8 are matrix multiplication and matrix addition, respectively. Not only are the final results of conventional serial algorithm and **Block** matrix multiplication algorithm identical, but so are the total numbers of scalar additions and multiplications performed by each. Conventional serial algorithm performs n^3 additions and multiplications, and block matrix multiplication algorithm performs q^3 matrix multiplications, each involving (n/q) x (n/q) matrices and requiring $(n/q)^3$ additions and multiplications. We can use p processes to implement the block version of matrix multiplication in parallel by choosing $q = \sqrt{p}$ and computing a distinct $C_{i,j}$ block at each process.

Henceforth, we describe a few ways of parallelizing Block matrix multiplication algorithm. Each of the following parallel matrix multiplication algorithms uses a block 2-D partitioning of the matrices.

Simple Parallel Algorithm

Consider two n x n matrices A and B partitioned into p blocks $A_{i,j}$ and $B_{i,j}$ $0 \leq k < \sqrt{p}$ of size $\left(n = \sqrt{p}\right) \times \left(n / \sqrt{p}\right)$ each. These blocks are mapped onto a $\sqrt{p} \times \sqrt{p}$ logical mesh of processes. The processes are labeled from $P_{0,0}$ to $P_{\sqrt{p}-1,\sqrt{p}-1}$. Process $P_{i,j}$ initially stores $A_{i,j}$ and $B_{i,j}$ and computes block $C_{i,j}$ of the result matrix. Computing submatrix $C_{i,j}$ requires all submatrices $A_{i,k}$ and $B_{k,j}$ for $\left(0 \leq i, j < \sqrt{p}\right)$ To acquire all the required blocks, an all-to-all broadcast of matrix A's blocks is performed in each row of processes, and an all-to-all broadcast of matrix B's blocks is performed in each column. After $P_{i,j}$ acquires $A_{i,0}, A_{i,1}....A_{i,\sqrt{p}-1}$ and $B_{0,j}, B_{1,j},...., B_{\sqrt{p}-1,j}$, it performs the submatrix multiplication and addition step of lines 7 and 8 in Block matrix multiplication algorithm.

Performance and Scalability Analysis

The algorithm requires two all-to-all broadcast steps (each consisting of $\sqrt{p}$ concurrent broadcasts in all rows and columns of the process mesh) among groups of $\sqrt{p}$ processes. The messages consist of submatrices of n^2/p elements. The total communication time is $2\left(t_s + \log\left(\sqrt{p}\right)\right) + t_w\left(n^2\sqrt{p}\right)\left(\sqrt{p}-1\right)$. After the communication step, each process computes a submatrix $C_{i,j}$, which requires $\sqrt{p}$ multiplications of $\left(n = \sqrt{p}\right) \times \left(n / \sqrt{p}\right)$ submatrices (lines 7 and 8 of Block matrix multiplication algorithm with $q = \sqrt{p}$. This takes a total of time $\sqrt{p} \times \left(n / \sqrt{p}\right)^3 = n^3 / p$. Thus, the parallel run time is approximately

$$T_P = \frac{n^3}{p} + t_s \log p + 2t_w \frac{n^2}{\sqrt{p}}.$$

The process-time product is $n^3 + t_s p \log p + 2 t_w n^2 \sqrt{p}$, and the parallel algorithm is cost-optimal for $p = O(n^2)$.

The isoefficiency functions due to t_s and t_w are $t_s\, p \log p$ and $8(t_w)^{3p3/2}$, respectively. Hence, the overall isoefficiency function due to the communication overhead is $\Theta(p^{3/2})$. This algorithm can use a maximum of n^2 processes; hence, $p \le n^2$ or $n^3 \ge p^3/2$. Therefore, the isoefficiency function due to concurrency is also $\Theta(p^{3/2})$.

A notable drawback of this algorithm is its excessive memory requirements. At the end of the communication phase, each process has $\sqrt{p}$ blocks of both matrices A and B. Since each block requires $\Theta(n^2/p)$ memory, each process requires $\Theta\left(n^2 / \sqrt{p}\right)$ memory. The total memory requirement over all the processes is $\Theta\left(n^2 / \sqrt{p}\right)$, which is $\sqrt{p}$ times the memory requirement of the sequential algorithm.

Cannon's Algorithm

Cannon's algorithm is a memory-efficient version of the simple parallel algorithm. To study this algorithm, we again partition matrices A and B into p square blocks. We label the processes from $P_{0,0}$ to

$P_{\sqrt{p}-1,\sqrt{p}-1}$, and initially assign submatrices $A_{i,j}$ and $B_{i,j}$ to process $P_{i,j}$. Although every process in the i th row requires all $\sqrt{p}$ submatrices $A_{i,k}\left(0 \le k < \sqrt{p}\right)$, it is possible to schedule the computations of the $\sqrt{p}$ processes of the ith row such that, at any given time, each process is using a different $A_{i,k}$. These blocks can be systematically rotated among the processes after every submatrix multiplication so that every process gets a fresh $A_{i,k}$ after each rotation. If an identical schedule is applied to the columns, then no process holds more than one block of each matrix at any time, and the total memory requirement of the algorithm over all the processes is $\Theta(n^2)$. Cannon's algorithm is based on this idea. The scheduling for the multiplication of submatrices on separate processes in Cannon's algorithm is illustrated in figure below for 16 processes.

(a) Initial alignment of A   (b) Initial alignment of B

(c) A and B after initial alignment   (d) Submatrix locations after first shift

$A_{0,2}$ $B_{2,0}$	$A_{0,3}$ $B_{3,1}$	$A_{0,0}$ $B_{0,2}$	$A_{0,1}$ $B_{1,3}$
$A_{1,3}$ $B_{3,0}$	$A_{1,0}$ $B_{0,1}$	$A_{1,1}$ $B_{1,2}$	$A_{1,2}$ $B_{2,3}$
$A_{2,0}$ $B_{0,0}$	$A_{2,1}$ $B_{1,1}$	$A_{2,2}$ $B_{2,2}$	$A_{2,3}$ $B_{3,3}$
$A_{3,1}$ $B_{1,0}$	$A_{3,2}$ $B_{2,1}$	$A_{3,3}$ $B_{3,2}$	$A_{3,0}$ $B_{0,3}$

$A_{0,3}$ $B_{3,0}$	$A_{0,0}$ $B_{0,1}$	$A_{0,1}$ $B_{1,2}$	$A_{0,2}$ $B_{2,3}$
$A_{1,0}$ $B_{0,0}$	$A_{1,1}$ $B_{1,1}$	$A_{1,2}$ $B_{2,2}$	$A_{1,3}$ $B_{3,3}$
$A_{2,1}$ $B_{1,0}$	$A_{2,2}$ $B_{2,1}$	$A_{2,3}$ $B_{3,2}$	$A_{2,0}$ $B_{0,3}$
$A_{3,2}$ $B_{2,0}$	$A_{3,3}$ $B_{3,1}$	$A_{3,0}$ $B_{0,2}$	$A_{3,1}$ $B_{1,3}$

(e) Submatrix locations after second shift   (f) Submatrix locations after third shift

The communication steps in Cannon's algorithm on 16 processes.

The first communication step of the algorithm aligns the blocks of A and B in such a way that each process multiplies its local submatrices. As figure (a) shows, this alignment is achieved for matrix A by shifting all submatrices $A_{i,j}$ to the left (with wraparound) by i steps. Similarly, as shown in figure (b), all submatrices $B_{i,j}$ are shifted up (with wraparound) by j steps. These are circular shift operations in each row and column of processes, which leave process $P_{i,j}$ with submatrices $A_{i,(j+i) \bmod \sqrt{p}}$ and $B_{(j+i) \bmod \sqrt{p}, j}$. Figure (c) shows the blocks of A and B after the initial alignment, when each process is ready for the first submatrix multiplication. After a submatrix multiplication step, each block of A moves one step left and each block of B moves one step up (again with wraparound), as shown in figure (d). A sequence of $\sqrt{p}$ such submatrix multiplications and single-step shifts pairs up each $A_{i,k}$ and $B_{k,j}$ for $k\left(0 \le k < \sqrt{p}\right)$ at $P_{i,j}$. This completes the multiplication of matrices A and B.

Performance Analysis

The initial alignment of the two matrices involves a rowwise and a columnwise circular shift. In any of these shifts, the maximum distance over which a block shifts is $\sqrt{p}-1$. The two shift operations require a total of time $2(t_s + t_w n^2/p)$. Each of the $\sqrt{p}$ single-step shifts in the compute-and-shift phase of the algorithm takes time $t_s + t_w n^2/p$. Thus, the total communication time (for both matrices) during this phase of the algorithm is $2\left(t_s + t_w n^2 / p\right)\sqrt{p}$. For large enough p on a network with sufficient bandwidth, the communication time for the initial alignment can be disregarded in comparison with the time spent in communication during the compute-and-shift phase.

Each process performs $\sqrt{p}$ multiplications of $\left(n/\sqrt{p}\right) \times \left(n/\sqrt{p}\right)$ submatrices. Assuming that a multiplication and addition pair takes unit time, the total time that each process spends in computation is n^3/p. Thus, the approximate overall parallel run time of this algorithm is

$$T_P = \frac{n^3}{p} + 2\sqrt{p}t_s + 2t_w \frac{n^2}{\sqrt{p}}.$$

The cost-optimality condition for Cannon's algorithm is identical to that for the simple parallel algorithm. As in the simple algorithm, the isoefficiency function of Cannon's algorithm is $\Theta(p^{3/2})$.

DNS Algorithm

The matrix multiplication algorithms presented so far use block 2-D partitioning of the input and the output matrices and use a maximum of n^2 processes for n x n matrices. As a result, these algorithms have a parallel run time of $\Omega(n)$ because there are $\Theta(n^3)$ operations in the serial algorithm. We now present a parallel algorithm based on partitioning intermediate data that can use up to n^3 processes and that performs matrix multiplication in time $\Theta(\log n)$ by using $\Omega(n^3/\log n)$ processes. This algorithm is known as the DNS algorithm because it is due to Dekel, Nassimi, and Sahni.

We first introduce the basic idea, without concern for inter-process communication. Assume that n^3 processes are available for multiplying two n x n matrices. These processes are arranged in a three-dimensional n x n x n logical array. Since the matrix multiplication algorithm performs n^3 scalar multiplications, each of the n^3 processes is assigned a single scalar multiplication. The processes are labeled according to their location in the array, and the multiplication $A[i, k]$ x $B[k,j]$ is assigned to process $P_{i,j,k}$ ($0 \le i, j, k < n$). After each process performs a single multiplication, the contents of $P_{i,j,0}$, $P_{i,j,1}$, ..., $P_{i,j,n-1}$ are added to obtain $C[i,j]$. The additions for all $C[i,j]$ can be carried out simultaneously in $\log n$ steps each. Thus, it takes one step to multiply and $\log n$ steps to add; that is, it takes time $\Theta(\log n)$ to multiply the n x n matrices by this algorithm.

We now describe a practical parallel implementation of matrix multiplication based on this idea. As figure below shows, the process arrangement can be visualized as n planes of n x n processes each. Each plane corresponds to a different value of k. Initially, the matrices are distributed among the n^2 processes of the plane corresponding to $k = 0$ at the base of the three-dimensional process array. Process $P_{i,j,0}$ initially owns $A[i,j]$ and $B[i,j]$.

In the figure below, the shaded processes in part (c) store elements of the first row of A and the shaded processes in part (d) store elements of the first column of B.

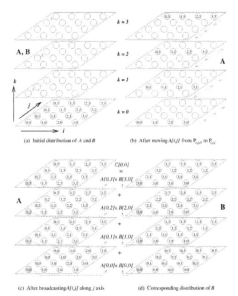

Communication steps in the DNS algorithm while multiplying 4 x 4 matrices A and B on 64 processes.

The vertical column of processes $P_{i,j,*}$ computes the dot product of row $A[i, *]$ and column $B[*, j]$. Therefore, rows of A and columns of B need to be moved appropriately so that each vertical column of processes $P_{i,j,*}$ has row $A[i, *]$ and column $B[*, j]$. More precisely, process $P_{i,j,k}$ should have $A[i, k]$ and $B[k, j]$.

The communication pattern for distributing the elements of matrix A among the processes is shown in figure (c). First, each column of A moves to a different plane such that the j th column occupies the same position in the plane corresponding to $k = j$ as it initially did in the plane corresponding to $k = 0$. The distribution of A after moving $A[i, j]$ from $P_{i,j,0}$ to $P_{i,j,j}$ is shown in figure (b). Now all the columns of A are replicated n times in their respective planes by a parallel one-to-all broadcast along the j axis. The result of this step is shown in figure (c), in which the n processes $P_{i,0,j}$, $P_{i,1,j}$, ..., $P_{i,n-1,j}$ receive a copy of $A[i,j]$ from $P_{i,j,j}$. At this point, each vertical column of processes $P_{i,j,*}$ has row $A[i, *]$. More precisely, process $P_{i,j,k}$ has $A[i, k]$.

For matrix B, the communication steps are similar, but the roles of i and j in process subscripts are switched. In the first one-to-one communication step, $B[i, j]$ is moved from $P_{i,j,0}$ to $P_{i,j,i}$. Then it is broadcast from $P_{i,j,i}$ among $P_{0,j,i}$, $P_{1,j,i}$, ..., $P_{n-1,j,i}$. The distribution of B after this one-to-all broadcast along the i axis is shown in figure (d). At this point, each vertical column of processes $P_{i,j,*}$ has column $B[*, j]$. Now process $P_{i,j,k}$ has $B[k,j]$, in addition to $A[i, k]$.

After these communication steps, $A[i, k]$ and $B[k, j]$ are multiplied at $P_{i,j,k}$. Now each element $C[i, j]$ of the product matrix is obtained by an all-to-one reduction along the k axis. During this step, process $P_{i,j,0}$ accumulates the results of the multiplication from processes $P_{i,j,1}$, ..., $P_{i,j,n-1}$. Figure above shows this step for $C[0, 0]$.

The DNS algorithm has three main communication steps:

(1) Moving the columns of A and the rows of B to their respective planes,

(2) Performing one-to-all broadcast along the j axis for A and along the i axis for B, and (3) all-to-one reduction along the k axis. All these operations are performed within groups of n processes and take time $\Theta(\log n)$. Thus, the parallel run time for multiplying two n x n matrices using the DNS algorithm on n^3 processes is $\Theta(\log n)$.

DNS Algorithm with Fewer than n^3 Processes

The DNS algorithm is not cost-optimal for n^3 processes, since its process-time product of $\Theta(n^3 \log n)$ exceeds the $\Theta(n^3)$ sequential complexity of matrix multiplication. We now present a cost-optimal version of this algorithm that uses fewer than n^3 processes.

Assume that the number of processes p is equal to q^3 for some $q < n$. To implement the DNS algorithm, the two matrices are partitioned into blocks of size (n/q) x (n/q). Each matrix can thus be regarded as a q x q two-dimensional square array of blocks. The implementation of this algorithm on q^3 processes is very similar to that on n^3 processes. The only difference is that now we operate on blocks rather than on individual elements. Since $1 \leq q \leq n$, the number of processes can vary between 1 and n^3.

Performance Analysis The first one-to-one communication step is performed for both A and B, and takes time $t_s + t_w(n/q)^2$ for each matrix. The second step of one-to-all broadcast is also performed for both matrices and takes time $t_s \log q + t_w(n/q)^2 \log q$ for each matrix. The final all-to-one reduction is performed only once (for matrix C) and takes time $t_s \log q + t_w(n/q)^2 \log q$. The multiplication of $(n/q) \times (n/q)$ submatrices by each process takes time $(n/q)^3$. We can ignore the communication time for the first one-to-one communication step because it is much smaller than the communication time of one-to-all broadcasts and all-to-one reduction. We can also ignore the computation time for addition in the final reduction phase because it is of a smaller order of magnitude than the computation time for multiplying the submatrices. With these assumptions, we get the following approximate expression for the parallel run time of the DNS algorithm:

$$T_P \approx \left(\frac{n}{q}\right)^3 + 3t_s \log q + 3t_w \left(\frac{n}{q}\right)^2 \log q$$

Since $q = p^{1/3}$, we get

$$T_P = \frac{n^3}{p} + t_s \log p + t_w \frac{n^2}{p^{2/3}} \log p.$$

The total cost of this parallel algorithm is $n^3 + t_s\, p \log p + t_w n^2\, p^{1/3} \log p$. The iso efficiency function is $\Theta(p(\log p)^3)$. The algorithm is cost-optimal for $n^3 = \Omega(p(\log p)^3)$, or $p = O(n^3/(\log n)^3)$.

Permissions

Index

CPSIA information can be obtained
at www.ICGtesting.com
Printed in the USA
BVHW011702270519
549358BV00002B/2/P